Biomathematics

Volume 13

John Impagliazzo

Deterministic Aspects of Mathematical Demography

An Investigation of the Stable Theory of Population
including an Analysis of the Population Statistics
of Denmark

With 52 Illustrations

Springer-Verlag
Berlin Heidelberg New York Tokyo

John Impagliazzo

State University of New York
Nassau Community College
Garden City, New York 11530
USA

Mathematics Subject Classification (1980): 92A15

ISBN 3-540-13616-9 Springer-Verlag Berlin Heidelberg New York Tokyo
ISBN 0-387-13616-9 Springer-Verlag New York Heidelberg Berlin Tokyo

Library of Congress Cataloging in Publication Data

Impagliazzo, John. Deterministic aspects of mathematical demography (Biomathematics; v. 13)
1. Population–Mathematical models. 2. Stable population model. 3. Denmark–Population.
I. Title. II. Series.

HB849.51.I46 1985   304,6'0724   84-24048
ISBN 0-387-13616-9 (U.S.)

Typesetting, Printing and Bookbinding:
Universitätsdruckerei H. Stürtz AG, Würzburg
2141/3140-543210

DEDICATED

to my children
Loretta and Stelio

to my wife
Annamaria

and to a friend
Betina Kjær Madsen

Preface

Mathematical Demography, the study of population and its analysis through mathematical models, has received increased interest in the mathematical community in recent years. It was not until the twentieth century, however, that the study of population, predominantly human population, achieved its mathematical character.

The subject of mathematical demography can be viewed from either a deterministic viewpoint or from a stochastic viewpoint. For the sake of brevity, stochastic models are not included in this work. It is, therefore, my intention to consider only established deterministic models in this discussion, starting with the life table as the earliest model, to a generalized matrix model which is developed in this treatise. These deterministic models provide sufficient development and conclusions to formulate sound mathematical population analysis and estimates of population projections. It should be noted that although the subject of mathematical demography focuses on human populations, the development and results may be applied to any population as long as the preconditions that make the model valid are maintained.

Information concerning mathematical demography is at best fragmented. From a mathematical point of view, the existing literature is either too shallow or overly specific. An individual with sound mathematical training will find that there does not exist a single source which consolidates the principal matter of this subject at a mature expository level. It is for this reason that this work is being presented. In the first chapter a broad discussion of demography is developed from the Stone Age to the twentieth century. Chapters Two through Five provide an in-depth mathematical discussion of the development of the stable theory of population, together with its three principal deterministic models. In chapters Six and Seven some of the comparisons and consequences of stable theory are shown. Chapter Eight discusses the population statistics of the Kingdom of Denmark to provide the reader with an actual demographic example of the subject discussed herein.

It is my hope that this work will fill the void that presently exists in the mathematical literature. It is my further hope that this work will provide a positive contribution to the development of mathematics.

November, 1984   J. Impagliazzo

Acknowledgments

I wish to thank the Department of Mathematics of Adelphi University, and in particular Dr. Walter Meyer for the time he had spent in developing my interest in this subject and for his many useful comments and suggestions. The professional courtesy he extended to me throughout the development of this work is most appreciated. I also wish to thank the editorial staff of Springer-Verlag, and Dr. Simon A. Levin for their guidance.

I wish to extend my further thanks to Lene Skotte of Danmarks Statistik, and to her staff particularly Kirsten Frandsen and Hanne Spøhr for their untiring efforts in helping me acquire information on the population statistics of Denmark. In addition I wish to thank professors Poul Matthiessen, Otto Andersen and Anders Hald of Copenhagen University for their informative and personal conversations and for the assistance they have given me.

I am most grateful to Betina Kjær Madsen for her selfless attitude, and for the time she spent translating Danish documents and typing preliminary materials. I wish to also thank Irina Karabets for the time she spent editing the manuscript, and John G. Phillips for his encouragement and support. Finally, I am most thankful to my family, Annamaria, Loretta and Stelio, for their enduring patience and understanding.

Table of Contents

1. The Development of Mathematical Demography

1.1 Introduction

Demography is the study of population, primarily human population, in terms of its growth and decay, fertility and mortality, and its relative mobility, together with its impact on the economic, political and sociological components of society. Interest in this subject can be traced back to ancient times. Oriental legends and biblical references indicate that an enumeration or census of a population by age and by locality was not uncommon. This was done primarily for military records and manpower, as well as for taxation. Governments also used such information for administrative aids and to establish the socio-economic character of its people.

1.2 Demography Before the Eighteenth Century

Demography in its early stages consisted primarily as an enumeration of a population, and is documented as early as 3800 B.C. in Babylonia [1]. In addition, mortality was also a concern. One of the earliest accountings of mortality can be traced back to the Stone Age where, from stone etchings it was determined that only 54% of the population reached the age of five; interestingly, however, 3% of the population reached the age of seventy [2]. A similar pattern is demonstrated in the Bronze Age with the peak of mortality occurring at fifteen years of age [3].

The first published table of mortality or life expectancies is attributed to the Roman jurisconsulate Æmilius Macer, who authorized a table to capitalize annuities. The table dates to about the year 225 A.D. and appears in the Latin in a work by Trenerry [4] as follows:

Æmilius Macer, Lib. 2, ad legem vicesimam hereditatium. "Computationi in alimentis faciendæ hanc formam esse Ulpianus scribit, ut a prima ætate usque ad annum vicesimum quantitas alimentorum triginta annorum computetur, ejusque quantitatis Falcidia præstetur: ab annis vero viginti usque ad annum vicesimum-quintum annorum viginti octo: ab annis vigintiquinque usque ad annos triginta, annorum vigintiquinque: ab annis triginta usque ad annos trigintaquinque, annorum vigintiduo: ab annis trigintaquinque usque ad annos quadraginta, annorum viginti: ab annis quadraginta usque ad annos quinquaginta, (tot) annorum computatio fit, quot ætati ejus ad annum sexagesimum deerit, remisso uno anno: ab anno vero quinquagesimo usque ad annum

2

quinquagesimum quintum, annorum novem: ab annis quinquagentaquinque usque ad annum sexagesimum annorum septem: ab annis sexaginta cujuscunque ætatis sit, annorum quinque .... Solitum est tamen a prima ætate usque ad annum trigesimum computationem annorum triginta fieri, ab annis vero triginta, tot annorum computationem inire, quot ad annum sexagesimum deesse videntur, nunquam ergo amplius quam triginta annorum computatio initur."

The passage translates as follows [5]:

Æmilius Macer, Book 2, on the twentieth law of heredity.

"Ulpian wrote this form for the computation of provisions, from the first age to the age of twenty the quantity of provision is computed to be thirty years, this quantity is given by the Falcidia: from the actual age of twenty to the age of twenty-five, twenty eight years: from the age of twenty-five to the age of thirty, twenty-five years: from the age of thirty until the age of thirty-five, twenty-two years: from the age of thirty-five until the age of forty, twenty years: from the age if forty until the age of fifty, such computation is made as his age to the age of sixty is lacking, less one year: from the actual age of fifty to the age of fifty-five, nine years: from the age of fifty-five until the age of sixty, seven years: from the age of sixty to whatever age may be, five years ....

Usually however from the first age until the age of thirty, the computation of thirty is made, but from the age of thirty, such computation of years is established as would seem to be lacking to the age of sixty, never however is the computation established for more than thirty years."

The passage suggests two different schedules where the description in the latter part of the passage, attributed to Macer, is superceded by the description attributed to Ulpian. Macer's schedule is shown in Table 1.1.

Table 1.1. Table of Macer (first published table of mortality)

Age	Provision	Age	Provision	Age	Provision
0–30	30 years	41	19 years	52	8 years
31	29	42	18	53	7
32	28	43	17	54	6
33	27	44	16	55	5
34	26	45	15	56	4
35	25	46	14	57	3
36	24	47	13	58	2
37	23	48	12	59	1
38	22	49	11	60+	0
39	21	50	10		
40	20	51	9		

Macer's schedule, though used for its simplicity, was considered arbitrary. Apparently, Macer realized its weakness and sanctioned the use of a more correct schedule, the first part of the passage, whose authorship is credited to Ulpian. This schedule shown in Table 1.2 is called Ulpian's Table and was considered more accurate than that of Macer since it reflected actual life expectancies. In fact, Ulpian's table was so accurate for its time that it was used for over 1600 years. The columns labelled 'Provision' in both the tables of Macer and Ulpian can be interpreted as the expectancy of additional years of life for the indicated age category.

Table 1.2. Table of Ulpian

Age	Provision	Age	Provision	Age	Provision
0–19	30 years	41	18 years	47	12 years
20–24	28	42	17	48	11
25–29	25	43	16	49	10
30–34	22	44	15	50–54	9
35–39	20	45	14	55–59	7
40	19	46	13	60+	5

The first mathematical formula in demography can be attributed to Girolamo Cardano (Cardan) who, in 1570, proposed that the *expectancy of life, e,* is a linear decreasing function of age, *x*. In brief, if ω is the *ultimate age of life,* then for some suitable constant *k*,

$$e = k(\omega - x) \tag{1.1}$$

for $0 \leq x \leq \omega$. This conjecture, however, was not based on actual information concerning human mortality [6].

In 1662 the first substantive work in demography was published by John Graunt [7]. In this work Graunt shows the results of a study on the city of London in 1658 where the number of deaths that occur at various age groups are illustrated. Table 1.3 gives a contemporary interpretation of Graunt's results.

Table 1.3. Mortality Table of Graunt

Exact Age	Survivors	Age Category	Deaths
birth	100		–
6	64	(0– 6]	36
16	40	(6–16]	24
26	25	(16–26]	15
36	16	(26–36]	9
46	10	(36–46]	6
56	6	(46–56]	4
66	3	(56–66]	3
76	1	(66–76]	2
80	0	(76–80]	1

This table will now be used to establish some preliminary definitions.

4

A set of individuals having experienced a particular event during the same period of time is called a *cohort* [8]. The set of those individuals born during a particular time interval is called a *birth-cohort*. The size of this cohort is called the *radix* of the cohort and is symbolized as l_0. For a given age x, l_x represents the number of survivors of the l_0 persons who are now exactly age x. Then for $n \geq 0$, it is necessary that

$$l_{x+n} \leq l_x \qquad (1.2)$$

For practical purposes the values of x, n, and l are considered to be non-negative integers.

Thus from Table 1.3, $l_0 = 100$, $l_6 = 64$, $l_{16} = 40$, etc. Clearly, l_x represents a discrete monotonic decreasing function of exact age x.

The *number of deaths* occuring between ages x and $x+n$ is denoted $_n d_x$ and is defined as

$$_n d_x = l_x - l_{x+n}. \qquad (1.3)$$

From Table 1.3, $_6 d_0 = 36$, $_{10} d_6 = 24$, etc. For a person aged x the *probability of dying* in the next n years is denoted $_n q_x$ and is defined as

$$_n q_x = {}_n d_x / l_x \qquad (1.4)$$

or

$$_n q_x = (l_x - l_{x+n})/l_x. \qquad (1.5)$$

For a person aged x the *probability of surviving* to age $x+n$, denoted $_n p_x$, is defined as

$$_n p_x = 1 - {}_n q_x \qquad (1.6)$$

or upon rewriting,

$$_n p_x = l_{x+n}/l_x. \qquad (1.7)$$

Using the entries of Table 1.3, it is easily verified that $_{10} q_6 = 0.375$ while $_{10} p_{56} = 0.5$. Demographic work of this type was first introduced in 1671 by Johan De Wit [9] in the computation of annuities.

Table 1.3 was not the only result of Graunt's work. He also engaged in discussions on births, deaths, migration and the demographic differences between male and female vital rates. His work is regarded as a masterpiece in the field and Table 1.3 is considered to be the first table [10] on human mortality. Thus, John Graunt may justifiably be called the Father of Demography.

The first 'modern' mortality table is usually credited to Dr. Edmund Halley who, in 1693, constructed a life table based on data from the city of Breslau in Poland. Halley's Table, shown in Table 1.4, was thought to be "... the best, as well as the first of its kind" [11].

The entries of the column labelled "age" are interpreted as the age interval $[x-1, x)$. The entries of the column labelled "Living" are interpreted as the average number of people alive for the corresponding age intergal. Let L_x

5

Table 1.4. Mortality Table of Halley

Age	Living	Age	Living	Age	Living	Age	Living	Age	Living	Age	Living
1	1000	16	622	31	523	46	387	61	232	76	78
2	855	17	616	32	515	47	377	62	222	77	68
3	798	18	610	33	507	48	367	63	212	78	58
4	760	19	604	34	499	49	357	64	202	79	49
5	732	20	598	35	490	50	346	65	192	80	41
6	710	21	592	36	481	51	335	66	182	81	34
7	692	22	586	37	472	52	324	67	172	82	28
8	680	23	580	38	463	53	313	68	162	83	23
9	670	24	574	39	454	54	302	69	152	84	19
10	661	25	567	40	445	55	292	70	142	*	*
11	653	26	560	41	436	56	282	71	131		
12	646	27	553	42	427	57	272	72	120		
13	640	28	546	43	417	58	262	73	109		
14	634	29	539	44	407	59	252	74	98		
15	628	30	531	45	397	60	242	75	88		

denote the *average number of persons alive* on the age interval $[x, x+1)$. It is Halley's intent that on the interval $[x-1, x)$ there are L_{x-1} persons alive on the average. In particular on the interval $[0, 1)$ there are

$$L_0 = 1000$$

persons alive on the average.

Caution must be taken in that Halley's L_{x-1} values are not the same as the l_x values which represent the survivors of a hypothetical radix l_0 at exact age x [12]. Halley's value L_{x-1} is the average value of the survivorship function taken over the unit interval for each age x. A linear approximation showing the relationship between these two expressions is

$$L_{x-1} = (l_{x-1} + l_x)/2. \tag{1.8}$$

Note that L_0 can not be the radix of the cohort. This can be seen by rewriting (1.8) as

$$l_{x-1} = 2L_{x-1} - l_x \tag{1.9}$$

and for Halley's initial age $x = 1$, (1.9) becomes

$$l_0 = 2L_0 - l_1$$

where l_0 is the radix of the cohort. By (1.2), $l_1 \le l_0$, implying that

$$l_0 \ge L_0 \tag{1.10}$$

with equality holding only under zero mortality.

6

The accomplishments of John Graunt and Edmund Halley had marked a cornerstone in the field of demography at the end of the seventeenth century. Halley's Table had set the stage for a new era of applications which extended to annuities, pensions and insurance, and had replaced Ulpian's Table after 1600 years of use. Halley's Table became the accepted standard of its time.

1.3 The Life Table – Definitions and Consequences

It is the intent of this section to develop some mathematical structure for a life table as a mathematical model. Consider a single individual, aged 0, who lives through age x to an ultimate possible age ω. The probability that this individual attains exact age x is defined by the survival function p as $p(x)$, where p is assumed to be differentiable for $0 \le x \le \omega$ such that $p(0) = 1$, $p(\omega) = 0$ and where $0 \le p(x) \le 1$.

Definition 1.1. Let l_0 be some hypothetical value called a *radix* which represents the number of living individuals at exact age 0. The number of *individuals living* at exact age x is

$$l(x) = l_0 p(x) \tag{1.11}$$

and the number of *individuals dying* between exact ages x and $x+n$ for $n>0$ is

$$_n d_x = l(x) - l(x+n). \tag{1.12}$$

A table exhibiting $l(x)$ and $_n d_x$ as functions of age x is called a *life table* or *mortality table* [13].

It is clear that mortality ensures that $p(x) \ge p(x+n)$ and therefore, for $n>0$ and $0 \le x \le \omega$,

$$l(x+n) \le l(x). \tag{1.13}$$

Note that for discrete age values, the survivorship function l expresses the survivors at age x as l_x, in which case (1.12) becomes (1.3), while (1.13) becomes (1.2). Furthermore, when $n=1$, (1.12) is written as

$$d_x = l(x) - l(x+1). \tag{1.14}$$

Figure 1.1 shows a continuous approximation of the survivorship function l based on Graunt's Table, Table 1.3, while Fig. 1.2 shows the discrete function $_n d_x$ for the same table.

It should be noted that equations (1.4) through (1.7) retain their discrete character even when function l is continuous.

7

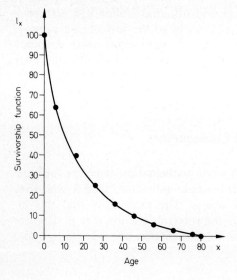

Fig. 1.1. Survivorship vs. age according to Graunt

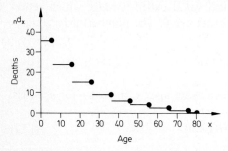

Fig. 1.2. Deaths vs. age according to Graunt

Definition 1.2. For a life at exact age x, its *probability of survival* to exact age $x + n$, $n \geq 0$, is denoted by $_np_x$ where

$$_np_x = l(x+n)/l(x). \qquad (1.15)$$

For a life at exact age x, its *probability of dying* within the next n years is denoted by $_nq_x$ where

$$_nq_x = 1 - {_np_x}. \qquad (1.16)$$

The expression p_x describes the ratio $l(x+1)/l(x)$, which is not the discrete counterpart of $p(x)$, but is the probability of surviving from birth to exact age x.

In this regard it is further noted that demographers sometimes treat $p(x)$ as a probability and sometimes as a relative frequency. If it is a probability, then $l_0 p(x)$ is, according to the binomial probability model, the expected number of survivors at age x. In most demographic models and in those discussed in this work, however, $p(x)$ is treated as a ratio, so the number of survivors at age x is exactly and definitely $l_0 p(x)$. This situation is occasionally confused by the fact

8

that demographers sometimes speak of it as a probability even while they treat it as a ratio.

In 1746 Antoine de Parcieux developed a series of life tables for the purpose of calculating annuities. One such table is shown in Table 1.5 [14]. Notice in particular that in comparing Table 1.5 to Table 1.4, the radix of 1000 begins at the age of 3. With respect to annuities, Table 1.5 is more representative of age structure due to the high infant mortality of the time.

Table 1.5. Life Table of de Parcieux

Age	Living	Age	Living	Age	Living	Age	Living	Age	Living
1	****	21	806	41	650	61	450	81	101
2	****	22	798	42	643	62	437	82	85
3	1000	23	790	43	636	63	423	83	71
4	970	24	782	44	629	64	409	84	59
5	948	25	774	45	622	65	395	85	48
6	930	26	766	46	615	66	380	86	38
7	915	27	758	47	607	67	364	87	29
8	902	28	750	48	599	68	347	88	22
9	890	29	742	49	590	69	329	89	16
10	880	30	734	50	581	70	310	90	11
11	872	31	726	51	571	71	291	91	7
12	866	32	718	52	560	72	271	92	4
13	860	33	710	53	549	73	251	93	2
14	854	34	702	54	538	74	231	94	1
15	848	35	694	55	526	75	211	95	0
16	842	36	686	56	514	76	192	96	*
17	835	37	678	57	502	77	173	97	*
18	828	38	671	58	489	78	154	98	
19	821	39	664	59	476	79	136	99	
20	814	40	657	60	463	80	118	100	

Halley's Table, Table 1.4, shows that more than twenty percent of the population died before the age of three. Also, the entries under "Living" in Table 1.5 are the survivorship values l_x, and not the L_x values of Halley. Consequently, after 53 years of prominence, Halley's table was replaced by that of de Parcieux as the standard of its time.

Although his life table achieved high acclaim, Monsieur de Parcieux is best known for his development and calculations on life expectancies.

Definition 1.3. The average future years of life expected of a person who is exact age x is called the *expectation of life* at age x. When calculated from a discrete life table it is the *average expectation of life*, denoted $\bar{e}_x$, or the *curtate expectation of life*, denoted e_x. When calculated from a continuous survivorship function $l(x)$ it is called the *complete expectation of life* and is denoted $\mathring{e}_x$.

The first discrete formulation was developed by de Parcieux as is now shown [15].

9

Theorem 1.4 (de Parcieux). Let l_x be the survivors of a radix at age x. Then

$$\bar{e}_x = \left(\sum_{k=x}^{\infty} l_k \right) \Big/ l_x - 1/2 \qquad (1.17)$$

where $\bar{e}_x$ is the *average* expectation of life.

Proof: Consider the l_x survivors of a cohort. One year later d_x of these will have died, having lived for an average of 0.5 additional years. Two years later d_{x+1} of these l_x survivors will have died, having lived for an average of 1.5 additional years. This process continues until all the l_x survivors will have died. The total person-years lived by the survivors of a cohort at age x is

$$0.5\,d_x + 1.5\,d_{x+1} + \ldots + (\omega - x + 0.5)d_\omega$$

or

$$\sum_{k=x}^{\omega} (k - x + 0.5)d_k. \qquad (1.18)$$

Hence, the average years yet to be lived by the survivors at age $x, \bar{e}_x$, is the ratio of (1.18) to l_x. Since $d_k = l_k - l_{k+1}$, then

$$l_x \bar{e}_x = 0.5\,(l_x - l_{x+1}) + 1.5\,(l_{x+1} - l_{x+2}) + \ldots + (\omega - x + 0.5)(l_\omega - l_{\omega+1})$$

which telescopes to

$$l_x \bar{e}_x = 0.5\,l_x + l_{x+1} + l_{x+2} + \ldots + l_\omega - (\omega - x + 0.5)l_{\omega+1}.$$

Since $l_{\omega+1} = 0$, then

$$l_x \bar{e}_x = 0.5\,l_x + \sum_{k=x+1}^{\omega} l_k$$

or

$$l_x \bar{e}_x = \left(\sum_{k=x}^{\omega} l_x \right) - 0.5\,l_x$$

from which (1.17) is immediate. □

    If in (1.17) it is assumed that people live in whole year intervals rather than half year averages, the second discrete formulation results.

Corollary 1.5. Let l_x be the survivors of a radix at age x. Then the *curtate* expectation of life is

$$e_x = \left(\sum_{k=x}^{\omega} l_k \right) \Big/ l_x - 1. \qquad (1.19)$$

Proof. The proof is similar to that of Theorem 1.4. □

10

The result of Corollary 1.5 is called curtate in the sense that it ignores the actual or averaged years really lived.

For the case when the survivorship function is continuous, with $l(x)$ the survivors of a radix at age x, then the expectation of life is [16]

$$\mathring{e}_x = (1/l(x)) \int_0^\infty l(x+u)\,du \qquad (1.20)$$

and is called the *complete* expectation of life. Clearly, this expression removes the approximations found in the curtate expectation of life, e_x, and the averaged expectation of life $\bar{e}_x$ of de Parcieux. It is true, however, that

$$\bar{e}_x = e_x + 1/2 \qquad (1.21)$$

and

$$\mathring{e}_x \doteq \bar{e}_x \qquad (1.22)$$

so that the complete expectation of life of (1.20) can be approximated as

$$\mathring{e}_x \doteq e_x + 1/2 \qquad (1.23)$$

For example, using Table 1.5 with $\omega = 95$, a person aged 85 is expected to live $\bar{e}_{85} = (178/48) - 1/2 = 3.208$ years which approximates the complete expectation of life of the person. Figure 1.3 shows the expectation of life as calculated by prominent demographers.

Consider now the survivors of a cohort at age x compared to the survivors of the same cohort at age $x+n$. The survivors at age $x+n$ are the survivors at

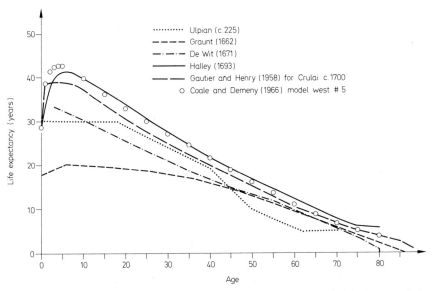

Fig. 1.3. Life expectancies according to various demographers (courtesy of Springer-Verlag)

age x, less the deaths that occur over the n-year interval. Then from (1.12)

$$l(x+n)=l(n)-{}_nd_x. \tag{1.24}$$

In turn these deaths can be interpreted as a value directly proportional to the survivors at exact age x, $l(x)$, and the interval width, n, over which these deaths occurred. This leads to the following concept due to the author.

Definition 1.6. Let $l(x)$ be the survivors of a cohort at exact age x, and ${}_nd_x$ the deaths over the age interval $[x, x+n)$. Then for $x=0, 1, 2, \ldots$

$$_n\bar{\mu}_x={}_nd_x/nl_x \tag{1.25}$$

is called *the average force of mortality* of the cohort at exact age x. For non-integer x, ${}_n\bar{\mu}_x$ is defined by the requirement that ${}_n\bar{\mu}_x$ is constant on the interval $[x, x+n)$.

Substituting (1.25) into (1.24) gives

$$l(x+n)=l(x)-{}_n\bar{\mu}_xnl(x) \tag{1.26}$$

and leads to the following:

Lemma 1.7. Let $l(x)$ be the survivors of a cohort at exact age x. Then on the interval $[x, x+n)$ the average force of mortality at exact age x is

$$_n\bar{\mu}_x=(1-l(x+n)/l(x))/n. \tag{1.27}$$

Proof: From (1.26) factor out $l(x)$ from each term on the right and the result is immediate. □

Lemma 1.8. The average force of mortality at exact age x on the interval $[x, x+1)$ is just the probability that a life aged x will die in the next year. That is, for $n=1$,

$$\bar{\mu}_x=q_x. \tag{1.28}$$

Proof: Substitute $n=1$ in (1.27), and recalling from (1.7) that $l(x+1)/l(x)$ is p_x, the result is immediate. □

For example, using Table 1.5, the average force of mortality at age 75 is ${}_1\bar{\mu}_{75}=-(192-211)/211=0.090$, while ${}_1\bar{\mu}_{85}=0.208$ and ${}_1\bar{\mu}_{90}=0.364$. Figure 1.4 shows a graph of the average force of mortality at five year intervals, $n=5$, for the date in Table 1.5.

In 1766 Daniel Bernoulli developed the force of mortality as a continuous function of age, μ, by investigating the interval of age $[x, x+h)$ with $h \to 0$ [17].

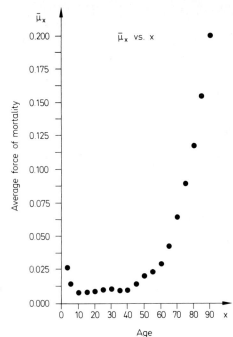

Fig. 1.4. Average force of mortality using the table of de Parcieux

Definition 1.9. The mortality index which expresses mortality at an annual rate at the precise moment of attaining age x is called the *force of mortality* at exact age x and is denoted $\mu(x)$.

Theorem 1.10 (Bernoulli). The force of mortality is the negative derivative of the natural logarithm of the survivorship function. That is,

$$\mu(x) = -[\ln(l(x))]' \qquad (1.29)$$

where $l(x) = l_0 p(x)$ is differentiable on $[0, \omega]$ because p is differentiable.

Proof: From (1.27) let $h = n$. Then on the interval $[x, x+h)$ the average force of mortality is

$$\bar{\mu}_x = (1 - l(x+h)/l(x))/h$$

which can be rewritten as

$$\bar{\mu}_x = -(1/l(x)) \frac{l(x+h) - l(x)}{h}.$$

In taking the limit as $h \to 0$, $\bar{\mu}_x \to \mu(x)$ from which

$$\mu(x) = \frac{-1}{l(x)} \frac{d}{dx}(l(x)). \qquad \Box \quad (1.30)$$

13

Unlike the expression for the probability of death, $_nq_x$, the force of mortality function, μ, may exceed unity, depending upon the definition of the function [18]. Indeed, it will now be shown that μ is an unbounded function when μ is defined according to Theorem 1.10.

Theorem 1.11. Let μ be the force of mortality function defined by (1.29). Then $\mu(x)$ is unbounded in any neighborhood $[a, \omega)$ for $0 \le a < \omega$.

Proof. Suppose the theorem is false, that is, $\mu(x)$ is bounded on the interval $[a, \omega)$. Then the integral of $\mu(x)$ over this interval must also be bounded.

$$\int_a^\omega \mu(x)dx = -\int_a^\omega \frac{d}{dx}[\ln(l(x))]dx = -\lim_{b \to \omega^-} \int_a^b \frac{d}{dx}[\ln(l(x))]dx$$

an improper integral since $l(\omega) = 0$. Therefore,

$$\int_a^\omega \mu(x)dx = \lim_{b \to \omega^-} [\ln(l(a)) - \ln(l(b))] = \infty$$

which is a contradiction. Hence, the theorem is true. $\qquad\qquad\square$

In Sect. 1.2 it was mentioned that Halley considered survivorship as an average value over an interval. This concept can be generalized with two interpretations. The first interpretation is as follows:

Definition 1.12. The number of *person-years* lived by the survivors of a cohort between exact ages x and $x + n$ is defined as

$$_nL_x = \int_x^{x+n} l(u)du \qquad\qquad (1.31)$$

where l is the survivorship function [19]. An alternate form of (1.31) is

$$_nL_x = \int_0^n l(x+u)du. \qquad\qquad (1.32)$$

For the special case where $n = 1$, the symbol $_1L_x$ is written simply as L_x, in which case

$$L_x = \int_0^1 l(x+u)du. \qquad\qquad (1.33)$$

This is now identical to Halley's meaning of survivorship as an average value of the $l(x)$ values on the unit interval.

The meaning of $_nL_x$ can have a second interpretation. Before this is investigated, however, the following is required.

Definition 1.13. Let a population be supported by l_0 annual births uniformly distributed over some time interval, say a calendar year. In addition, let the population have (a) no migration, (b) the same total size from each year to year, (c) the same age-specific birth rates each year, and (d) the same age-specific death rates each year. Such a population is called a *stationary population*.

In this respect, since each year the radix of the hypothetical population is the same and is subject to the same mortality, then every cohort must follow the given mortality or life table. Thus results in a second interpretation for the $_nL_x$ value as shown in the following:

Definition 1.14. Let $l(x)$ be the survivors of a cohort in a stationary population. Let the number of persons alive in the interval $[x, x+dx)$ be

$$l(x)dx.$$

Then the number of *persons alive* between the ages x and $x+n$ is defined as

$$_nL_x = \int_0^n l(x+u)\,du. \tag{1.34}$$

Clearly, $_nL_x$ represents the stationary population figure for $n-1$ completed years after age x at any point in time. This is the exact interpretation of Halley when $n=1$. In discrete form (1.34) becomes

$$_nL_x = \sum_{i=x}^{x+n} L_i. \tag{1.35}$$

For example, using Table 1.4,

$$_3L_6 = 692 + 680 + 670 = 2042 \text{ person-years}$$

When the survivorship function is discrete, the integral of (1.34) can be evaluated approximately using the trapezoidal rule from which

$$_nL_x = (l_x + l_{x+n})/2 + \sum_{i=x+1}^{x+n-1} l_i \tag{1.36}$$

where age is taken in annual increments.

The concepts generated from definitions 1.12 and 1.14 suggest the following definition [20].

Definition 1.15. Let $l(x)$ be the survivors of a cohort at exact age x. The *total person-years remaining* for the cohort who are now exact age x and number $l(x)$ is

$$T_x = \int_x^\omega l(u)\,du. \tag{1.37}$$

15

In other words, T_x describes the total future lifetime of the $l(x)$ lives which survive to age x. It is interesting to note the following:

Lemma 1.16. Given a stationary population where $l(x)$ represents the survivors of a cohort at exact age x. Then

$$\mathring{e}_x = T_x/l(x) \tag{1.38}$$

where $\mathring{e}_x$ is the complete expectation of life.

Proof: In (1.37) let $u = x + v$ which then transforms into

$$T_x = \int_0^{\omega - x} l(x+v)\, dv$$

Since $l(x+v) = 0$ for all $v \geq \omega - x$, it follows that:

$$\int_0^{\omega - x} l(x+v)\, dv = \int_0^{\infty} l(x+v)\, dv$$

and by (1.20) the lemma is demonstrated. $\square$

The total after lifetime function, T_x, is credited to Émmanauel Étienne Duvillard who, in 1806 presented it as the following [21]:

Lemma 1.17. The total person-years remaining for a cohort numbering $l(x)$ at exact age x is

$$T_x = \sum_{i=x}^{\omega - 1} L_i. \tag{1.39}$$

Proof: From (1.37)

$$T_x = \int_x^{\omega} l(u)\, du = \sum_{k=x}^{\omega - 1} \int_k^{k+1} l(u)\, du. \tag{1.40}$$

By letting $u = k + v$ in (1.54)

$$T_x = \sum_{k=x}^{\omega - 1} \int_0^1 l(k+v)\, dv$$

and using (1.33) the result is immediate. $\square$

Around the year 1800 the field of mathematical demography had focused on the development of life tables and their attendant extensions. Paramount in their development were the tables of Halley and de Parcieux. In addition, dynamic use of the survivorship function had taken place with the use of new

16

life table parameters such as life expectancy and the force of mortality. One must concede, however, that the motivation for these developments was mostly sociological rather than mathematical, with the concern over communicable diseases such as small-pox [17, 21] at the time.

1.4 The Life Table – Practical Considerations as a Population Model

In 1815 Joshua Milne proposed a method of generating a life table from the current data of a given population [22]. He gave little theoretical or empirical evidence for the formulations he derived. They are presented here primarily for historical purposes. Later in this section, conditions under which his formulations are exactly true are presented.

Milne's reasoning went as follows. Let l_x be the survivors of a cohort at exact age x, and let d_x be the number of deaths between ages x and $x+1$ at time t, where t is the time in the middle of a given calendar year. Let P_x be the number of observed individuals at time t, whose age lies on the interval $[x, x+1)$. Let D_x be the ratio of the observed number of deaths that occurred over the same calendar year to persons whose age lay on the interval $[x, x+1)$ at the time of death. Milne assumed that at age x, the arithmetic mean of the survivorship function to the deaths as obtained from a life table, is in the same ratio as the observed population to the observed deaths. That is,

$$\frac{P_x}{D_x} \doteq \frac{(l_x + l_{x+1})/2}{l_x - l_{x+1}} = \frac{l_x - 0.5 d_x}{d_x}. \tag{1.41}$$

Expansion and consolidation yields

$$l_x D_x \doteq P_x d_x + 0.5 d_x D_x$$

whereby

$$d_x \doteq \left[\frac{D_x}{P_x + 0.5 D_x}\right] l_x. \tag{1.42}$$

Statement (1.42) is known as Milne's formula. This formula will be justified later in this section and again in Sect. 2.2. This leads to the following [23]:

Definition 1.18. Let d_x and L_x be the usual life table values at age x. The *central death rate* at age x, denoted m_x, is the ratio

$$m_x = d_x / L_x. \tag{1.43}$$

Another meaning of m_x is the *age-specific death rate* at age x.

Lemma 1.19. Let $l(x)$ be the survivorship function at age x and let $\mu(x)$ be the force of mortality function at age x. Then

$$m_x = \frac{\int_0^1 l(x+u)\mu(x+u)\,du}{\int_0^1 l(x+u)\,du}. \tag{1.44}$$

Proof: By the definition of μ the number of deaths on the interval $[x, x+dx)$ is

$$l(x)\mu(x)\,dx.$$

Then on the interval $[x, x+1)$ the number of deaths is

$$d_x = \int_0^1 l(x+u)\mu(x+u)\,du.$$

Combining this with (1.33), the result of (1.44) is immediate. $\square$

A generalization of Definition 1.18 is

$$_nm_x = {_nd_x}/{_nL_x} \tag{1.45}$$

with obvious interpretation. The extension of this concept to observed information leads to the following:

Definition 1.20. Let $_nP_x$ be the number of observed individuals whose age falls on the interval $[x, x+n)$ in the middle of calendar year. Let $_nD_x$ be the number of observed deaths that occurred for that same calendar year to the individuals aged x to $x+n$ at the time of death. The *observed death rate* at age x, denoted $_nM_x$, is defined as

$$_nM_x = {_nD_x}/{_nP_x}. \tag{1.46}$$

The difference between (1.45) and (1.46) is that $_nM_x$ is the observed value while $_nm_x$ is the hypothetical life table value. Milne's assertion given by (1.42) assumes that when $n=1$ these two values are approximately equal. Clearly, $_nM_x$ is an age-specific death rate.

Milne's assertion can now be extended for any integer age x on the discrete interval $[0, \omega - n]$. Extending statement (1.41) gives

$$_nP_x/{_nD_x} \doteq [n(l_x + l_{x+n})/2]/(l_x - l_{x+n}). \tag{1.47}$$

Upon rewriting, this gives

$$_nP_x \, {_nd_x} \doteq nl_x \, {_nD_x} - (n/2){_nD_x} \, {_nd_x}$$

which yields

$$_nd_x \doteq \left[\frac{n \cdot {}_nD_x}{_nP_x + (n/2)_nD_x}\right] l_x.$$ (1.48)

Since $l_{x+n} = l_x - {}_nd_x$, substitution of (1.48) and expansion gives

$$l_{x+n} \doteq \left[\frac{2_nP_x + n_nD_x - 2n \cdot {}_nD_x}{2_nP_x + n_nD_x}\right] l_x.$$

Dividing by $_nP_x$ results in

$$l_{x+n} \doteq \left[\frac{2 - n_nM_x}{2 + n_nM_x}\right] l_x.$$ (1.49)

A special case of (1.49) occurs when $n = 1$ and leads to

$$l_{x+1} \doteq \left[\frac{2 - M_x}{2 + M_x}\right] l_x$$ (1.50)

where $M_x = {}_1M_x$.

The recursive form of (1.49) enables one to construct a life table solely from the observed values of population and deaths over the specified age interval. Thus, given a radix, l_0, the remaining values of l_x can be found, whereby $_nd_x$, $_nP_x$ and $_nq_x$ are quickly obtainable. Then by using a linear approximation for $_nL_x$, T_x and $\mathring{e}_x$ can be obtained. Table 1.6 shows the results of the calculation of the life table parameters based on observed age-specific values of $_nP_x$ and $_nD_x$ of Danish females for the year 1967 [24]. From these the value of $_nM_x$ is calculated. The quantity

$$\left[\frac{2 - n_nM_x}{2 + n_nM_x}\right]$$

is an approximation to the value $_nP_x$ from which the l_x values are calculated along with the $_nq_x$ and the $_nd_x$. The $_nL_x$ values are obtained by

$$_nL_x = n(l_x + l_{x+n})/2.$$ (1.51)

Letting $T_x = \sum_x {}_nL_i$ results in $\mathring{e}_x = T_x/l_x$.

Some of the previous results were based on the assumption that the survivorship function, l, was piecewise linear. In general this is not the case. Suppose the observed population distribution was represented by a continuous function, f, defined on the age interval $[x. x+n)$ at time t. If the population distribution at time t is $f(x, t)$, then between ages x and $x+dx$ at time t, the population is $f(x, t)dx$. Let the force of mortality be a function of age alone given as $\mu(x)$ at age x. Then the deaths between times t and $t+dt$, occurring to persons aged between x and $x+dx$ at time t, is $\mu(x)f(x, t)dx\,dt$. Therefore, the

19

Table 1.6. Life Table, Danish Females, 1967, calculated by author

Age x	Age interval $[x, x+n)$	Observed values $_nP_x$	$_nD_x$	$_nM_x$	Life table calculations* l_x	$_nd_x$	$_np_x$	$_nq_x$	$_nL_x$	T_x	e_x
0	[0, 1)	41 642	493	0.01184	100 000	1177	0.98823	0.01177	99 412	7 540 320	75.40
1	[1, 5)	159 930	102	0.00064	98 823	253	0.99744	0.00256	394 786	7 440 908	75.30
5	[5, 10)	180 365	71	0.00039	98 570	192	0.99805	0.00195	492 370	7 046 122	71.48
10	[10, 15)	180 908	48	0.00027	98 378	133	0.99865	0.00135	491 558	6 553 752	66.62
15	[15, 20)	188 736	72	0.00038	98 245	187	0.99810	0.00189	490 758	6 062 194	61.70
20	[20, 25)	203 913	71	0.00035	98 058	172	0.99825	0.00175	489 860	5 571 436	56.82
25	[25, 30)	156 365	70	0.00045	97 886	220	0.99775	0.00225	488 880	5 081 576	51.91
30	[30, 35)	141 936	103	0.00073	97 666	356	0.99636	0.00364	487 440	4 592 696	47.02
35	[35, 40)	141 216	199	0.00141	97 310	684	0.99297	0.00703	484 840	4 105 256	42.19
40	[40, 45)	150 789	362	0.00240	96 626	1153	0.98807	0.01928	480 248	3 620 416	37.47
45	[45, 50)	154 932	544	0.00351	95 473	1661	0.98260	0.01740	473 213	3 140 168	32.89
50	[50, 55)	148 112	725	0.00489	93 812	2266	0.97584	0.02415	463 395	2 666 955	28.43
55	[55, 60)	147 456	1104	0.00749	91 546	3366	0.96323	0.03676	449 315	2 203 560	24.07
60	[60, 65)	130 470	1589	0.01218	88 180	5211	0.94090	0.05910	427 873	1 754 245	19.89
65	[65, 70)	112 351	2243	0.01996	82 969	7887	0.90494	0.09506	395 128	1 326 372	15.99
70	[70, 75)	88 519	3140	0.03547	75 082	12 232	0.83709	0.16290	344 830	931 244	12.40
75	[75, 80)	60 066	3662	0.06097	62 850	16 626	0.73547	0.26453	272 685	586 414	9.33
80	[80, 85)	34 413	3708	0.10775	46 224	19 618	0.57558	0.42442	182 075	313 729	6.78
85+	[85, ω]	17 759	3589	0.20209	26 606	26 606	0.32870	0.67130	131 654	131 654	4.95

* Calculated by the author.

deaths bounded by ages x and $x+n$ and by times t and $t+1$ is

$$_nD_x = \int_t^{t+1} \int_x^{x+n} \mu(x) f(x, t) \, dx \, dt. \tag{1.52}$$

It is common to suppose that f is essentially constant with respect to time whereby (1.52) reduces to

$$_nD_x = \int_0^n f(x+u) \mu(x+u) \, du. \tag{1.53}$$

By similar reasoning, the number of individuals bounded by ages x and $x+n$ and by times t and $t+1$ is

$$_nP_x = \int_t^{t+1} \int_x^{x+n} f(x, t) \, dx \, dt$$

which reduces to

$$_nP_x = \int_0^n f(x+u) \, du. \tag{1.54}$$

This results in the following:

Theorem 1.21. Let f be a continuous population distribution function for a given population and let μ be the force of mortality function for the population. The *age-specific death rate* is given by

$$_nM_x = \frac{\int_0^n f(x+u)\mu(x+u)\,du}{\int_0^n f(x+u)\,du}. \tag{1.55}$$

Proof: By substituting (1.53) and (1.54) into (1.46), the result follows immediately. □

The result of Theorem 1.21 is considered the fundamental equation relating observed values to that of the table [25].

The population distribution function f may take many forms. For example, suppose $f(x)$ was proportional to $l(x)$; that is, for some constant c,

$$f(x+u) = c\,l(x+u). \tag{1.56}$$

From (1.29)

$$\mu(z)\,dz = (-1/l(z))\,d(l(z)). \tag{1.57}$$

Substituting (1.56) and (1.57) into (1.55) yields

$$_nM_x = \left[-\int_0^n d(l(x+u)) \right] \bigg/ \left[\int_0^n l(x+u)\,du \right]$$

which reduces to

$$_nM_x = {}_nd_x/{}_nL_x = {}_nm_x. \tag{1.58}$$

If in addition it is assumed that l is linear on the interval $[x, x+n)$ then $_nL_x = n(l_x + l_{x+n})/2$, and

$$l_{x+n} = [(2 - n\,{}_nM_x)/(2 + n\,{}_nM_x)]\,l_x \tag{1.59}$$

which is the same as Milne's generalized formula of (1.49). Of course, without the assumption of (1.56), the aforementioned results would not be so convenient. Table 1.7 shows the construction of a life table [26] for the same observed data of Table 1.6, where the survivorship function is approximated by a cubic polynomial rather than by a piecewise linear approximation, as was used for Table 1.6. A comparison of these tables shows a remarkable closeness in the life table parameters.

The construction of life tables has become more of an art than a science. Some noteworthy contributors are Reed and Merrell [27] and Greville [28]. Greville's work was later criticized by Fergany [29] who was then counter-criticized by Mitra [30]. More recent contributors include Mitra [31], McCann [32] and Schoen [33].

21

Table 1.7. Life Table, Danish Females, 1967, published results

Observed values $_nP_x$	$_nD_x$	$_nM_x$	Age x	Life table values $_nq_x$	l_x	$_nd_x$	$_nL_x$	$_nm_x$	$\cdot T_x$	$\mathring{e}_x$
41642	493	0.01184	0	0.01170	100000	1170	99141	0.01181	7541451	75.41
159930	102	0.00064	1	0.00254	98830	251	394595	0.00064	7442310	75.30
180365	71	0.00039	5	0.00196	98579	193	492410	0.00039	7047716	71.49
180908	48	0.00027	10	0.00133	98385	130	491599	0.00027	6555305	66.63
188736	72	0.00038	15	0.00191	98255	187	490815	0.00038	6063706	61.71
203913	71	0.00035	20	0.00174	98068	171	489918	0.00035	5572892	56.83
156356	70	0.00045	25	0.00225	97897	220	488972	0.00045	5082974	51.92
141936	103	0.00073	30	0.00363	97677	355	487593	0.00073	4594001	47.03
141216	199	0.00141	35	0.00702	97322	684	485067	0.00141	4106409	42.19
150789	362	0.00240	40	0.01194	96638	1154	480512	0.00240	3621342	37.47
154932	544	0.00351	45	0.01741	95485	1663	473500	0.00351	3140830	32.89
148112	725	0.00489	50	0.02420	93822	2270	463792	0.00489	2667330	28.43
147456	1104	0.00749	55	0.03683	91552	3372	449951	0.00749	2203538	24.07
130470	1589	0.01218	60	0.05955	88180	5251	428728	0.01225	1753588	19.89
112351	2243	0.01996	65	0.09598	82929	7959	396224	0.02009	1324860	15.98
88519	3140	0.03547	70	0.16462	74970	12341	345823	0.03569	928636	12.39
60066	3662	0.06097	75	0.26718	62628	16733	272855	0.06133	582813	9.31
34413	3708	0.10775	80	0.43045	45896	19756	182048	0.10852	309958	6.75
17759	3589	0.20209	85+	*1.00000	26140	26140	127910	0.20436	127910	4.89
2439869	21895									

The life table is considered to be the cornerstone of mathematical demography. It describes the mortality aspects of a population at a particular time. When the population is a stationary population, that is, it exhibits no growth or decay in the population age distribution, then the life table will remain fixed through the passage of time. The idealism of a stationary population may seem to detract from the importance of the life table. This is not the case. In fact, the life table provides demographers with an invaluable tool which can be continually updated by a periodic census, and thereby describes a mortality profile over a relatively short period of time. In this respect, the life table is an appropriate model of the mortality of a population. Figures 1.5 through 1.8 show illustrations of life table parameters based on the data of Table 1.7.

1.5 Early Models of Population Projections

At the end of the eighteenth century William Godwin, a respected English economist, promoted the philosophy that man was able to control his own destiny [34]. In particular, he argued that the increase of population growth did not threaten the happiness of mankind in that its pressures on society lie only in the future. Mathematically speaking, Godwin professed that the population growth of man was directly proportional to the needs of man.

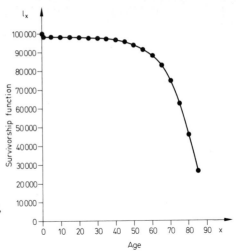

Fig. 1.5. Survivorship vs. age, Danish females, 1967

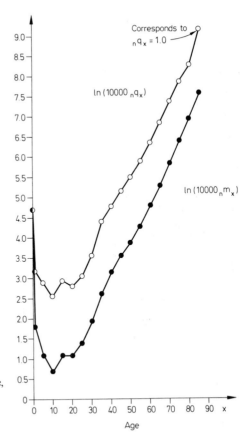

Fig. 1.6. Comparison of $_nq_x$ and $_nm_x$ vs. age, Danish females, 1967

23

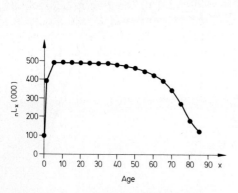

Fig. 1.7. a $_nL_x$ vs. age, Danish females, 1967.

b T_x vs. age, Danish females, 1967

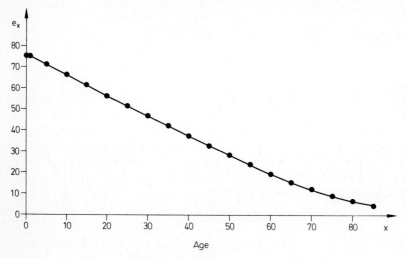

Fig. 1.8. Life expectancy, Danish females, 1967

Stimulated by Godwin's philosophy, Thomas Malthus published a work [35] in 1798 which hypothesized that:

i) food is necessary for existence with only a finite amount of land on which to grow it;

ii) the rate of human reproduction remained constant.

From this and other less explicit assumptions, Malthus deduced that the food supply of man would increase arithmetically while the growth of the population would increase geometrically. If the supportable population is the maximum population that can be supported by the existing food supply, then it would only be a matter of time until the population would reach a supportable level.

24

Mathematically, Malthus argued that if P is the population function as a function of time t, and S is the supportable population function as a function of time t, then P and S are increasing functions such that P has geometric (exponential) growth and S exhibits arithmetic (linear) growth. At some point in time, the population $P(t)$ will equal the supportable population $S(t)$, as is shown in the following.

Theorem 1.22. Let the population and supportable functions of time t be respectively defined as

$$P(t) = kc^t \qquad (1.60)$$

and

$$S(t) = at + b \qquad (1.61)$$

where k, c, a and b are constants such that to ensure growth

$$k > 0, \quad c > 1, \quad \text{and} \quad a > 0.$$

Then there exists some $t_1 > 0$ such that $P(t_1) = S(t_1)$ and for all $t > t_1$

$$P(t) > S(t). \qquad (1.62)$$

Proof: The time derivatives of P and S after letting $c = e^r$ are

$$\dot{P}(t) = rP = kre^{rt} \quad \text{and} \quad \dot{S}(t) = a$$

for all $t \geq 0$. Consider the case where initially the supportable population exceeds the population itself, but the rate of growth of the population is less than the supportable population. That is,

$$P(0) < S(0) \quad \text{and} \quad \dot{P}(0) < \dot{S}(0)$$

implying that a $t = 0$, see Figure 1.9,

$$k < b \quad \text{and} \quad rk < a$$

The population at time t

$$P(t) = kc^t = k \exp(rt)$$

is an increasing function with upward concavity. As such it will always lie above its tangent line. Since $P(0) < S(0)$, and $P(t)$ is increasing, then for sufficiently large t, say t',

$$a = \dot{S}(t') = \dot{P}(t') = rt' \exp(rt').$$

Then for all $t > t'$,

$$\dot{P}(t) = rk \exp(rt) > rk \exp(rt') = \dot{P}(t') = \dot{S}(t') = a \qquad (1.63)$$

25

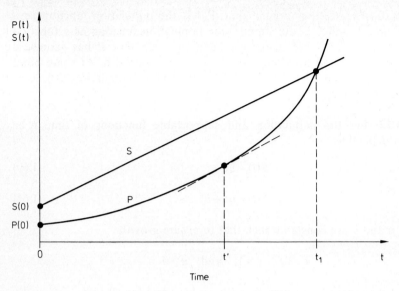

Fig. 1.9. Illustration of proof of Theorem 1.22

By the concavity of P and from (1.63), the curves of P and S will cross at some time $t_1 > t'$. Then for all $t > t_1$, $P(t) > S(t)$, which was to be demonstrated. $\square$

The significance of this theorem is that in reality, $P(t)$ cannot exceed the value of $S(t)$ for any time t by definition. Thus, at some point in time, $t = t_1$, some catastrophic event would have to occur to the population. In essence, Malthus claimed that for all $t > t_1$, man would no longer be able to control his destiny. This sparked a clash between Malthus and Godwin [36] which even today their theories have yet to be resolved. Malthus truly believed that for a constant birth rate, which is greater than the death rate, there is a continuous compounding of human population contributing to its growth.

The Godwin-Malthus feud persisted [37, 38] and centered on the claim that a population would grow exponentially unless checked by human intervention or resource limits. In 1838 Pierre-Francois Verhulst proposed that the rate of growth of a population is a linearly decreasing function of the population itself [3]. Symbolically,

$$dP/dt = mP - \phi(P). \tag{1.64}$$

For the case when $\phi(P) = nP$, the solution to (1.64) reduces to a simple exponential. A more general case leads to the following for $\phi(P) = nP^a$.

Theorem 1.23 (Verhulst). Let a population be described according to the differential equation

$$dP/dt = mP - nP^a. \tag{1.65}$$

26

Then the population satisfies the equation

$$[P(t)]^{a-1} = \frac{m \exp((a-1)mt)}{Cm + n \exp((a-1)mt)} \tag{1.66}$$

for arbitrary constant C.

Proof: Equation (1.65) is a Bernoulli equation of the form

$$P^{-a}\frac{dP}{dt} - mP^{1-a} = -n. \tag{1.67}$$

Upon substitution of $u = P^{1-a}$ into (1.67), the equation becomes

$$u' + (a-1)mu = (a-1)n$$

which is first order linear and solves as

$$u = \frac{n + Cm \exp(-(a-1)mt)}{m}.$$

Since $P^{a-1} = 1/u$, the result is immediate. □

The result of Verhulst's theorem is called the *generalized logistic* equation. For the case when $a = 2$, the differential equation becomes

$$dP/dt = mP - nP^2 \tag{1.68}$$

which has the solution

$$P(t) = \frac{A}{1 + B \exp(-mt)} \tag{1.69}$$

for $A = m/n$ and $B = CA$. Equation (1.68) is the *classical logistic* diffetential equation from population biology whose solution graphs into a curve known as a *sigmoid*. Figure 1.10 shows an example with properties derived from the following [40]:

Corollary 1.24. The logistic equation of (1.69) for $m, n > 0$ has properties of a lower asymptote of $P = 0$, an upper asymptote of $P = A$, and a single inflection point (t_1, P_1) where

$$t_1 = (\ln B)/m \quad \text{and} \quad P_1 = A/2. \tag{1.70}$$

Furthermore, P is positive and monotonically increasing for all t.

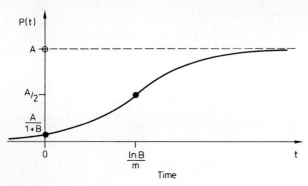

Fig. 1.10. Logistic curve

Proof: By taking limits as $t \to -\infty$ and as $t \to +\infty$, the two asymptotes are established. Ordinary differentiation shows that

$$P'(t) = \frac{mAB \exp(-mt)}{[1 + B \exp(-mt)]^2} \tag{1.71}$$

and

$$P''(t) = \frac{m^2 AB \exp(-mt)[B \exp(-mt) - 1]}{[1 + B \exp(-mt)]^3}.$$

From (1.71) it is clear that $\exp(mt_1) = B$, from which

$$t_1 = \ln B/m \quad \text{and} \quad P_1 = A/2.$$

To show that P is monotonic and increasing, consider (1.69) where the denominator and $\exp(-mt)$ are obviously positive. At $t = 0$, $P(0) = A/(1 + B)$, from which

$$B = (A - P(0))/P(0)$$

is always positive since $P(0) > 0$ and $A > 0$ is an upper bound for the function P. Hence, P is monotonically increasing for all t. The fact that P is strictly positive is obvious. □

The Logistic function satisfies the two biological assumptions concerning population growth. In its early stage of growth a population grows uninhibitedly as an exponential; in its later stage of growth, inhibiting factors cause it to grow at a decreasing rate to a saturation level determined by the "carrying capacity" of the environment [41, 42].

The population projection models of Malthus and Verhulst are global models in that they ignore the age structure of the population, as well as age-specific mortality and fertility and their possible change over age and time. These models have their proper place. But population projection can be viewed from a different perspective – one involving *age structure*, the number of individuals in each age interval at time t. Basically speaking, if the age structure of a population is known at time t, then at time $t+n$ much of the age structure of the population is also known as demonstrated by the following approximation.

Theorem 1.25. Given a life table at time t from which $_nL_x$ has its usual definition. If $_nF_t(x)$ represents the total number of people alive on the age interval $[x, x+n)$ at time t, then

$$_nF_{t+n}(x+n) \doteq \left[\frac{_nL_{x+n}}{_nL_x}\right] {_nF_t(x)}. \tag{1.72}$$

Proof: Let the observed population distribution be represented at time t by a continuous function, f, of age x. Let y be an element of the age interval $[x, x+n)$. Then at time t the number of individuals alive between ages y and $y+dy$ is $f(y)dy$, and on the interval $[x, x+n)$ the number of individuals alive is

$$_nF_t(x) = \int_x^{x+n} f(y)dy. \tag{1.73}$$

At time $t+n$ the surviving individuals have aged n years and find themselves on the age interval $[x+n, x+2n)$ of another population distribution function, g, of age x which total in number

$$_nF_{t+n}(x+n) = \int_x^{x+n} g(y+n)dy \tag{1.74}$$

as shown in Fig. 1.11. If the given life table is maintained at time $t+n$, then the population at time t and $t+n$ is subject to the same mortality and

$$g(y+n)dy = {_np_y} f(y)dy \tag{1.75}$$

where $_np_y$ is the life table parameter defined as $_np_y = l(y+n)/l(y)$ for survivorship function l. But in the life table $l(y)$, is known only for $y=x$, $y=x+n$, $y=x+2n$, etc. If $l^*(x)$ represents the average value of the survivorship function on the interval $[x, x+n)$, then by the mean value theorem

$$l^*(x) = (1/n) \int_x^{x+n} l(y)dy$$

and by definition

$$l^*(x) = (1/n) {_nL_x}. \tag{1.76}$$

An approximation to $_np_y$ is $l^*(x+n)/l^*(x)$, defined as $_np_x^*$, which when substituted into equation (1.75) for $y \in [x, x+n)$ becomes

$$g(y+n)dy \doteq {_np_x^*} f(y)dy$$

29

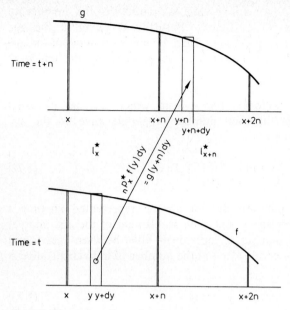

Fig. 1.11. Illustration of proof of Theorem 1.25

showing the average transport of survivors from time t to time $t+n$. Upon integrating with respect to y and recalling equations (1.73) and (1.74), this expression becomes

$$_nF_{t+n}(x+n) \doteq {}_np_x^* {}_nF_t(x).$$

But from (1.76) and the definition of $_np_x^*$, one obtains

$$_np_x^* = {}_nL_{x+n}/{}_nL_x$$

from which the theorem is proved. $\qquad\qquad\qquad\qquad\qquad\qquad\square$

The result of Theorem 1.25 justifies the long-standing practice used by demographers to formulate projections over small time intervals for a given life table. Consult Keyfitz and Flieger [43] for a concrete example of this practice. An extension of Theorem 1.25 is now shown.

Corollary 1.26. Given a life table at time t from which $_nL_x$ has its usual definition. If the life table applies at time $t+kn$, for k a non-negative integer, then

$$_nF_{t+kn}(x+kn) = \left[\frac{_nL_{x+kn}}{_nL_x}\right]{}_nF_t(x). \qquad (1.77)$$

30

Proof: By successive application of (1.72) where for $i = 1, 2, \ldots, k$

$$_nF_{t+in}(x+in) = \left[\frac{_nL_{x+in}}{_nL_{x+(i-1)n}}\right] {_nF_{t+(i-1)n}(x+(i-1)n)}$$

the individuals at time $t + kn$ number

$$_nF_{t+kn}(x+kn) = \left[\frac{_nL_{x+kn}}{_nL_{x+(k-1)n}}\right]\left[\frac{_nL_{x+(k-1)n}}{_nL_{x+(k-2)n}}\right] \cdots \left[\frac{_nL_{x+2n}}{_nL_{x+n}}\right]\left[\frac{_nL_{x+n}}{_nL_x}\right] {_nF_t(x)}$$

which gives the required result. $\qquad\square$

1.6 Mortality and Survival Revisited

The ability to avoid the ultimate destruction of death has always been a philosophical paradox of mankind. From a mathematical standpoint, the function which describes man's ability to survive is l, the survivorship function. The simplest and perhaps the earliest function describing l was proposed in 1725 by Abraham de Moivre [44], who conjectured that for age x,

$$l(x) = c(\omega - x) \tag{1.78}$$

where ω is the ultimate age of life. In reality the survivorship function is more complicated than a decreasing linear function, as shown in Fig. 1.1 and Fig. 1.5.

In the nineteenth century, however, the Godwin-Malthus feud generated much interest in man's survivability. In 1825 Benjamin Gompertz [45] proposed that

the average exhaustion of a man's power to avoid death to be such that at the end of equal infinitely small intervals of time, he lost equal portions of his remaining power to oppose destruction which he had at the commencement of these intervals.

In essence, it is Gompertz's assumption that if the force of mortality, $\mu(x)$, is a measure of man's susceptibility to death, then the measure of man's resistance to death is just $1/\mu(x)$, and that man's power to resist death decreases at a rate proportional to itself. This leads to the following assertion known as *Gompertz's Law of Mortality*.

Lemma 1.27 (Gompertz). Let μ be the force of mortality function such that

$$\frac{d}{dx}\left[\frac{1}{\mu(x)}\right] = -k\left[\frac{1}{\mu(x)}\right] \tag{1.79}$$

for constant k. Then for $0 < x < \omega$,

$$\mu(x) = ac^x \tag{1.80}$$

for constants a and c.

Proof: Separating variables in (1.79) and integrating leads to

$$\ln(1/\mu(x)) = -kx - \ln a$$

for arbitrary constant $-\ln a$. Then

$$a/\mu(x) = e^{-kx}.$$

By letting $c = e^k$ the result is immediate. $\qquad\square$

A typical force of mortality curve is shown in Fig. 1.12. Notice that Gompertz's result is not applicable for very young ages. However, it did provide a means to determine the survivorship function as is now shown.

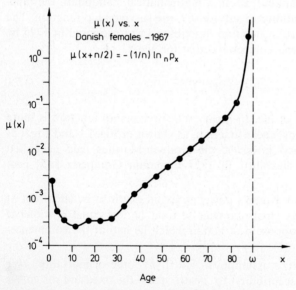

Fig. 1.12. Force of mortality vs. age, Danish females, 1967

Theorem 1.28 (Gompertz). Let the force of mortality be defined as $\mu(x) = ac^x$ for constants a and c. Then there exist constants h and b such that

$$l(x) = hb^{c^x} \tag{1.81}$$

where l is the survivorship function.

32

Proof. By representing $\mu(x)$ from (1.80), and recalling the definition of μ from (1.29) with $k = \ln c$, then

$$\frac{d}{dx}[\ln(l(x))] = -ae^{kx}$$

and for arbitrary constant $\ln(h)$

$$\ln(l(x)) = -(a/k)e^{kx} + \ln(h)$$

from which

$$l(x) = h\exp(-(a/k)e^{kx}).$$

Letting $b = e^{-a/k}$, and since $e^k = c$, the theorem is demonstrated. $\qquad\square$

In relation to this theorem Gompertz stated,

It is possible that death may be the consequence of two generally coexisting causes: the one, chance, without previous disposition to death or deterioration; the other, a deterioration, or an increased inability to withstand destruction.

Gompertz's Law considers only the second cause.

In 1860, W.K. Makeham [46] attempted to accommodate Gompertz's first cause of death, chance, by modifying Gompertz's representation for the force of mortality function. This was done by adding a positive constant to the force of mortality of (1.80), and leads to the following:

Theorem 1.29 (Makeham). Let the force of mortality be represented as

$$\mu(x) = ac^x + G \qquad (1.82)$$

where $G > 0$ is a constant. Then the survivorship function for $0 < x < \omega$, is

$$l(x) = hb^{c^x}g^x \qquad (1.83)$$

for constants h, b, c and g.

Proof: As in Theorem 1.28,

$$\frac{d}{dx}\ln(l(x)) = -ac^x - G.$$

Integrating with arbitrary constant $\ln(h)$ and $c = e^k$ yields

$$l(x) = h\exp(-(a/k)e^{kx} - Gx).$$

After letting $b = e^{-a/k}$ and $G = -\ln(g)$, the result asserted by Theorem 1.29 is obtained. $\qquad\square$

33

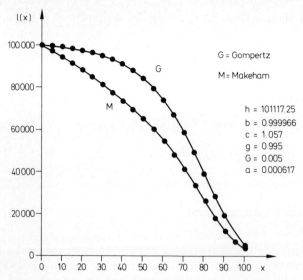

Fig. 1.13. Survivorship vs. age, comparison of Gompertz's Law and Makeham's Law

Theorem 1.29 is known as *Makeham's Law* and results in an improvement over Gompertz's Law. Figure 1.13 shows a typical graph for the $l(x)$ function for each of these laws. Both laws have prominence even today as they are used in the fields of insurance and biology.

1.7 Conclusion

As the nineteenth century came to a close, the status of mathematical demography consisted of work in two basic areas:

    i) construction and refinements of the life table;

    ii) population projection.

One preoccupation of demographers was the development of actuarial calculations, such as life insurance premiums and annuities, based on the life table. Another was the realization that a population may reach its supportable limit. In all cases mathematical demography was concerned primarily with the macro-analysis of population both in structure and in growth.

Mathematical demography, however, was still in its infancy. The life table, as important as it may be, ignored fertility and all its implications. The life table is a model of mortality, nothing more. But fertility is of greater importance to a population, for without it the population must become extinct. Mathematical demography must consider the dynamic interrelation of fertility and mortality, as well as other aspects that affect a population. The quest of finding a suitable model to portray a population has led to the stable theory of population, which is the salient subject of this work.

34

1.8 Notes for Chapter One

[1] Spiegelman, M. (1968), Introduction to demography. p. 1ff.

[2] Acsadi and Nemeskeri (1970), History of human life span and mortality. Cited from the Royal Statistical Society, News and Notes, Rosamund Weatherall, Editor, June, 1982, London, vol. 8, no. 10, p. 7.

[3] Ibid.

[4] Trenerry, C.F. (1926), The origin and early history of insurance. pp. 151–152. Taken from Digest, vol. 35, no. 2, p. 68.

[5] Translated from the Latin by the author.

[6] Smith, D. and Keyfitz, N. (1977), Mathematical demography-selected papers. p. 1.

[7] Graunt, J. (1662), Natural and political observations mentioned in a following index and made upon the bills of mortality. Republished in the Journal of the Institute of Actuaries, vol. 90, pp. 44–47, 1964.

[8] Wunsch, G. and Tremote, M. (1978, Introduction to demographic analysis – Principles and methods. p. 7.

[9] DeWit, J. (1671), Waardye von Lyf-renten naer proportie van Losrenten. English translation in Hendriks (1852), Contributions to the History of Insurance, with a Restoration of the Grand Pensionary DeWit's treatise on Life Annuities, vol. 2, p. 232ff.

[10] Pollard, J.H. (1973), Mathematical models for the growth of human populations. p. 3.

[11] DeMoivre, A. (1738), The doctrine of chances. Third Ed., p. 347.

[12] Westergaard, H. (1932), Contributions to the history of statistics. p. 34. Cited in Smith and Keyfitz, op. cit.

[13] Jordan, C.W. (1967), Society of Actuaries' textbook on life contingencies. Second Ed., p. 9.

[14] DeMoivre (1738), op. cit., p. 346.

[15] de Parcieux, A. (1746), Essai sur les probabilités de la Durée de la vie humaine. Cited in Smith and Keyfitz, op. cit., p. 2.

[16] Pollard (1973), op. cit., p. 10.

[17] Bernoulli, D. (1766), Essai d'une nouvelle analyse de la mortalité causée par la petite vérole et les avantages de l'inoculation pour la prévenir. Histoire de l'Académie Royale des Sciences. pp. 1–45. Cited in Smith and Keyfitz, op. cit., p. 2.

[18] Jordan (1967), op. cit., p. 16.

[19] Wunsch, G. and Termote, M. (1978), op. cit., p. 94.

[20] Jordan (1967). op. cit., p. 170.

[21] Duvillard, É.É. (1806), Analyse et tableaux de l'influence de la petite vérole sur la mortalité a chaque age. Cited in Smith and Keyfitz, op. cit., p. 2.

[22] Milne, J. (1815), A treatise on the valuation of annuities and assurances on lives and survivorships. Art. no. 177.

[23] Jordan (1967), op. cit., p. 172.

[24] Keyfitz, N. and Flieger, W. (1971), Population – facts and methods of demography. p. 426.

[25] Ibid., p. 134.

[26] Ibid., p. 426.

[27] Reed, L.J. and Merrell, M. (1939), A short method for constructing a abridged life table. American Journal of Hygiene, vol. 30, pp. 33–38.

[28] Greville, T.N.E. (1943), Short methods of constructing abridges life tables. Record of the American Institute of Actuaries, vol. 32, pp. 34–40.

[29] Fergany, N. (1971), On the human survivorship function and life table construction. Demography, vol. 8, no. 3, pp. 331–334.

[30] Mitra, S. (1972), Comment on N. Fergany's On the human survivorship function and life table construction. Demography, vol. 9, no. 3, p. 515.

[31] Mitra, S. (1973), On the efficiency of the estimates of life table functions. Demography, vol. 10, no. 3, pp. 421–426.

[32] McCann, J.C. (1976), A technique for estimating life expectancy with crude vital rates. Demography, vol. 13, no. 2, pp. 259–272.

[33] Schoen, R. (1978), Calculating life tables by estimating Chiang's *a* from observed rates. Demography, vol. 15, no. 4, pp. 625–635.

[34] Godwin, W. (1793), Enquiry concerning political justice and its influence on morals and happiness.

[35] Malthus, T.R. (1798), An essay in the principles of population as it affects the future improvement of society with remarks on the speculations of Mr. Godwin.

[36] Godwin, W. (1820), Of population: An enquiry concerning the power of increase in the numbers of Mankind, being an answer to Mr. Malthus's essay on that subject.

[37] Spengler, J.J. (1971), Malthus on Godwin's "Of population". Demography, vol. 8, no. 1, pp. 1–12.

[38] Petersen, W. (1971), The Malthus-Godwin debate, then and now. Demography, vol. 8, no. 1, pp. 13–26.

[39] Verhulst, P.F. (1838), Notice sur la loi que la population suit dans son accroissement. Correspondance Mathématique et Physique Publiée par A. Quetelet, vol. 10, pp. 113–117.

[40] Davis, H.T. (1962), Introduction to nonlinear differential and integral equations. p. 97.

[41] Pielou, E.C. (1969), An introduction to mathematical ecology. p. 19.

[42] May, R.M. (1978 (1975)), Mathematical aspects of the dynamics of animal populations. Studies in Mathematical Biology — Populations and Communities, Part II, edited by S.A. Levin, p. 317ff.

[43] Keyfitz, N. and Flieger, W., op. cit., p. 131.

[44] DeMoivre, A. (1725), Annuities on lives: Or, the valuation of annuities upon any number of lives. p. 4.

[45] Gompertz, B. (1825), On the nature of the function expressive of the law of mortality. Philosophical Transactions, vol. 27, pp. 513–519.

[46] Makeham, W.M. (1860), On the law of mortality and the construction of annuity tables. Assurance Magazine, vol. 8, pp. 301–310.

2. An Overview of the Stable Theory of Population

2.1 Introduction

At the turn of the twentieth century the life table was the dominant model that was used to represent a population. This model, however, was and still is only a picture of mortality of a given population at a given time. The life table does not take into account fertility, and as a result, is not an effective tool that can be used to thoroughly analyze and project a population. The mathematical attempts that had been made to project populations, such as the exponential and logistic curves, represented simple models based on conjectures concerning the behavior of a population.

Demographic analysis requires sound working models. One may concede the fact that a perfect mathematical model which will exactly portray a given population cannot be constructed. The model one constructs, however, must be founded on fundamental premises that can be attributed to a population, not just on conjecture. The effective use of such a model is possible only if the model used accurately reflects the population and if the conditions under which the model is formed are maintained. Furthermore, the valid use of a model is governed by the time domain on which it is constructed. This is particularly true if the model is used in forming predictions.

The Malthusian theory of population which maintains the assumption that the time rate of change of a population is proportional to the population itself, is an oversimplification. Populations, in particular human populations, do not necessarily compound continuously as in the case of monetary growth or radioactive decay. To say that a population described by the time function P is

$$P(t) = P_0 \exp(r(t - t_0)) \tag{2.1}$$

requires very strong justification. Indeed there exists no realistic accounting of births and deaths of a population in such a model.

The growth or decay of a population is the net result of births and deaths. For example, in the Malthusian model, if births and deaths changed in such a manner that the difference between the birth rate and the death rate was a constant, there would be no change in the value of r in (2.1), and the expression for $P(t)$ would stay the same. Experience shows, however, that if such a change would occur, the age distribution of the population would be different [1]. Such a phenomenon is not predicted by this equation. Furthermore,

38

experience shows that the rates of births and deaths do vary with age and perhaps even with time. Needless to say, none of these concepts are reflected in the Malthusian model.

It suffices to say that populations can not be viewed merely as a whole. Further investigation is required to determine how each of its parts, age categories, affects the whole. A good mathematical model must reflect these and other important components which give rise to population analysis and projection.

2.2 Duration of Events Compared to Time

The consideration of the concept of time is usually viewed in the following two ways: location of events according to the calendar period during which they occur, or, the measure of elapsed duration since the origin of an event first occurred. For example, the former consideration was used in determining the size of a population at a particular time t, as was illustrated by the logistic equation; the latter consideration was used in determining the number of deaths between ages x and $x+n$ in the life table. If these two considerations of time are combined, then demographic events can be located in time in two different ways: by their calendar period and by their elapsed duration.

In 1875 the noted demographer Wilhelm Lexis proposed a two-dimensional diagram which would illustrate events in the two measures of time [2], which is now called the *Lexis diagram* or the *Lexis grid*. If the event is the birth of a cohort, for example, the calendar periods are referenced along the abscissa while age is referenced along the ordinate. Suppose the birth cohort consists of all individuals born between relative time $t=t_0-n$ and $t=t_0$, that is, one the time interval $(t_0-n, t_0]$ where the age is exactly zero, as shown in Fig. 2.1. Each newborn is represented by a ray of unit inclination called a *lifeline* which relates age as a function of time. In the absence of mortality the ray would extend indefinitely. Since mortality exists, each lifeline terminates when the individual dies, and by age ω, all lifelines will have terminated.

Consider Fig. 2.2 with lifelines L_i. Rectangle ABCD represents all occurrences of life or death that happen on the time calendar interval $(t, t+n]$, and where the age falls between ages x and $x+n$. Lifelines L_1, L_2, L_3 and L_4 are related to this rectangle. For this dual time consideration, lifelines L_1 and L_4 are survivors while lifelines L_2 and L_3 are deceased. However, the four lifelines do not come from the same cohort. An individual whose exact age is x at exact time t, was born exactly $t-x$ years ago. In this respect, lifelines L_3 and L_4 are members of the birth cohort born on the interval $(t-x, t-x+n]$, while L_1 and L_2 are members of the birth cohort born on the interval $(t-x-n, t-x]$. Lifelines L_1 and L_2 both died on the time interval $(t, t+n]$ but on different age intervals. Lifelines L_3 and L_4 died on the same age interval $[x, x+n)$ but on different time intervals. Lifeline L_5 belongs to the same birth cohort as L_3 and L_4, and died on the time interval $(t, t+n]$ and age interval $[x-n, x)$.

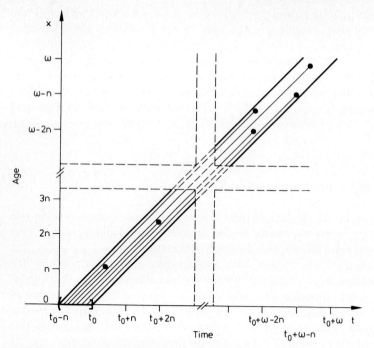

Fig. 2.1. Age vs. time, Lexis grid for a single cohort

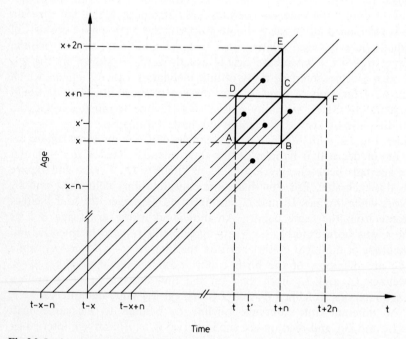

Fig. 2.2. Lexis grid showing life table equivalencies

40

When viewed from the standpoint of mortality, the Lexis grid can provide a geometric interpretation of the life table. Consider once more Fig. 2.2 where time t' means any time on the interval $(t, t+n]$ and where age x' means any age on the interval $[x, x+n)$. Then rectangle ABCD represents all individuals of age x' who died at time t'. The congruent triangles ABC and ACD making up this rectangle indicate that the deaths come from two different cohorts.

Parallelogram ACED represents all individuals of the same cohort who died at time t'; congruent triangles ACD and CED making up this parallelogram represent the deaths that occur at ages x' and $x'+n$ respectively. Parallelogram ABFC represents all individuals of the same cohort who died at age x'; congruent triangles ABC and BFC making up this parallelogram represent the deaths that occur at times t' and $t'+n$ respectively. Assume that for any cohort, the births are distributed uniformly over time, and the deaths are distributed uniformly over age and time, that is, between t and $t+2n$ and between x and $x+2n$. Consider the cohort born in the interval $(t-x, t-x+n]$. The survivors of the cohort at exact age x, l_x, are lifelines that cross line segment AB; then l_{x+n} is represented by the lifelines crossing line segment CF. At time $t+n$, the survivors of the cohort between ages x and $x+n$, P_x, are the lifelines crossing line segment BC. Because deaths are distributed uniformly, regions having the same geometric area represent an equal number of deaths. In particular, if D_x is the number of deaths in rectangle ABCD, and since the area of rectangle ABCD equals the area of parallelogram ABFC, then D_x and $_nd_x = l_x - l_{x+n}$ are the same. Furthermore, since triangles ABC and BFC are congruent with common segment BC representing P_x, then $P_x = (l_x + l_{x+n})/2$. This leads to the following:

Lemma 2.1. Let P_x, D_x, l_x and $_nd_x$ be defined as presented. Then

$$P_x/D_x = (l_x - 0.5\,_nd_x)/_nd_x. \tag{2.2}$$

Proof: By definition of $_nd_x$, $l_{x+n} = l_x - _nd_x$. Since $_nd_x$ and D_x are the same, the result follows by simple substitution. $\square$

The reader should recognize this result as a version of Milne's formula of statement (1.41).

While the Lexis diagram does not provide the tool to construct a life table, it does give a good geometric illustration of the age-time relationship concerning births and deaths. Although the focus of this discussion has been mortality, the Lexis diagram can be applied to other areas of demography such as fertility, morbidity and nuptuality. Indeed, it has even been extended to multiple dimensions to take into account multiple cohorts [3].

2.3 Population Pyramids and Age-Specific Considerations

In the year 1967 the population of Denmark numbered 4,838,772, of which 2,398,903 were male and 2,439,869 were female. While this information may be important, it provides no information on the age structure of the Danish people for that year. If, however, the population was presented not only according to male and female, but also by age category in intervals of 5 years, for example, then there would be a new dimension of interpretation for this population. Table 2.1 [4] shows such an age structure. Let i be a non-negative integer that indexes each age category to which is assigned the age interval $[ih, (i+1)h)$, where $h = 5$, and let P_i be the population size for each age category with M_i and F_i the respective male and female population size. The table shows eighteen strata belonging to this particular population. Demographers display population strata such as this one as a *population pyramid*, as shown in Fig. 2.3. Population pyramids need not be stratified in five-year intervals which is used for convenience only. Actual information on demographic studies may be given in one-year intervals, such as information on a person's age. Indeed, the strata may even be viewed as a limiting case on the age interval $[x, x + \Delta x)$, forming an age continuum. Figures 2.4a and 2.4b show population pyramids displayed in this manner. For further interesting observations, consult Pick [5].

Table 2.1. Population Age Structure, Denmark, 1967

Age Category	Age Index	Age Interval	Population				
			Total	Males		Females	
$x-x+4$	i	$[ih, (i+1)h]$	P_i	M_i	%	F_i	%
0– 4	0	[0, 5)	403776	212204	8.8	201572	8.3
5– 9	1	[5, 10)	368785	188420	7.9	180365	7.4
10–14	2	[10, 15)	371062	190154	7.9	180908	7.4
15–19	3	[15, 20)	386434	197698	8.2	188736	7.7
20–24	4	[20, 25)	418746	214833	9.0	203913	8.4
25–29	5	[25, 30)	318006	161650	6.7	156356	6.4
30–34	6	[30, 35)	284363	142427	5.9	141936	5.8
35–39	7	[35, 40)	280727	139511	5.8	141216	5.8
40–44	8	[40, 45)	297736	146947	6.1	150789	6.2
45–49	9	[45, 50)	306154	151222	6.3	154932	6.4
50–54	10	[50, 55)	291378	143266	6.0	148112	6.1
55–59	11	[55, 60)	288183	140727	5.9	147456	6.0
60–64	12	[60, 65)	248759	118289	4.9	130470	5.3
65–69	13	[65, 70)	207575	95224	4.0	112351	4.6
70–74	14	[70, 75)	159458	70939	3.0	88519	3.6
75–79	15	[75, 80)	106604	46538	1.9	60066	2.5
80–84	16	[80, 85)	60349	25936	1.1	34413	1.4
85+	17	[85, ω]	30677	12918	0.5	17759	0.7
			4838772	2398903		2439869	

When doing any analysis in the demographic field of population, it is customary to consider only the female segment of the population [6]. There is sound reason for this. During the course of one year, a woman can be responsible for at most two birth cycles, while a man may be responsible for several

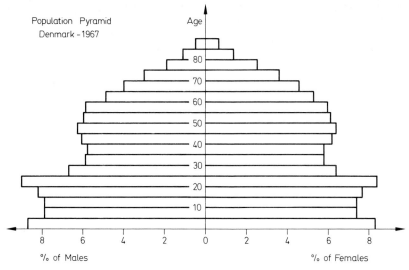

Fig. 2.3. Population pyramid, Denmark, 1967, five-year intervals

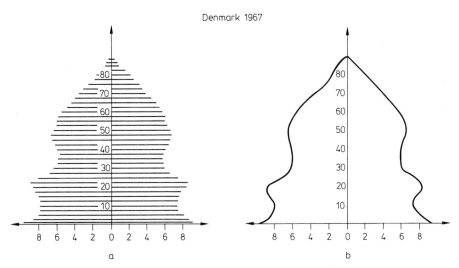

Fig. 2.4. a Population pyramid, Denmark, 1967, small age intervals. **b** Population pyramid, Denmark, 1967, continuous age distribution

hundred. Furthermore, the childbearing years for a woman range approximately from 15 to 50 years of age, while that of a man may range approximately from 15 to 80 years of age. In addition, registration of births more often includes the age of the mother than that of the father, especially in the case of illegitimate births. For these and other considerations, the demographic study is confined to the one-sex female model, as will be adopted in this work. This does not preclude that the male model is inappropriate. It is just that the demographic data on females is more complete when the study includes births. In this regard, unless otherwise noted, the word "population" implies female population, and population pyramids will include only their right portion.

The right segment of a population describes a discrete function of age at a particular time. For example, consider the right segment of the population pyramid of Fig. 2.3. The lowest stratum indexed by $i=0$ forms a birth cohort of the female population of Denmark for ages ranging 0 through 4 in the reference year $t_0 = 1967$. The cohort indexed by $i=2$ was born 10 to 15 years before 1967, and in 1977 this same cohort will be indexed by $i=4$. Thus, both the ancestry and posterity of a cohort can be investigated.

Consider a population at two time periods, t and $t+h$. The birth cohort at time t with age index i after aging h years will find itself in the age stratum indexed by $i+1$ at time $t+h$. Let $F_i(t)$ represent the size of a cohort with age index i at time t. At time $t+h$ this same cohort will number $F_{i+1}(t+h)$. But not all the $F_i(t)$ may survive to time $t+h$, implying that

$$F_{i+1}(t+h) \le F_i(t). \tag{2.3}$$

This leads to the following:

Definition 2.2. Let a female cohort number $F_i(t)$ at time t and $F_{i+1}(t+h)$ at time $t+h$. Let w be the index of the last age stratum. Then for $0 \le i \le w$ the *survivorship ratio* is

$$g_{i+1} = F_{i+1}(t+h)/F_i(t). \tag{2.4}$$

Clearly, $0 \le g_{i+1} \le 1$ is a function of both age and time. The value of g_{i+1} may be computed by taking a census at two different time periods. Note that the value of g_{w+1} must be zero since all members of the cohort have died. Figure 2.5 illustrates how a cohort moves between strata.

The $F_i(t)$ members of a cohort alive at time t are the survivors of the $F_{i-1}(t-h)$ members of the same cohort who were alive at time $t-h$. From (2.4) for $1 \le i \le w+1$

$$F_i(t) = g_i F_{i-1}(t-h). \tag{2.5}$$

The progress of a cohort as its size changes from $F_{i-1}(t-h)$ to $F_{i+1}(t+h)$ can now be followed as shown in Fig. 2.6. Successive application of (2.5) yields

$$F_{i+1}(t+h) = g_{i+1} g_i F_{i-1}(t-h). \tag{2.6}$$

This results in the following:

Lemma 2.3. Let $F_i(t)$ be the size of a cohort indexed by i at time t, and g_i the corresponding survivorship ratio. Then

$$F_k(t) = \left(\prod_{j=1}^{k} g_j \right) F_0(t - kh) \tag{2.7}$$

for $1 \le k \le w+1$.

44

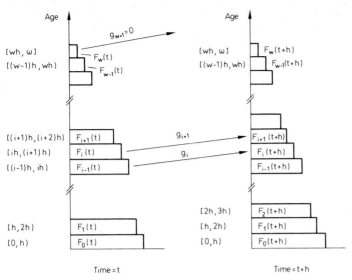

Fig. 2.5. Cohort mobility between two contiguous time periods

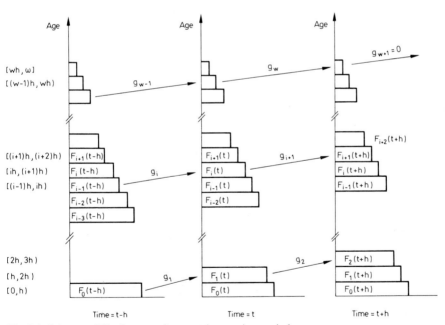

Fig. 2.6. Cohort mobility between three contiguous time periods

Proof: The result follows immediately from successive application of expression (2.6) for $0 \leq i \leq w$. □

Thus, a cohort of age index k at time t is related to its size at birth at time $t - kh$ by expression (2.7). For example, with respect to Table 2.1, the cohort in

45

the 40–44 age category having age index 8 on age interval $[40, 45)$ is composed of the survivors born $kh = 40$ years ago on the time interval $(1922, 1927]$ according to survivorship values g_1 through g_8. A generalization of Lemma 2.3 follows.

Theorem 2.4. Let $F_i(t)$ be the size of a cohort indexed by i at time t, and g_i the corresponding survivorship ratio. Then for $0 \le i < w$

$$F_{i+k}(t + kh) = \left[\prod_{j=i+1}^{i+k} g_j \right] F_i(t) \tag{2.8}$$

where $1 \le k \le w - i + 1$.

Proof: From (2.5) successive applications yield

$$F_{i+k}(t + kh) = g_{i+k} F_{i+k-1}(t + (k-1)h)$$
$$= g_{i+k} g_{i+k-1} F_{i+k-2}(t + (k-2)h)$$
$$= g_{i+k} g_{i+k-1} g_{i+k-2} \cdots g_{i+2} g_{i+1} F_i(t)$$

from which the result follows. $\qquad\qquad\qquad\qquad\qquad\qquad\qquad\qquad\square$

For example, for the data in Table 2.1, one can determine the size of the 50–54 age cohort in 1987 from 30–34 age cohort in 1967; in this case, $t = 1967$, $t + kh = 1987$, $kh = 20$, $h = 5$, $k = 4$, and $i = 6$, so

$$F_{10}(1987) = g_{10} g_9 g_8 g_7 F_6(1967)$$

It is assumed, of course, that the values of g are the same for the time period 1967 to 1987.

In order for any population to avoid extinction, the population must exhibit a reproductive or maternity factor. It is believed that human populations do possess such a factor. Indeed, the age interval $[0, h)$ at exact time t, is composed of those females born in the time interval $(t - h, t]$ and who actually survive to time t. This leads to the following:

Definition 2.5. Let $B_h(t)$ be the number of female births on the time interval $(t - h, t]$ and let $F_0(t)$ be the number of females on the age interval $[0, h)$ at exact time t. Then the probability of surviving birth to the age category indexed by 0 at time t is

$$g_0 = F_0(t) / B_h(t). \tag{2.9}$$

Figure 2.7 illustrates the justification for this definition. However, the total births occurring in the time interval $(t - h, t]$ result from many sources. Specifically, each stratum in the population at time $t - h$ makes a non-negative contribution to the births $B_h(t)$. This leads to the following:

Definition 2.6. Let $B_{h,i}(t)$ be the number of female births in the time interval $(t - h, t]$ produced by those females in the age category indexed by i at time $t - h$.

46

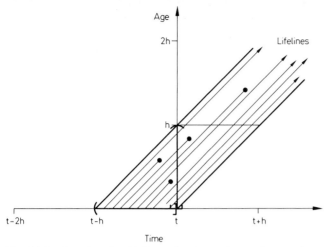

Age

2h —

Lifelines

h

t−2h   t−h   t   t+h

Time

Fig. 2.7. Portion of Lexis grid illustrating that g_0 is not always unity

Then

$$m_i = B_{h,i}(t)/F_i(t-h)h \qquad (2.10)$$

is the *unit maternity rate* for the age category indexed by i.

In this sense, m_i represents the annual maternity rate when t is measured in years for the ith age category, and is called the *age-specific fertility rate*. Clearly,

$$B_{h,i}(t) = m_i F_i(t-h)h. \qquad (2.11)$$

The total births on the time interval $(t-h, t]$ is the aggregate of these contributions, as illustrated in Fig. 2.8 [7]. Thus,

$$B_h(t) = \sum_{i=0}^{w} B_{h,i}(t) \qquad (2.12)$$

or from (2.11),

$$B_h(t) = \sum_{i=0}^{w} m_i F_i(t-h)h. \qquad (2.13)$$

Each contribution to be births at time t from the females in the ith age category at time $t-h$, results from the survivors of those females born on the time interval $(t-(i+2)h,\ t-(i+1)h]$. Thus for each age category i, $B_{h,i}(t)$ belongs to a different maternal birth cohort. For example, in the case when $i = 2$, the contribution of births to $B_h(t)$ made by the female cohort having age interval $[2h, 3h)$ at time $t-h$ is $B_{h,2}(t)$, where $B_{h,2}(t) = m_2 F_2(t-h)h$. However, the $F_2(t-h)$ members of the cohort are the survivors of this same cohort whose size was $F_1(t-2h)$. In turn, these females are the survivors of the same cohort whose size was $F_0(t-3h)$, which are the survivors of the $B_h(t-3h)$ births. This

47

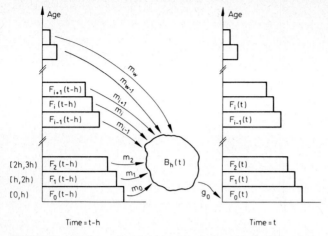

Fig. 2.8. Contribution to births at time t (credit to Walter Meyer)

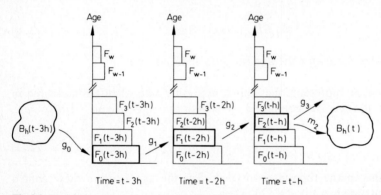

Fig. 2.9. Population pyramid model showing how births at time t are related to the births at time t $-ih$

process is illustrated in Fig. 2.9 [8]. Therefore,

$$B_{h,2}(t) = m_2 g_2 g_1 g_0 B_h(t - 3h)h. \tag{2.14}$$

A generalization of this concept is shown in Fig. 2.10. The figure is an extension of the Lexis grid which shows the accumulation of births on the interval $(t-h, t]$ from each cohort [9]. In particular, the females on age interval $[ih, (i+1)h)$ at time $t-h$, were born on the time interval $(t-(i+2)h, t-(i+1)h]$ and make a birth contribution on the interval $(t-h, t]$ numbering $B_{h,i}(t)$. This results in the following:

Theorem 2.7. For age-specific maternity rate m_i and survivorship ratio g_j let

$$\phi_{i+1} = m_i \left[\prod_{j=0}^{i} g_j \right] h. \tag{2.15}$$

48

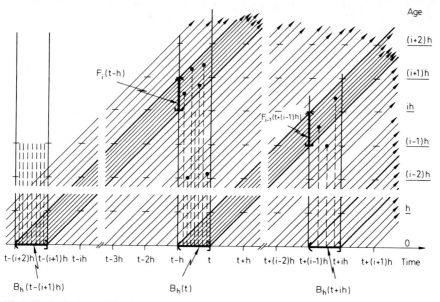

Fig. 2.10. Author's modification of Lexis grid showing two generations of births

Then

$$B_{h,i}(t) = \phi_{i+1} B_h(t-(i+1)h)h. \tag{2.16}$$

Proof: From (2.11) $B_{h,i}(t) = m_i F_i(t-h)h$. From (2.7) of Lemma 2.3

$$B_{h,i}(t) = m_i \left[\prod_{j=1}^{i} g_j \right] F_0(t-(i+1)h)h. \tag{2.17}$$

Combining (2.17) with (2.9) gives

$$B_{h,i}(t) = m_i \left[\prod_{j=1}^{i} g_j \right] g_0 B_h(t-(i+1)h)h. \tag{2.18}$$

After combining (2.18) with (2.15) the result is immediate. □

Note that the function ϕ of (2.15) is called the *net maternity function* since the contribution of births comes from the net survivors of the original birth cohort. In this respect, the net survivorship from birth to the age category indexed by i, denoted p_i, is the probability of surviving birth to age index i; that is,

$$p_i = \prod_{j=0}^{i} g_j. \tag{2.19}$$

Note that $p_0 \leq 1$ since g_0 is not necessarily unity, and $p_w \geq 0$ since g_w is not necessarily zero.

The aggregation of the $B_{h,i}(t)$ as was shown in (2.12), forms the basis of discussion for the models to be presented. This aggregation, as well as the other results of this section, was an outgrowth of the study of population pyramids. Thus, population pyramids provide the demographer with a useful tool, not only to demonstrate the age structure of a population, but to develop the mathematical mechanism from which the ancestry and posterity of a cohort can be investigated.

2.4 Classical Formulation of the Stable Theory of Population

The first cornerstone of mathematical demography is understood to be the life table. The second cornerstone of mathematical demography is considered to be the Stable Theory of Population formulated in the classical sense, which exhibits the property of *strong ergodicity* [10] for the population model. Some of the premises which make the stable theory of population a plausible approach to the study of population will now be investigated [11].

One of the major handicaps incurred in studying a population is the external flow of people into and out of the population under question. This flow is called *migration*. Migration disrupts the structure of a population and causes the mathematical analysis of it to be very difficult if not impossible. In order to circumvent this difficulty, it is assumed that the population under question is free from migration. In this case the population is said to be *closed*. This becomes the first assumption of stable theory [12].

The stable theory of population confines itself to the study of a single sex only. While either sex may be used in the demographic study, consideration is predominantly given to the female in human population due to the reasons mentioned earlier. Specifically, it is assumed that human females are capable of reproduction between the ages of 15 and 49. The symbols α and β are respectively assigned to represent the minimum and maximum age of reproductive capability.

The maternity function is non-negative through all ages of life, that is, $m_i \geq 0$ for all age indices i such that $0 \leq i \leq w$. Furthermore, for all ages outside the age interval (α, β), the maternity function will vanish. In addition, while it is possible for the maternity function to be a function of time as well as age, the stable theory of population assumes that this function is independent of time. The probability of surviving birth to age index i is assumed to be independent of time. In addition, stable theory assumes that there exists an ultimate age of life, ω, such that for all $i > w$, where w is the last age index which includes ω, the probability of survival, p_i, is zero. This is summarized in the following:

Lemma 2.8. Let $\alpha \in [jh, (j+1)h)$ and let $\beta \in [kh, (k+1)h)$, where h is the interval width of each age interval, and where

$$0 \leq \alpha < \beta \leq \omega. \tag{2.20}$$

The net maternity function ϕ defined as $\phi_{i+1} = m_i p_i$ by (2.15) is a non-negative function of compact support.

Proof: Since $0 \le p_i \le 1$ and since m_i is obviously bounded and non-negative, then ϕ is also. Since $m_i = 0$ for all $i < j$ and for all $i > k$, the result follows immediately. $\qquad\qquad\qquad\qquad\qquad\qquad\qquad\qquad\qquad\qquad\qquad\qquad\square$

In summary, the stable theory of population in the classical sense rests upon the following fundamental premises:

1. The population is closed to migration
2. The age-specific birth rate is time invariant
3. The age-specific death rate is time invariant

together with

4. The models are of the one sex type
5. There exists an ultimate, finite age of life, ω
6. The reproductive period occurs on a finite age interval (α, β).

It will be shown that models obeying these premises demonstrate an asymptotic behavior which will *stabilize* a population to fixed age distribution and have an exponential growth pattern.

It is possible to allow certain modifications, perturbations and extensions of the aforementioned premises and still preserve the stable theory of population, albeit in the non-classical sense. One such variation is to consider the case where the age-specific death rate is allowed to have slight variations in time while age-specific birth rate is time invariant; a model of this type is called *quasi-stable* as suggested by Coale [13]. Another variation is to consider environmental and economic constraints such as the affects of cohort size or the size of the labor force on fertility as demonstrated by Lee [14]. Strong deviation from the given premises, however, nullifies the use of stable theory as a valid population model.

2.5 An Overview of Deterministic Models in Stable Population Theory

The concept of Stable Population Theory is not a recent innovation. Historically, the roots of stable theory can be traced to a 1760 publication of Leonhard Euler [15]. The concern of Euler was the ability to make a projection of a population even though it was based on incomplete data. In it Euler introduces the concept of 'stable' age structures in which the proportions of all age categories would remain fixed if the population experienced no abrupt changes or migration, and if mortality rates were constant and births increased exponentially over time.

In 1761 in an article by Johann Peter Süssmilch [16], Süssmilch expounds on some of Euler's earlier unpublished works on population, and shows that an initial population of two may grow to eight million in three hundred years.

Particular reference is made to one of Euler's earlier works [17], which had given glimpses of the first signs of a recurrence equation. In it Euler postulates a situation where a couple were married at age 20 and had one child when their ages were 22, 24 and 26. The births at time t would follow an equation of the form

$$B(t) = B(t-22) + B(t-24) + B(t-26).$$ (2.21)

This equation would have a solution of the form

$$B(t) = B_0 s^t$$ (2.22)

where s would satisfy the constraint

$$1 = s^{26} - s^4 - s^2$$

from which it is possible to determine that $s = 1.047$. Proof supporting these expressions is lacking. However, it cannot be denied that Euler's assumptions are the fundamental premises of stable population theory, and that the attempt at formulating and solving a problem on these assumptions make Euler the "father of the stable theory of population". It is ironic that over one and one-half centuries elapsed since Euler, before mathematicians again addressed this theory.

Models of the stable theory of population fall into two categories: *deterministic* models, and *stochastic* models. In addition, models from these categories can be developed from a *discrete time* approach or from a *continuous time* approach. It is the intent of this work to present and further develop those stable models of the deterministic kind and show how they lead to the conclusions of stable theory of population. Deterministic discrete time models are of two basic types: recurrence models and matrix models. Deterministic continuous time models are usually based on a calculus approach due to Lotka [18, 19], although other attempts have been made, such as von Foerster [20]. The deterministic discrete time matrix model is primarily due to Bernardelli [21], Lewis [22] and Leslie [23]. Deterministic discrete time recurrence models have received some attention, such as Dobbernack and Tietz [24], and Meyer [25].

The discrete time recurrence model, the continuous time model, and the discrete time matrix model will be discussed in detail in the subsequent chapters. However, to give some insight on stable population theory, some of the highlights of the discrete time recurrence model will be presented here. In Sect. 2.3 it was already mentioned that the births on the interval $(t-h, t]$, $B_h(t)$, is the aggregation of the individual age contribution of the births $B_{h,i}(t)$ as described in expression (2.16). Thus,

$$B_h(t) = \sum_{i=0}^{w} \phi_{i+1} B_h(t-(i+1)h)h$$ (2.23)

where some of the terms in the summation may be zero from Lemma 2.8. By appropriate substitution, (2.23) is normalized and rewritten as

$$B(t) = \sum_{k=1}^{n} \phi'_k B(t-k). \tag{2.24}$$

If it is assumed that a solution to (2.24) is of the form

$$B(t) = B_0 s^t \tag{2.25}$$

then (2.25) will satisfy (2.24) subject to the constraint

$$\sum_{k=1}^{n} \phi'_k s^{-k} = 1 \tag{2.26}$$

which is called the *characteristic equation* of the recurrence equation of (2.24). The characteristic equation can be written as an nth degree characteristic polynomial equation of the form

$$s^n - \phi'_1 s^{n-1} - \phi'_2 s^{n-2} - \cdots - \phi'_{n-1} s - \phi'_n = 0 \tag{2.27}$$

which admits exactly one positive real root, s_1, which dominates in magnitude all other $n-1$ roots of (2.27), that is,

$$|s_i| < s_1 \tag{2.28}$$

for $2 \leq i \leq n$. The dominance of this principal root is the salient feature which leads to the stability of a population. Each of the n distinct roots of (2.27) provides a solution of (2.24) of the form s_i^t which is linearly independent of any of the remaining $n-1$ solutions. Because of the homogeneity of (2.24), a linear combination of the n solutions is a solution, so

$$B(t) = \sum_{i=1}^{n} a_i s_i^t \tag{2.29}$$

is the complete solution of (2.24) provided the s_i are distinct. If the s_i are not distinct and σ_i is the algebraic multiplicity of s_i, then after letting $s = e^r$, the solution takes the form for appropriate n'

$$B(t) = a_1 \exp(r_1 t) + \sum_{i=2}^{n'} \sum_{j=1}^{\sigma_i} a_{ij} t^{j-1} \exp(r_i t). \tag{2.30}$$

This is the general solution to the recurrence equation of (2.24) and reduces to (2.29) when all the $\sigma_i = 1$.

53

The significance of the stable theory of population can now be outlined. From (2.30)

$$\exp(-r_1 t)B(t) = a_1 + \sum_{i=2}^{n'} \sum_{j=1}^{\sigma_i} a_{ij} t^{j-1} \exp(-(r_1-r_i)t). \qquad (2.31)$$

But because of (2.28), r_1 dominates all other r_i where for sufficiently large t,

$$\exp(-r_1 t)B(t) = a_1 + o(e^{-r_1 t}) \qquad (2.32)$$

which is asymptotically equivalent to

$$B(t) \cong a_1 \exp(r_1 t). \qquad (2.33)$$

Demographic conditions ensure that a_1 is positive [26]. Care must be taken here not to interpret this as a reduction to the Malthusian model for two reasons: first, the result of (2.33) is true only for very large values of t, namely as $t \to \infty$; second, r_1 is not simply the difference between the current birth rate and the current death rate, but a culmination of the total interaction of the age-specific birth and death rates promulgated from the characteristic equation. For this reason r_1 is called the *intrinsic rate of growth*. Figure 2.11 shows a sketch of a possible solution of the general solution of (2.30); the oscillations are a result of the complex nature of the r_i values.

It is now possible to pursue the consequences of (2.33) for the age structure of a population. Before doing so, some preliminaries are necessary.

Lemma 2.9. Let $F_i(t)$ be the number of females of age category i at time t. Let $B_h(t)$ be the number of births on the interval $(t-h, t]$, and let p_i be the rate at which the survivors of birth survive to age category i. Then

$$F_i(t) = p_i B_h(t-ih). \qquad (2.34)$$

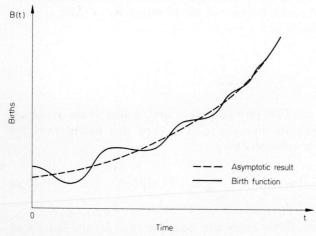

Fig. 2.11. Graph demonstrating a typical solution to the discrete time recurrence model

54

Proof: From (2.9)

$$F_0(t) = g_0 B_h(t).$$

Substitution into (2.7) yields

$$F_k(t) = \left(\prod_{j=1}^{k} g_j \right) g_0 B_h(t - kh).$$

Utilizing (2.19) the result is immediate. $\qquad\square$

This lemma substantiates what was understood from Fig. 2.10. Also, the total number of females at time t is the sum of all the females in each age category, that is,

$$\sum_{i=0}^{w} F_i(t) = \sum_{i=0}^{w} p_i B_h(t - ih). \qquad (2.35)$$

The ratio of (2.34) to (2.35) leads to the following.

Definition 2.10. The *fraction of the population* in the age interval indexed by i at time t is the ratio defined by

$$c_i(t) = F_i(t) \left/ \sum_{j=0}^{w} F_j(t). \right. \qquad (2.36)$$

Lemma 2.11. Let $B_h(t)$ and p_i be defined as in Lemma 2.9. Then

$$c_i(t) = p_i B_h(t - ih) \left/ \sum_{j=0}^{w} p_j B_h(t - jh). \right. \qquad (2.37)$$

Proof: The proof is an immediate consequence of expression (2.35) and the result of Lemma 2.9. $\qquad\square$

Corollary 2.12. Let $B_h(t)$ and ϕ_{i+1} be defined as usual and let $B(t)$ and ϕ'_k have their normalized meaning. The expressions for $B_h(t)$ and $B(t)$ are equivalent.

Proof. From (2.23) and using Lemma 2.8

$$B_h(t) = \sum_{i=0}^{w} \phi_{i+1} B_h(t - (i+1)h) h = 0 + \sum_{i=j}^{k} \phi_{i+1} B_h(t - (i+1)h) h + 0$$

Letting $t' = t/h$, $u = i + 1$, $\phi'_u = \phi_{i+1} h$ and $n = k - j + 1$, then

$$B_h(t') = \sum_{u=1}^{n} \phi'_u B_h(t' - u) = B(t')$$

by (2.24) which was to be demonstrated. $\qquad\square$

This leads to the following important consequence of the stable theory of population.

Theorem 2.13. Let $c_i(t)$ be defined as in Lemma 2.11 and c_i a constant. Then for sufficiently large values of t, $c_i(t) \to c_i$; that is, the fraction of the population whose age is indexed by i will asymptotically approach a fixed value.

Proof. Using the conclusions of Lemma 2.11 and Corollary 2.12 results in the expression

$$c_i(t) = p_i B(t - ih) \left/ \sum_{j=0}^{w} p_j B(t - jh). \right.$$

Substituting (2.33), the asymptotic equivalent of $B(t)$, into this equation results in

$$c_i(t) = a_1 \exp(r_1 t) p_i \exp(-r_1(ih)) / a_1 \exp(r_1 t) \sum_{j=0}^{w} p_j \exp(-r_1(jh))$$

which reduces to

$$c_i(t) = p_i \exp(-r_1(ih)) \left/ \sum_{j=0}^{w} p_j \exp(-r_1(jh)) \right. \tag{2.38}$$

a function of age category alone, independent of time. $\qquad\qquad \square$

The effect of this theorem is that a population under the premises of stable population theory will tend to 'forget' its past history and approach a fixed age distribution. Demographers refer to this as the property of *strong ergodicity*, which is the salient result of stable population theory and is fully expressed in (2.38). Lotka was the first to demonstrate [27] this property after it was conjectured by Euler about 150 years earlier. Under relaxed hypotheses of fertility and mortality, demographers also refer to the property of *weak ergodicity* as coined by Hajnal [28] which will be discussed in Sect. 7.5.

2.6 Conclusion

The twentieth century has brought the subject of mathematical demography out of seclusion into a dymamic and respected branch of mathematics. The subject is built upon two pillars of strength: the life table, and the stable theory of population in the classical sense. An in-depth discussion on the three stable models of the discrete time recurrence, continuous time integral, and the discrete time matrix models appear in chapters 3, 4 and 5 respectively.

The subject of mathematical demography has many unexplored possibilities. Concepts such as quasi-stability and weak ergodicity have already been investigated; time variation in both birth and death rates demonstrate interesting extensions, and the problem of migration has yet to be addressed in its full context. Therefore, the subject remains open to innovative mathematical ideas which can extend beyond the topic of population.

2.7 Notes for Chapter Two

[1] Coale, A.J. (1972), The growth and structure of human populations: A mathematical investigation. p. 117 ff.

[2] Lexis, W. (1875), Einleitung in die Theorie der Bevölkerungs-Statistik. pp. 5–7.

[3] Wunsch, G. (1968), La théorie des événements réduits: application aux principaux phénomènes démographiques. Recherches Economiques de Louvain, vol. 34, no. 4, pp. 391–409.

[4] Keyfitz, N. and Flieger, W. (1971), Population, facts and methods of demography. p. 426.

[5] Pick, J.B. (1974), Computer display of population age structure. Demography, vol. 11, no. 4, pp. 673–682.

[6] Keyfitz, N. (1977), Applied mathematical demography. p. 114.

[7] Meyer, W. (1978), Notes on mathematical demography: Stable population theory. p. 6.

[8] Ibid., p. 8.

[9] This modification of the Lexis grid is due solely to the author.

[10] McFarland, D.D. (1969), On the theory of stable populations: A new and elementary proof of the theorem under weaker assumptions. Demography, vol. 6, no. 3, pp. 301–322.

[11] Lopez, A. (1961), Problems in stable population theory. pp. 16–18.

[12] For an interesting account on migration consult: Zuev, G.M. and Soroko, E.L. (1978), Mathematical description of migration processes. Avtomatika i Telemekhanika (USSR), vol. 39, no. 7, pp. 94–101.

[13] Coale, A.J. (1963), Estimates of various demographic measures through the quasi-stable age distribution. Emerging Techniques in Population Research, 39th Annual Conference of the Milbank Memorial Fund, 1962, pp. 175–193.

[14] Lee, Ronald (1974), The formal dynamics of controlled populations and the echo, the boom and the bust. Demography, vol. 11, no. 4, pp. 563–585.

[15] Euler, L. (1760), Recherches générales sur la mortalité et la multiplication du genre humaine. Mémoires de l'Académie Royale des Sciences et Belles Lettres, vol. 16, pp. 144–164.

[16] Süssmilch, J.P. (1761), Die göttliche Ordnung. vol. 1, pp. 291–299.

[17] Euler, L. (1748), Introductio in analysin infinitorum.

[18] Lotka, A.J. (1907), Relation between birth rates and death rates. Science, N.S., vol. 26, pp. 21–22.

[19] Sharpe, F.R. and Lotka, A.J. (1911), A problem in age distribution. Philosophical Magazine, ser. 6, vol. 21, pp. 435–438.

[20] Foerster, H. von (1959), The kinetics of cellular proliferation.

[21] Bernardelli, H. (1941), Population waves. Journal of the Burma Research Society, vol 31, part 1, pp. 1–18.

[22] Lewis, E.G. (1942), On the generation and growth of a population. Sankhya, vol. 6, pp. 93–96.

[23] Leslie, P.H. (1945), On the use of matrices in certain population mathematics. Biometrika, vol. 33, pp. 183–212.

[24] Dobbernack, W. and Tietz, G. (1940), Twelfth International Congress of Actuaries, vol. 4, pp. 233ff.

[25] Meyer, W. (1978), op. cit.

[26] Meyer, W. (1982), Asymptotic birth trajectories in the discrete form of stable population theory. Theoretical Population Biology, vol. 21, no. 2, pp. 167–170.

[27] Lotka (1907), op. cit.

[28] Hajnal, J. (1958), Weak ergodicity in non-homogeneous markov chains. Proceedings of the Cambridge Philosophical Society, vol. 54, pp. 233–246.

3. The Discrete Time Recurrence Model

59

3.1 Introduction

As previously mentioned, the discrete time recurrence model in the study of population is credited to Euler, and has received sporadic and incomplete attention since his time. Indeed, the only development of this topic known to the author is an unpublished work by Meyer [1]. It is, therefore, in the best interest of the field of mathematical demography that this topic receive further exposure.

The important demographic results due to the discrete time recurrence model have already been highlighted in the previous chapter. It is the author's intent to demonstrate these results and to enhance the stature of this topic as a legitimate model in the field of mathematical demography, particularly as it applies to the stable theory of population. After more than two hundred years, its time is most certainly due.

3.2 Linear Recurrence Equations – A Pandect

Before investigating the involvement of population in the mathematical recurrence process, it is advantageous to examine some of the theory of difference equations, especially as it applies to the linear case. The functions involved in this discussion are assumed to be defined over a discrete domain of real numbers as opposed to being defined over a real interval.

Definition 3.1. Let f be a function of x defined for $x = a$, $a + h$, $a + 2h$, $a + 3h$, $a + 4h$, ... for $h > 0$. Let $\Delta f(x)$ denote the *forward difference* of $f(x)$ defined over increment h as

$$\Delta f(x) = f(x+h) - f(x) \qquad (3.1)$$

such that for positive integer n,

$$\Delta^n f(x) = \Delta[\Delta^{n-1} f(x)]. \qquad (3.2)$$

Then for some relation G,

$$G(\Delta^n f(x), \Delta^{n-1} f(x), \ldots, \Delta f(x), f(x), x) = 0 \qquad (3.3)$$

is an nth *order difference equation* (2).

60

For example, the well known Fibonacci sequence, defined recursively as

$$x_{n+2} = x_{n+1} + x_n$$

for $n = 0, 1, 2, \ldots$ with initial conditions $x_0 = x_1 = 1$ is a simple example of a second order recursive equation [3]. In addition, under appropriate conditions the existence and uniqueness of a solution to (3.3) can be established [4].

A special case of the difference equation occurs when no nonlinear functions of function f appear in the equation. This leads to the following:

Definition 3.2. Let r and g_i be functions of x defined for $x = a$, $a+h$, $a+2h$, $a+3h$, ... for $h > 0$. If $g_0(x)$ does not vanish at each of these x values, then the equation

$$\sum_{i=0}^{n} g_i(x) f(x - (n-i)h) = r(x) \tag{3.4}$$

is an nth *order linear difference equation.*

For the case where $r(x)$ is identically zero for each value of x of its definition, then the equation of (3.4) is called a *homogeneous* n^{th} order linear difference equation, otherwise it is *non-homogeneous*. It can be shown [5 and 6] that under appropriate conditions a unique solution does exist for (3.4). In addition it is clear that if $f_1(x)$ and $f_2(x)$ are solutions to the homogeneous equation, then for constants c_1 and c_2 the expression $c_1 f_1(x) + c_2 f_2(x)$ is also a solution; that is, the solutions to the homogeneous equation form a vector space. The significance of having a vector space for the set of solutions to (3.4) is that it can be demonstrated that the dimension of the vector space is n, the order of the linear difference equation. Before this is highlighted, it is important to give some insight to the meaning of linearly independent functions as they relate to difference equations as shown in the following:

Lemma 3.3. Let F_1 and F_2 be two functions defined for $x = a$, $a+h$, $a+2h$, $a+3h$, $a+4h$, ... If there exists at least one $x = a$, $a+h$, $a+2h$, $a+3h$, ... on this interval such that the determinant

$$\begin{vmatrix} F_1(x) & F_2(x) \\ F_1(x+h) & F_2(x+h) \end{vmatrix} \neq 0 \tag{3.5}$$

then the functions F_1 and F_2 are linearly independent.

Proof: Suppose F_1 and F_2 are linearly dependent. Then there exist constants c_1 and c_2 such that for all values of x for which the functions are defined,

$$c_1 F_1(x) + c_2 F_2(x) = 0$$

and

$$c_1 F_1(x+h) + c_2 F_2(x+h) = 0.$$

Thus, the system

$$\begin{bmatrix} F_1(x) & F_2(x) \\ F_1(x+h) & F_2(x+h) \end{bmatrix} \begin{bmatrix} c_1 \\ c_2 \end{bmatrix} = \begin{bmatrix} 0 \\ 0 \end{bmatrix}$$

has non-trivial solutions and so the determinant of the coefficient matrix is zero for all x. This contradicts the assumption of the statement. Therefore, F_1 and F_2 are linearly independent. $\qquad\square$

The previous theorem can be generalized to n discrete functions. However, the following is required.

Definition 3.4. Let F_1, F_2, F_3, ..., F_n be n functions of x defined for $x=a$, $a+h$, $a+2h$, $a+3h$, ... The determinant

$$\begin{vmatrix} F_1(x) & F_2(x) & F_3(x) & \cdots & F_n(x) \\ F_1(x+h) & F_2(x+h) & F_3(x+h) & \cdots & F_n(x+h) \\ F_1(x+2h) & F_2(x+2h) & F_3(x+2h) & \cdots & F_n(x+2h) \\ \cdots & \cdots & \cdots & \cdots & \cdots \\ F_1(x+(n-1)h) & F_2(x+(n-1)h) & F_3(x+(n-1)h) & \cdots & F_n(x+(n-1)h) \end{vmatrix} \quad (3.6)$$

is called the nth *order Casorati*.

The Casorati is analogous to the Wronskian in differential equations.

Theorem 3.5. Let F_1, F_2, ..., F_n be n functions of x defined for $x=a$, $a+h$, $a+2h$, ... The functions are linearly independent only if the nth order Casorati is not zero for at least one of these x values.

Proof: The proof is similar to that shown in Lemma 3.3. $\qquad\square$

The establishment of linear independence of a set of discrete functions leads to the following important theorem concerning homogeneous linear difference equations with constant coefficients.

Theorem 3.6. For real constants k_i such that $k_0 \neq 0$ and $k_n \neq 0$, let

$$\sum_{i=0}^{n} k_i f(x+(n-i)h) = 0 \qquad (3.7)$$

be an nth order linear difference equation with constant coefficients defined for $x=a$, $a+h$, $a+2h$, ... Then

(a) there exist n linearly independent solutions $F_1, F_2, F_3, ..., F_n$ of equation (3.7);

(b) the number of linearly independent solutions is at most n;

(c) the n linearly independent solutions form a basis of a vector space of dimension n.

62

Proof: (a) An abstract existence proof may be found in Miller [7]. It is also possible to exhibit a set of such functions as will be demonstrated in Theorems 3.9 and 3.10.

(b) Suppose there were $n+1$ linearly independent solutions to equation (3.7). This can occur only if the $(n+1)^{th}$ order Casorati is not zero for at least one x for which the functions are defined. The Casorati is

$$
\begin{vmatrix}
F_1(x) & F_2(x) & \cdots & F_n(x) & F_{n+1}(x) \\
F_1(x+h) & F_2(x+h) & \cdots & F_n(x+h) & F_{n+1}(x+h) \\
\cdots & \cdots & \cdots & \cdots & \cdots \\
F_1(x+(n-1)h) & F_2(x+(n-1)h) & \cdots & F_n(x+(n-1)h) & F_{n+1}(x+(n-1)h) \\
F_1(x+nh) & F_2(x+nh) & \cdots & F_n(x+nh) & F_{n+1}(x+nh)
\end{vmatrix}.
$$

(3.8)

Let F_p be any one of the $n+1$ functions described in (3.8). Then by equation (3.7)

$$
F_p(x+nh) = - \sum_{i=1}^{n} g_i k_i(x) F_p(x+(n-i)h)
$$

which can be substituted for the last row of functions in (3.8) for values of p $=1, 2, 3, \ldots, n$, $n+1$. By means of row reduction, the last row of the determinant can be made to equal zero, whereby the determinant is zero. This implies that the $n+1$ functions are linearly dependent, which is a contradiction. Therefore, there are at most n linearly independent functions.

(c) It is easily shown that if f_1 and f_2 are two solutions to equation (3.7) then for arbitrary constants c_1 and c_2, the function $c_1 f_1 + c_2 f_2$ is also a solution. Thus, the entire solution set of equation (3.7) forms a vector space. From parts (a) and (b) of this theorem, the dimension of the vector space must be n. ☐

Theorem 3.7. A function F satisfying the nth order linear difference equation of (3.7) can be written as

$$
F(x) = \sum_{i=1}^{n} c_i F_i(x)
$$

(3.9)

for arbitrary constants c_i and where the F_i are elements of the fundamental set of solutions of (3.7).

Proof: Since there are n linearly independent functions on a vector space of dimension n, the functions must span the space. ☐

A special case of the nth order non-homogeneous linear difference equation expressed by (3.4) occurs when the coefficients are real constants. That is, for $h>0$ and for $x=a, a+h, a+2h, a+3h, a+4h, \ldots$

$$
g_i(x) = k_i
$$

where k_i is a real constant. This leads to the following:

Lemma 3.8. Given the non-homogeneous linear difference equation of nth order with constant coefficients expressed as

$$\sum_{i=1}^{n} k_i f(x+(n-i)h) = r(x). \tag{3.10}$$

Let $\{F_i(x)\}$ be a basis of the vector space of solutions for the homogeneous case of (3.10). If $G(x)$ is a particular solution, then the general solution of (3.10) is

$$f(x) = F(x) + G(x) \tag{3.11}$$

where $F(x)$ is defined by (3.9).

Proof: Substitution of (3.9) into (3.11), which is again substituted into (3.10) produces $n^2 + n$ terms equal to $r(x)$ in the form

$$\sum_{i=1}^{n} \sum_{j=1}^{n} k_i c_j F_j(x+(n-i)h) + \sum_{i=1}^{n} k_i G(x+(n-i)h) = r(x)$$

in which the double summation is the homogeneous part which vanishes and the second summation satisfies (3.10) by hypothesis. $\square$

The homogeneous n^{th} order linear recurrence equation with constant coefficients of (3.7) can be rewritten. Since $k_0 \neq 0$ let

$$b_i = -k_i/k_0$$

for $i = 1, 2, \ldots, n$. Then

$$f(x+nh) = \sum_{i=1}^{n} b_i f(x+(n-i)h) \tag{3.12}$$

which enables one to evaluate f at $x+nh$ from its prior values as far back as x. In the next section it will be shown that the discrete form of (3.12), which is equivalent to (3.7), is the desired representation for the population model. However, what is now required is a method to solve the recursive equation of (3.12) which is shown in the following:

Theorem 3.9. Let s be any complex number. The function

$$f(x) = s^x \tag{3.13}$$

is a solution to the linear homogeneous recurrence equation

$$f(x+nh) = b_1 f(x+(n-1)h) + b_2 f(x+(n-2)h) + \ldots + b_n f(x) \tag{3.14}$$

if and only if $s=0$, or s is a zero of the *characteristic polynomial*

$$\Psi(s)=s^{nh}-b_1 s^{nh-h}-b_2 s^{nh-2h}-\dots-b_n. \qquad (3.15)$$

Proof: Without loss of generality let $h=1$. Assume that s^x is a solution to (3.14). Then by direct substitution

$$s^x s^n=(b_1 s^{n-1}+b_2 s^{n-2}+\dots+b_{n-1}s+b_n)s^x$$

from which the *characteristic equation*

$$\Psi(s)=s^n-b_1 s^{n-1}-b_2 s^{n-2}-\dots-b_n=0 \qquad (3.16)$$

is obtained. For $s=0$ the result is trivial.

Now assume that (3.16) is true. Then by multiplying through by s^x and combining exponentials yields

$$s^{x+n}-b_1 s^{x+n-1}-b_2 s^{x+n-2}-\dots-b_n s^x=0$$

from which it is clear that s^x is a solution to (3.14) for $h=1$. $\qquad\square$

The fundamental theorem of algebra ensures that the characteristic equation of (3.16) will have exactly n roots, multiplicities considered. Furthermore, if the coefficients b_i are real, then complex roots must occur in conjugate pairs. This results in the following:

Theorem 3.10. Let s_i be a root of multiplicity σ_i for the characteristic equation of (3.16) where $\sum \sigma_i=n$. Then a solution to the homogeneous linear recursive equation (3.14) is

$$f(x)=[C_{i1}+C_{i2}x+\dots+C_{i\sigma_i}x^{\sigma_i-1}]s_i^x \qquad (3.17)$$

where the set of functions $\{C_{ij}x^{j-1}s_i^x\}$ for $j=1, 2, \dots, \sigma_i$ is linearly independent.

Proof (sketch): An application of the σ_i^{th} order Casorati will show that it does not vanish for the functions $x^{j-1}s_i^x$ for $1 \le j \le \sigma_i$. Hence, these functions are linearly independent. Direct substitution of these σ_i functions into (3.14) will show that each is a solution. Since any linear combination of these solutions is also a solution, the assertion of the theorem is demonstrated. $\qquad\square$

Theorem 3.11. Given the homogeneous linear recursive equation

$$f(x+n)=\sum_{i=1}^{n} b_i f(x+n-i) \qquad (3.18)$$

whose characteristic equation has a root s_i with algebraic multiplicity σ_i, where $\sum_1^{n'} \sigma_i = n$, and where the b_i are real constants. Then

$$f(x) = \sum_{i=1}^{n'} \sum_{j=1}^{\sigma_i} C_{ij} x^{j-1} s_i^x \tag{3.19}$$

is the general solution of the recursive equation.

Proof: By Theorem 3.6 it has already been shown that the n linearly independent solutions of equation (3.7) form a vector space of dimension n. Since the sum of all the multiplicities of the roots of the characteristic equation is n, then there exist n linearly independent solutions of the form $C_{ij} x^{j-1} s_i^x$ for each of the characteristic roots s_i. Thus, these n solutions form a basis for the vector space. Since these solutions necessarily span the vector space, the assertion of the theorem is demonstrated. $\square$

There are concluding aspects worth mentioning. First of all, when $\sigma_i = 1$, then the root s_i is obviously a simple root. In addition, the roots s_i may not be real, and when they are complex they occur in complex conjugate pairs, $s_k = u_k + iv_k$ and $\bar{s}_k = u_k - iv_k$ for $u_k, v_k \in \mathbb{R}$ if the coefficients b_i of (3.18) are assumed to be real. In this situation a term of (3.19) of the form

$$C_{kj} x^{j-1} s_k^x = C_{kj} x^{j-1} (u_k + iv_k)^x$$

will always be accompanied by one of the form

$$C'_{kj} x^{j-1} \bar{s}_k^x = C'_{kj} x^{j-1} (u_k - iv_k)^x.$$

Under certain conditions the imaginary contribution to the summation of (3.19) will cancel, as is now shown.

Theorem 3.12. Let a linear homogeneous recursive equation be defined and have a solution as prescribed by Theorem 3.11. If the recursive equation is subjected to the constraint of having n initial conditions each of which is real, then the solution must be real. That is, the imaginary parts of the solution will cancel.

Proof: Consider the case where $n=2$, where the characteristic equation has complex roots, and where the initial conditions y_0 and y_1 are real valued. Then (3.18) and (3.19) become respectively

$$f(x+2) = b_1 f(x+1) + b_2 f(x)$$

and

$$f(x) = cs_1^x + ds_2^x \tag{3.20}$$

where by hypothesis c and d are arbitrary complex constants, and s_1 and s_2 are complex conjugate roots of the characteristic equation

$$\Psi(s) = s^2 - b_1 s - b_2 = 0.$$

Let $y_0 = f(0)$, $y_1 = f(1)$, $s_1 = u + vi$ and $s_2 = u - vi$. Then from (3.20),

$$y_0 = c + d \quad \text{and} \quad y_1 = c(u + vi) + d(u - vi) \tag{3.21}$$

from which a unique solution for c and d can be found. If the complex conjugate of the equations in (3.21) is taken, then

$$y_0 = \bar{c} + \bar{d} \quad \text{and} \quad y_1 = \bar{c}(u - vi) + \bar{d}(u + vi) \tag{3.22}$$

By equating y_1 of (3.21) and (3.22) it is clear that $c = \bar{d}$, and $d = \bar{c}$. The solution of (3.20) then takes the form for positive discrete $x = m$

$$f(m) = c(u + vi)^m + \bar{c}(u - vi)^m$$

and after expanding binomially and rearranging becomes

$$f(m) = (c + \bar{c}) \left[\binom{m}{0} u^m + \binom{m}{2} u^{m-2}(vi)^2 + \binom{m}{4} u^{m-4}(vi)^4 + \cdots \right]$$
$$+ (c - \bar{c}) \left[\binom{m}{1} u^{m-1}(vi) + \binom{m}{3} u^{m-3}(vi)^3 + \cdots \right].$$

The first bracket is real while the second bracket is imaginary. Since $c + \bar{c} = 2\,\mathrm{Re}(c)$ while $c - \bar{c} = 2\,\mathrm{Im}(c)$, then the solution function f is strictly real, which was to be demonstrated. □

Theorems 3.11 and 3.12 provide the necessary ingredients required for the study of the discrete time recursive model in the stable theory of population. This will be discussed in the next section. It should be noted, however, that many other applications are possible such as income and inventory analysis [8]. Also, the subject of differential equations with all its applications provides a close analogy to the subject of finite recursive equations. It is unfortunate that this subject has been deprived of the recognition it truly deserves.

3.3 The Discrete Time Recursive Stable Population Model

In the discussion of population pyramids in Chapter Two it was shown that the contribution of births on the time interval $(t - h, t]$ from the females in age category indexed by i, denoted $B_{h,i}(t)$, is directly related to the births that occurred $t - (i + 1)h$ years ago. The relationship was expressed by equation

(2.16), which is again presented here in modified form for $t' = 0, h, 2h, 3h, \dots$ as

$$B'_{h', i}(t') = \phi'_{i+1} B'_{h'}(t' - (i+1)h')h' \tag{3.23}$$

where ϕ' is the net maternity function defined by (2.15) and where $B'_{h'}$ is the total birth function over a time interval of width h'. The total births at time t', that is, on the interval $(t' - h', t']$, is the aggregation of the births expressed by (3.23), as demonstrated by Fig. 2.10, and written for $t' = 0, h, 2h, 3h, \dots$ as

$$B'_{h'}(t') = \sum_{i=0}^{w} \phi'_{i+1} B'_{h'}(t' - (i+1)h')h' \tag{3.24}$$

which is similar to (2.23). This expression can assume a simpler form as is shown by the following:

Lemma 3.13. The expression

$$B(t) = \sum_{k=1}^{n} \phi_k B(t - k) \tag{3.25}$$

is equivalent to the expression of (3.24) for $t = 0, 1, 2, \dots$.

Proof: By setting $t = t'/h'$ the time intervals of width h' are converted to unit time intervals, that is, the time interval $(t' - h', t']$ is transformed to the time interval $(t - 1, t]$. Let $k = i + 1$ so that the $w + 1$ age intervals vary over index k for $k = 1, 2, \dots, n$ where $n = w + 1$. Redefine functions ϕ' and $B'_{h'}$ as

$$\phi_k = \phi'_{i+1} h' \quad \text{and} \quad B(t) = B'_{h'}(th')$$

respectively. Rewriting (3.24) yields

$$B'_{h'}(th') = \sum_{i+1=1}^{w+1} [\phi'_{i+1} h'] B'_{h'}((t'/h' - (i+1))h')$$

which, after appropriate substitution, results in (3.25). $\qquad\square$

Thus, (3.24) has been normalized so that each unit of t represents the equivalent of h' years.

The values of the net maternity function ϕ_k are assumed known for all k, and by virtue of Lemma 2.8 may vanish for some values of k. By the premises of classical stable theory, function ϕ is time invariant. As a result, the expression of (3.25) is a homogeneous n^{th} order linear recurrence equation with constant coefficients, and at time $t + n$

$$B(t + n) = \sum_{k=1}^{n} \phi_k B(t + n - k) \tag{3.26}$$

which parallels (3.18). Furthermore, a solution to this equation, by virtue of previous discussions, must be subject to a characteristic equation similar to (3.16) which takes the form

$$\Psi(s) = s^n - \phi_1 s^{n-1} - \phi_2 s^{n-2} - \ldots - \phi_n = 0. \tag{3.27}$$

Then by Theorem 3.11 the solution to the equation of (3.26) is

$$B(t) = \sum_{i=1}^{n'} \sum_{j=1}^{\sigma_i} a_{ij} t^{j-1} s_i^t \tag{3.28}$$

where n' is the number of distinct roots s_i having multiplicity σ_i of the characteristic equation of (3.27). If n initial conditions are given at a particular time t_0 defined as

$$B_1 = B(t_0), \, B_2 = B(t_0 + 1), \, B_3 = B(t_0 + 2), \, \ldots, \, B_n = B(t_0 + n - 1) \tag{3.29}$$

then the constants a_{ij} can be uniquely calculated. Demographic considerations ensure that the initial conditions of (3.29) are real valued, and by Theorem 3.12 the birth function of (3.28) is a real function of time for all t.

The demographic nature of the net maternity function ϕ guarantees that it is never negative as shown by Lemma 2.8. This leads to the following:

Theorem 3.14. The characteristic equation (3.27) of the population renewal equation of (3.26) admits exactly one simple positive real root, provided that the coefficients ϕ_i are non-negative real values.

Proof: Since $\phi_i \geq 0$ for $i = 1, 2, \ldots, n$, the polynomial $\Psi(s)$ is a real polynomial. By Descartes' Rule of Signs [9], it can have at most one positive real zero; if the number of positive real zeros, counted according to multiplicity, is less than the number of sign changes, then the difference of these quantities would be even. This is impossible when the number of sign changes is one. Therefore, exactly one positive root exists. □

The unique positive root is called the *principal root* of the characteristic equation (3.27) and is denoted s_1. This leads to the following:

Theorem 3.15. The birth function of the population renewal equation (3.26) is

$$B(t) = a_1 s_1^t + \sum_{i=2}^{n'} \sum_{j=1}^{\sigma_i} a_{ij} t^{j-1} s_i^t \tag{3.30}$$

where $n = 1 + \sum_{2}^{n'} \sigma_i$ and where the constants a_1 and a_{ij} are obtained by the n initial conditions B_i of (3.29).

69

Proof: Expression (3.28) is the general solution of the population renewal equation (3.26). By Theorem 3.14 the coefficients $a_{1j}=0$ for all $j>1$ since $\sigma_1 = 1$. Letting $a_1 = a_{11}$ the result is obtained. $\qquad\square$

It must be emphasized that the birth function of (3.30) is the general solution since the functions contained within it form a basis of the vector space of all possible solutions.

Corollary 3.16. An alternate form of the birth function of the population renewal equation is

$$B(t)=a_1 \exp(r_1 t)+ \sum_{i=2}^{n'} \sum_{j=1}^{\sigma_i} a_{ij} t^{j-1} \exp(u_i t) \cos(v_i t) \qquad (3.31)$$

where $r_k = u_k + iv_k = \ln(s_k)$.

Proof: Using $s_i = \exp(r_i) = \exp(u_i + iv_i)$ in (3.30) yields

$$B(t)=a_1 [\exp(r_1)]^t + \sum_{i=2}^{n'} \sum_{j=1}^{\sigma_i} a_{ij} t^{j-1} [\exp(u_i)]^t [\exp(iv_i)]^t$$

where the coefficient of v_i is $i = \sqrt{-1}$. Since $[\exp(m)]^t = \exp(mt)$, the use of Euler's Identity yields

$$B(t)=a_1 \exp(r_1 t)+ \sum_{i=2}^{n'} \sum_{j=1}^{\sigma_i} a_{ij} t^{j-1} \exp(u_i t) \cos(v_i t)$$

$$+ i \sum_{i=2}^{n'} \sum_{j=1}^{\sigma_i} a_{ij} t^{j-1} \exp(u_i t) \sin(v_i t). \qquad (3.32)$$

But by Theorem 3.12 the imaginary part of (3.32) vanishes, from which the result is immediate. $\qquad\square$

The result of Corollary 3.16 clearly demonstrates that the solution of the population renewal equation (the birth function) is composed of exponential, algebraic and trigonometric functions of time. One may speculate the obvious possibility that because of the trigonometric terms, the birth function B could have oscillations which are significant even for asymptotically large values of t, as shown in Fig. 3.1.

Theorem 3.17. The birth function (3.31) is such that for $i = 2, 3, ..., n'$

$$r_1 > u_i = \text{Re}(r_i) \qquad (3.33)$$

and as a result

$$s_1 > |s_i| \qquad (3.34)$$

that is, the principal root of the characteristic polynomial dominates all other roots in magnitude.

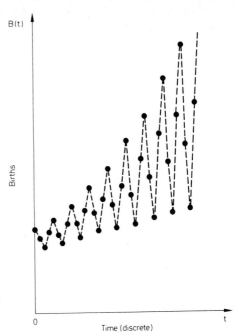

B(t)

Births

0

Time (discrete)   t

Fig. 3.1. Graph of possible birth function with no dominance of principal root

Proof: Suppose the assertion of (3.33) is not true, that is, suppose for some i value, $2 \leq i \leq n'$, that $u_i \geq r_1$. Then for any $t \geq 0$

$$\exp(-u_i t) \leq \exp(-r_1 t). \qquad (3.35)$$

Furthermore, since $\cos(v_i t) \leq 1$, then for $t = 0, 1, 2, 3, \ldots$

$$\exp(-u_i t) \cos(v_i t) \leq \exp(-u_i t).$$

Since v_i is not a multiple of 2π, there exists at least one $t = k$ where $1 \leq k \leq n$, and n is the degree of the recursive equation, such that

$$\exp(-u_i k) \cos(v_i k) < \exp(-u_i k)$$

and by (3.35)

$$\exp(-u_i k) \cos(v_i k) < \exp(-r_1 k). \qquad (3.36)$$

But the characteristic equation of (3.27) can be rewritten as

$$1 = \sum_{k=1}^{n} \phi_k s_i^{-k} = \sum_{k=1}^{n} \phi_k \exp(-r_i k) \qquad (3.37)$$

for each of its n' roots. Since imaginary parts must cancel for the real equation (3.37), then for all $i = 1, 2, \ldots, n'$

$$1 = \sum_{k=1}^{n} \phi_k \exp(-u_i k) \cos(v_i k) \qquad (3.38)$$

71

for the specific i value for which (3.36) holds. From (3.36), (3.37) and (3.38) one obtains

$$1 = \sum_{k=1}^{n} \phi_k \exp(-u_i k) \cos(v_i k) < \sum_{k=1}^{n} \phi_k \exp(-r_1 k) = 1$$

forcing a contradiction. Thus, the assertion of (3.33) is true.

In order to show (3.34), observe that for $i = 2, 3, \ldots, n'$ the magnitude of the roots of the characteristic equation is

$$|s_i| = |\exp(r_i)| = |\exp(u_i + i v_i)| = |\exp(u_i)| |\exp(i v_i)| = |\exp(u_i)|.$$

From (3.33) $u_i < r_1$ and since $|\exp(u_i)| = \exp(u_i)$, the assertion of (3.34) is an immediate consequence. □

The significance of Theorem 3.17 is that for large values of time t, the term $a_1 \exp(r_1 t)$ will overpower all other terms of the birth function described in (3.31) of Corollary 3.16. This is shown in the following:

Theorem 3.18. Let the birth function of the population renewal equation be described as in (3.31). Then

(a) The coefficient a_1 is real and positive, that is,

$$a_1 > 0. \tag{3.39}$$

(b) In the limit as time t approaches infinity, $B(t)$ reduces to its leading term, that is, asymptotically,

$$B(t) \approx a_1 \exp(r_1 t). \tag{3.40}$$

Proof: (a) A detailed proof of this assertion is found in Meyer [10].

(b) Multiplying both sides of (3.31) by $\exp(-r_1 t)$ yields

$$\exp(-r_1 t) B(t) = a_1 + \sum_{i=2}^{n'} \sum_{j=1}^{\sigma_i} a_{ij} t^{j-1} \cos(v_i t) \exp(-(r_1 - u_i)t)$$

where a_1 is positive by (3.39) and $\exp(-(r_1 - u_i)t) \to 0$ as $t \to \infty$ as a result of Theorem 3.17. Thus,

$$\exp(-r_1 t) B(t) \approx a_1 \tag{3.41}$$

from which the result is immediate. Equation (3.41) is described in Fig. 3.2. □

The asymptotic result of Theorem 3.18 can then be used to show that there is an asymptotic age distribution, which is the heart of the stable theory of population. This was demonstrated in the latter part of Sect. 2.5 of the previous chapter.

72

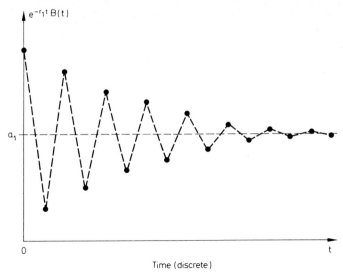

Fig. 3.2. Graph showing asymptotic behavior resulting from dominance of principal root

3.4 Conclusion

It has been previously mentioned that the discrete time recursive model in the stable theory of population has received little mathematical attention since its inception over two centuries ago. The development presented in this chapter is an attempt to rectify that neglect and to show that it is founded on a sound mathematical basis, which can be used not only to study population under stable premises, but as a useful mathematical tool that can be used in a variety of applications.

One of the advantages of the discrete time model is that a problem can be formulated and solved by simple calculation. The electronic calculator or the computer are perfect tools to execute the theory presented. Another important advantage of the discrete format is that the overall level of mathematics is more elementary when compared to the continuous model. While elements from analysis have been hinted at, such aspects have been circumvented deliberately in order to maintain the discrete nature of the model. The antithesis of this approach is treated in the next chapter, after which the development of both the discrete time and continuous time models can be better appreciated.

3.5 Notes for Chapter Three

[1] Meyer, W. (1978), Notes on mathematical demography: Stable population theory. Unpublished, available from author.
[2] Hildebrand, F.B. (1968), Finite-difference equations and simulations. p. 1 ff.

[3] Miller, K.S. (1960), An introduction to the calculus of finite differences and difference equations. p. 127 ff.

[4] Sherbert, D.R. (1979), Difference equations with applications. Applications of Difference Equations to Economics and Social Sciences, UMAP. p. 2.

[5] Goldberg, S. (1958), Introduction to difference equations. p. 61.

[6] Miller, K.S. (1968), Linear difference equations. pp. 3–4.

[7] Miller (1960), op. cit., pp. 135–137.

[8] Goldberg (1958), op. cit., p. 153 ff.

[9] Hall, H.S. and Knight, S.R. (1957 (1887)), Higher algebra. p. 459.

[10] Meyer, W. (1982) Asymptotic birth trajectories in the dicrete form of stable population theory. Theoretical Population Biology, vol. 21, no. 2, pp. 167–170.

4. The Continuous Time Model

4.1 Introduction

In Chapters Two and Three, attention was given to the female population stratified in a finite number of $w+1$ age intervals that were indexed by i for $0 \le i \le w$. In addition, the female births were considered on discrete time intervals of the form $(t-h, t]$. This led to the discrete time population renewal equation (2.23) of the form

$$B_h(t) = \sum_{i=0}^{w} \phi_{i+1} B_h(t-(i+1)h)h \qquad (4.1)$$

and its attendant solution.

In this chapter an investigation of population renewal will be undertaken from the standpoint that the number of age stratifications between birth and the ultimate age of death is allowed to increase without bound. This results in births being considered on time intervals whose lengths become infinitesimally small whereby time is considered as a continuum, and the birth function is a continuous function of time.

4.2 The Development of the Continuous Time Model

Let B be a continuous function of time t. Let F be a continuous function of both age x and time t. The interpretation of functions B and F are given according to the following [1]:

Definition 4.1. The *female birth rate* at time t, that is, the total number of females born per unit time, calculated instantaneously at time t, is denoted $B(t)$. The total *number of females* at time t whose age is between x and $x+h$ is given by $F(x, t)h$, for $h > 0$.

The value h denotes a small increment of age, as well as a corresponding increment of time. On the time interval $(t-h, t]$ there are approximately $B(t)h$ births. By the Mean Value Theorem for integrals, the *mean birth rate* on the

76

interval $(t-h, t]$ is

$$B^*(t)=(1/h) \int_{t-h}^{t} B(z)dz. \tag{4.2}$$

Likewise, on the age interval $[x, x+h)$ at time t, the *mean number of females* can be represented by the average value F^* as

$$F^*(x, t)=(1/h) \int_{x}^{x+h} F(y, t)dy \tag{4.3}$$

as illustrated in Fig. 4.1 (a) and Fig. 4.1 (b) respectively. Then the following is true:

1. $B^*(t)h$ is the exact number of births on the time interval $(t-h, t]$, and
2. $F^*(x, t)h$ is the exact number of females at time t on the age interval $[x, x+h)$ for all $t \in \mathbb{R}$ and for all x such that $x \in [0, \omega]$, where ω is the ultimate age of life.

The $F^*(x, t)h$ females at time t are the survivors of those females who were born between $x-h$ and x years prior to time t. That is, they are the survivors of the $B^*(t-x)h$ births on the time interval $(t-x-h, t-x]$. This is shown in Fig. 4.2, which is the continuous analog to the discrete version shown in Fig. 2.10. This leads to the following:

Definition 4.2. Let functions B^* and F^* be defined as (4.2) and (4.3) respectively. Then the *probability of surviving birth to age x* is

$$p^*(x, t)=F^*(x, t)/B^*(t-x). \tag{4.4}$$

From the premises of classical stable theory it is assumed that this probability is time invariant. Then rewriting $p^*(x, t)$ as $p^*(x)$, the expression of (4.4) can be rewritten as

$$F^*(x, t)h=p^*(x)B^*(t-x)h \tag{4.5}$$

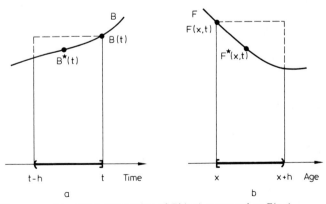

Fig. 4.1. a Illustration of $B^*(t)$ compared to $B(t)$. **b** Illustration of $F^*(x, t)$ compared to $F(x, t)$

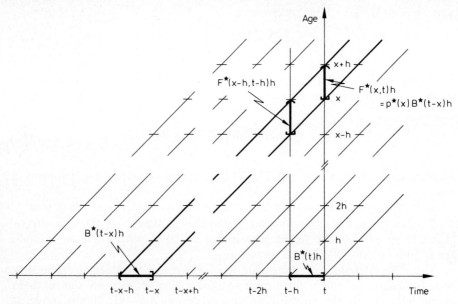

Fig. 4.2. Illustration showing the relation between $B^*(t)$ and $B^*(t-x)$

which is true for $x \in [0, \omega]$, and describes the mortality aspects of a birth cohort. Note that the function p^* is directly related to the survivorship function of the life table by the relation $p^*(x) = l(x)/l_0$ for radix l_0.

It is customary to select time relative to some base year such that for the specified point in time for that year, $t = 0$. Then when considering births over the interval $(t-h, t]$ for $t \geq 0$, two separate contributions occur:

1. Births from females who are already alive at $t = 0$, and
2. Births from females who themselves were born at a time $t > 0$.

This results in two disjoint age categories represented by the age intervals $[t, \omega)$ and $[0, t)$ respectively. Figure 4.3 illustrates this situation, which results in the following:

Theorem 4.3. Relative to time $t = 0$ for F^*, B^* and p^* previously defined,

$$F^*(x, t)h' = \begin{cases} B^*(t-x)p^*(x)h & \text{for } 0 \leq x < t \quad (4.6) \\ F^*(x-t, 0)p^*(x)h/p^*(x-t) & \text{for } x \geq t \end{cases} \quad . \quad (4.7)$$

Proof: For $x \in [0, t)$ the result is an immediate consequence of the reasoning leading to (4.5).

For $x \in [t, \omega)$ observe from Fig. 4.3 that the females numbering $F^*(x, 0)h$ and those females numbering $F^*(x+t, t)h$, belong to the same birth cohort which originally numbered $B^*(-x)h$. Then using Definition 4.2.

$$B^*(-x)h = F^*(x, 0)h/p^*(x) = F^*(x+t, t)h/p^*(x+t)$$

78

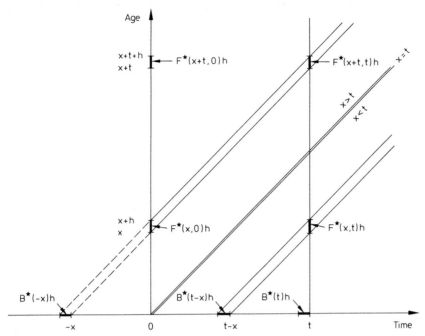

Fig. 4.3. Illustration of $F^*(x, t)$ for $0 < x \leq t$ and $x > t$

from which
$$F^*(x + t, t)h = [p^*(x + t)/p^*(x)] F^*(x, 0)h.$$

Since p^* is time invariant, and since $x \geq t$, subtracting t from each age yields the required result. Consult Fig. 4.3. $\qquad\square$

From the standpoint of fertility one must consider that the births at time t is an aggregate of all the female births contributed by the females at each age. However, before this can be done, the following is necessary [2].

Definition 4.4. The *number of female births per unit of time* calculated instantaneously at time t due to the $F^*(x, t)h$ females whose age lies on the interval $[x, x + h)$ is

$$F^*(x, t)m^*(x, t)h \tag{4.8}$$

where m^* is the age-specific birth rate at time t.

By premise of the stable theory of population it is assumed that m^* is time invariant, and as a result this *age-specific birth rate* is written simply as $m^*(x)$. Since time is assumed a continuum in this model, age is also a continuum and as a result age $x \in \mathbb{R}$ such that $x \in [0, \omega]$. From Fig. 4.4 the age axis is partitioned into n equal parts having boundaries x_i for $i = 0, 1, 2, \ldots, n$ and with interval width $h = \omega/n$. For each interval the age-specific birth rate is approxi-

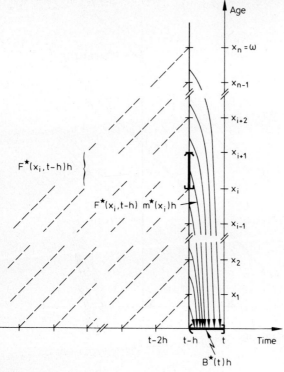

Fig. 4.4. Age contribution to the births $B^*(t)h$

mately $m^*(x_i)$. The contribution to the births at time t comes from the females who survived beyond time $t-h$. Then over time increment h this is expressed as

$$B^*(t)h = \sum_{i=1}^{n} [F^*(x_i, t-h)h] m^*(x_i)h. \tag{4.9}$$

This results in the following:

Lemma 4.5. Let B and F be defined as in Definition 4.1. Then

$$B(t) = \int_0^\omega F(x, t)m(x)dx \tag{4.10}$$

where $m(x)$ is the limit of $m^*(x)$ as $h \to 0$.

Proof: Since age is a continuum, the number of age stratifications n can be increased without bound. As $n \to \infty$, $h = (\omega/n) \to 0$. Then by definition

$$\lim_{h \to 0} [B^*(t)] = \lim_{h \to 0} (1/h) \int_{t-h}^{t} B(z)dz = B(t).$$

80

Thus, from (4.9) taking the limit as $n \to \infty$ and by definition of the integral,

$$B(t) = \lim_{n \to \infty} \sum_{i=1}^{n} F^*(x_i, t-h)m^*(x_i)h. \qquad (4.11)$$

As $n \to \infty$ the right side of (4.11) is just a Riemann sum which gives the desired integral of (4.10). □

Theorem 4.6. For the functions as defined herein, where $p^*(x) \to p(x)$ as $h \to 0$,

$$B(t) = G(t) + \int_0^t B(t-x)p(x)m(x)dx \qquad (4.12)$$

where

$$G(t) = \begin{cases} \int_t^\omega F(x-t, 0)\dfrac{p(x)m(x)}{p(x-t)}\,dx, & t \le \omega \\ 0, & t > \omega. \end{cases} \qquad (4.13)$$

Proof: From expressions (4.6) and (4.7) the limiting process results in

$$F(x,t)dx = \begin{cases} B(t-x)p(x)dt & \text{for } 0 \le x < t \\ F(x-t, 0)[p(x)/p(x-t)]dx & \text{for } x \ge t. \end{cases} \qquad (4.14)$$

Substituting these expressions for $F(x, t)$ into (4.10), the assertion of the theorem is demonstrated. □

The time function G of (4.13) is interpreted as the rate per unit time of the female births at time t to all females who were also alive at time $t=0$. Theorem 4.6 demonstrates the *fundamental integral equation* for the continuous, one-sex, deterministic population model which is essentially due to Lotka [3, 4]. The functions m and p are assumed continuous and known for all $x \in [0, \omega]$. Thus $G(t)$ can be tabulated or otherwise obtained from known statistics. Furthermore, the product of the functions m and p can combined.

Definition 4.7. Let m and p be continuous functions as previously defined. The *net maternity function*, ϕ, is defined as

$$\phi(x) = p(x)m(x). \qquad (4.15)$$

Clearly, ϕ is continuous for all $x \in [0, \omega]$.

Corollary 4.8. The fundamental integral equation for the continuous, one-sex, deterministic population model for $t \le \omega$ is

$$B(t) = \int_0^t B(t-x)\phi(x)dx + G(t) \qquad (4.16)$$

where

$$G(t) = \int_t^\omega F(x-t,0)[\phi(x)/p(x-t)]dx. \tag{4.17}$$

Proof: After substituting (4.15) into (4.12) and (4.13), the result is immediate.

□

The reader may recognize (4.16) as a linear Volterra equation of the second kind; based on the demographic nature of the functions ϕ, G and B, a solution always exists [5]. The solution of this equation is the subject of the next sections.

4.3 Solution of the Continuous Model According to Lotka

The question now remains: For which function B is the fundamental equation of (4.16) satisfied? In demographic circles the first response to this question was given by Sharpe and Lotka [6] in 1911. In their terse but enlightening article, Sharpe and Lotka proposed, without complete justification, that the solution to the fundamental equation is an infinite series of exponentials. That is, the form:

$$B(t) = \sum_{i=1}^\infty c_i s_i^t. \tag{4.18}$$

It is the intent of the author to develop the missing ideas and mathematics which led Sharpe and Lotka to arrive at such a conclusion.

As an initial simplification, assume that the time t exceeds the value of β, the ultimate age of reproduction. This leads to the following:

Lemma 4.9. Let G be defined as in (4.17). Then for $t \geq \beta$

$$G(t) \equiv 0 \tag{4.19}$$

and for $t < \beta$

$$G(t) = \int_t^\beta F(x-t,0)[\phi(x)/p(x-t)]dx. \tag{4.20}$$

Proof: By ordinary analysis $G(t)$ can be written as

$$G(t) = \int_t^\beta F(x-t,0)\phi(x)/p(x-t)dx + \int_\beta^\omega F(x-t,0)\phi(x)/p(x-t)dx. \tag{4.21}$$

But for ages beyond β the age-specific maternity function is zero and by Definition 4.7, $\phi(x) = 0$ when $x > \beta$. In this case the second integral of (4.21) vanishes and (4.20) is demonstrated. When $t \geq \beta$ it is clear that both integrals must vanish, which was to be demonstrated.

□

Theorem 4.10. Let $t \geq \beta$, the ultimate age of reproduction. Then

$$B(t) = \int_0^t B(t-x)\phi(x)dx. \tag{4.22}$$

Proof: The proof follows immediately from Lemma 4.9. □

Equation (4.22) is the homogeneous form of the fundamental equation. A solution to (4.22) is assumed to take the form cs^t. However, before investigating the ramifications of this proposal, observe the following:

Corollary 4.11. Let α and β represent the initial and ultimate age of reproduction. Then

$$B(t) = \int_\alpha^\beta B(t-x)\phi(x)dx \tag{4.23}$$

for time $t \geq \beta$.

Proof: The maternity function m is zero for all ages x except those that lie on the interval $[\alpha, \beta]$. As a result

$$\phi(x) = \begin{cases} 0 & \text{for } x < \alpha \\ m(x)p(x) & \text{for } \alpha \leq x \leq \beta \\ 0 & \text{for } x > \beta. \end{cases}$$

Since $t \geq \beta$, the result is immediate. □

Theorem 4.12. The function f defined by

$$f(t) = c \exp(rt) \tag{4.24}$$

is a solution to the fundamental equation of (4.23) if and only if the value r satisfies the equation

$$\int_\alpha^\beta \exp(-rx)\phi(x)dx = 1. \tag{4.25}$$

Proof: Assume f provides a solution to (4.23). Then by direct substitution

$$c \exp(rt) = c \exp(rt) \int_\alpha^\beta \exp(-rx)\phi(x)dx$$

from which (4.25) follows.

Assume r satisfies (4.25). Multiplying (4.25) by the expression $c \exp(rt)$ is sufficient to demonstrate that it is a solution to (4.23). □

The equation (4.25) is called the *characteristic equation* of the fundamental integral equation of (4.23). The solution for r in this equation will generate a spectrum of complex values for r. From this spectrum, however, only one value will be real, as shown in the following:

Theorem 4.13. The characteristic equation

$$\int_\alpha^\beta \exp(-rx)\phi(x)dx - 1 = 0 \tag{4.26}$$

admits exactly one real root for r.

Proof: Let Ψ be a characteristic function defined by

$$\Psi(r) = \int_\alpha^\beta \exp(-rx)\phi(x)dx. \tag{4.27}$$

Demographic conditions ensure that $\phi(x)$ is non-negative. Let $r \in \mathbb{R}$. Since age x is a non-negative real number, then $\exp(-rx)$ is real and positive. Since $\phi(x) > 0$ on some open subinterval of $[\alpha, \beta]$, then

$$\Psi(r) > 0 \quad \text{for all } r \in \mathbb{R}$$

$$\lim_{r \to -\infty} \Psi(r) = \infty$$

$$\lim_{r \to \infty} \Psi(r) = 0.$$

Recalling that $x \geq 0$, and knowing that the integrand of (4.27) is well-behaved, use of ordinary calculus and Leibnitz' Rule shows that

$$\Psi'(r) = -\int_\alpha^\beta x \exp(-rx)\phi(x)dx$$

demonstrating that $\Psi'(r) < 0$ for all $r \in \mathbb{R}$. (It is interesting to note that

$$\Psi''(r) = \int_\alpha^\beta x^2 \exp(-rx)\phi(x)dx$$

demonstrating that $\Psi''(r) > 0$ for all $r \in \mathbb{R}$, or that Ψ is a concave-up function.) It is clear that for all $r \in \mathbb{R}$, Ψ is a positive, monotonically decreasing function of r. Using this information concerning the function Ψ, it is clear from Fig. 4.5 that it takes on the value of 1 exactly once at $r = r'$, that is,

$$\Psi(r) = 1$$

for only one $r = r' \in \mathbb{R}$. $\qquad\qquad\square$

The unique real root of the characteristic equation (4.26) is called the *characteristic root* or *principal root* of the equation. This leads to the following:

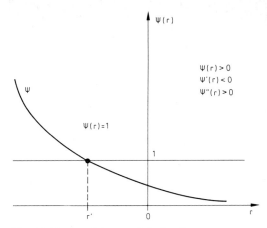

Fig. 4.5. Nature of characteristic function

Theorem 4.14. All roots of the characteristic equation (4.26), save the principal root, are complex and occur in complex conjugate pairs.

Proof: That the roots of the characteristic equation are complex, excluding the principal root, is an immediate deduction from Theorem 4.13.

Suppose one root of the characteristic equation was $r = u + iv$. Substitution into (4.26), after using Euler's Identity, gives

$$1 = \int_\alpha^\beta \exp(-ux) \cos(vx) \phi(x) dx - i \int_\alpha^\beta \exp(-ux) \sin(vx) \phi(x) dx. \qquad (4.28)$$

Since the complex conjugate of 1 is itself, the complex conjugate of (4.28) leads to

$$1 = \int_\alpha^\beta \exp(-ux) \cos(-vx) \phi(x) dx - i \int_\alpha^\beta \exp(-ux) \sin(-vx) \phi(x) dx$$

implying that $r = u - iv$ is also a root, which was to be demonstrated. □

The principal (real) root of the characteristic equation will dominate the real part of all other complex roots, as shown in the following:

Theorem 4.15. Let r' denote the principal root of the characteristic equation and let $r = u + iv$ denote any other complex root of that equation. Then

$$r' > \mathrm{Re}(r). \qquad (4.29)$$

Proof: Substitution of $r = u + iv$ into the characteristic equation gives the result expressed by (4.28). Equating real and imaginary parts yields

$$\int_\alpha^\beta \exp(-ux) \cos(vx) \phi(x) dx = 1 \qquad (4.30)$$

which must also equal

$$\int_\alpha^\beta \exp(-r'x)\phi(x)dx = 1. \tag{4.31}$$

Since x is any real number on the interval $[\alpha, \beta]$, then $\cos(vx) < 1$ for at least one such x value, and as a result

$$\int_\alpha^\beta \exp(-ux)\cos(vx)\phi(x)dx < \int_\alpha^\beta \exp(-ux)\phi(x)dx. \tag{4.32}$$

Equating (4.30) and (4.31) and substituting into (4.32) gives

$$\int_\alpha^\beta \exp(-r'x)\phi(x)dx < \int_\alpha^\beta \exp(-ux)\phi(x)dx$$

implying

$$\exp(-r'x) < \exp(-ux)$$

whereby $r' > u$ from which the result is immediate. $\square$

The homogeneous case of the fundamental equation exhibits the property that a linear combination of any two solutions satisfying (4.23) is also a solution. This is shown in the following:

Lemma 4.16. Let r_i and r_j be roots of the characteristic equation (4.26) whose corresponding solutions are $\exp(r_i t)$ and $\exp(r_j t)$. Then for arbitrary constants c_i and c_j

$$c_i \exp(r_i t) + c_j \exp(r_j t) \tag{4.33}$$

is also a solution.

Proof: Substitution of (4.33) into (4.23) yields

$$c_i \exp(r_i t) + c_j \exp(r_j t) = c_i \exp(r_i t) \int \exp(-r_i x)\phi(x)dx$$
$$+ c_j \exp(r_j t) \int \exp(-r_j x)\phi(x)dx. \tag{4.34}$$

Since the two integrals of (4.34) equal unity by virtue of (4.26) the assertion of the theorem is demonstrated. $\square$

The solution of the fundamental equation (4.16) must also satisfy its homogeneous counterpart (4.23) for $t \geq \beta$. One approach to solving the fundamental equation is to find all possible solutions of the homogeneous case, and then to seek among them for the particular one that will satisfy (4.16). This is precisely the strategy that Lotka followed. Lotka assumed, without any proof or justification, that every solution of the homogeneous equation (4.23) is of the form

$$B(t) = \sum_{i=1}^\infty c_i \exp(r_i t). \tag{4.35}$$

Once this is granted, the c_i can be determined so that $B(t)$ will satisfy not only (4.23) but also the fundamental equation (4.16).

It is at this point that the biologist Lotka and mathematicians have parted company. Lotka assumed that for any arbitrary time function G of the fundamental equation (4.16), and for any arbitrary net maternity function ϕ that might be demographically reasonable, there will be some choice of the coefficients in (4.35) so that the renewal equation is satisfied. As Feller [7] and others have pointed out, this is surely not true if G and ϕ are arbitrary continuous functions. The upshot is that for demographically reasonable functions G and ϕ, the fundamental equation (4.16) does have a solution of the form (4.35).

4.4 Considerations on the Continuous Model According to Feller

The arguments produced by Lotka in the previous section are less than perfect. The mathematical discrepencies caused Lotka to receive much criticism concerning his method for almost thirty years. It was not until Wilhelm Feller published his landmark work in 1941 on population renewal theory [8] that Lotka's method received some justification and was placed on a sound mathematical basis. Feller indicated [9] that

> Lotka's method rests essentially on the fundamental assumption that the characteristic equation ... has infinitely many distinct simple roots $s_0, s_1, \ldots$, and that the solution $(B(t))$ of $((4.16))$ can be expanded into a series
> $$B(t) = \sum_k A_k e^{s_k t} \qquad (4.36)$$
> where the A_k are complex constants.

For example, there exist functions ϕ for which the roots of the characteristic equation are finite in number. Therefore, the solution set to the homogeneous equation (4.23) will be a finite dimensional vector space whereas the space of possible functions G is not finite dimensional. Lotka gives no reason to believe that there must be infinitely many roots. Furthermore, Feller points out that Lotka's approach contains a further assumption, namely that the infinitely many roots of the characteristic equation must be simple. Feller shows that in the case of multiple roots, Lotka's solution is not valid, but that a closely related solution exists. Feller further indicates [10] that

> The main limitation of Lotka's theory can be formulated in the following way: Lotka's method depends only on the function $G(t)$ and in the roots of (the characteristic equation). Now two different functions (ϕ) can lead to characteristic equations having the same roots. Lotka's method would be applicable to both only if the corresponding two integral equations (4.16)

had the same solution $(B(t))$. This, however, is not necessarily the case. Thus, if Lotka's method is applied, and if all computations are correctly performed, and if the resulting series for $(B(t))$ converges uniformly, there is no possibility of telling which equation is really satisfied by the resulting $(B(t))$: it can happen that one unwittingly solved some unknown equation of type $((4.16))$ which, by chance, leads to a characteristic equation having the same roots as the characteristic equation of the integral equation with which one was really concerned.

That is, two different functions ϕ can have the same characteristic roots even though the solutions of the integral equations are not the same. Lotka's method would give the same solution for both.

Feller settled all these points in his 1941 paper in which he gave mathematical conditions under which Lotka's method is valid. In this section some of the salient features of Feller's paper are presented which in effect allows a solution to be fundamental equation (4.16) to represented as an expansion of the type shown in (4.35). Before demonstrating this, the following is necessary.

Lemma 4.17. Given the general population renewal equation of (4.16). Let the functions $*B(s)$, $*G(s)$ and $*\phi(s)$ denote the Laplace Transforms of $B(t)$, $G(t)$ and $\phi(t)$ respectively. Then

(a) the Laplace transforms of each of these functions exist, and

(b) the Laplace Transform of the birth function is

$$*B(s) = *G(s)/(1 - *\phi(s)). \qquad (4.37)$$

Proof: (a) The functions G and ϕ are each bounded and of compact support. Thus, they are of exponential order and as such their Laplace transforms exist. For the case of the birth function B, the solution of the fundamental equation, it has been shown by Feller [11] in his Theorem 1 that the Laplace transform also exists.

(b) The integral of the the non-homogeneous renewal equation of (4.16) suggests a convolution of two functions whereby the Laplace Transform is a reasonable approach in an attempt at a solution. Taking the transform of (4.16) results in

$$\int_0^\infty e^{-st}B(t)dt = \int_0^\infty \int_0^t e^{-st}B(t-x)\phi(x)dxdt + \int_0^\infty e^{-st}G(t)dt. \qquad (4.38)$$

The double integral of (4.38) is easily recognized as the convolution of Laplace transforms [12] which enables one to write

$$*B(s) = *B(s)*\phi(s) + *G(s) \qquad (4.39)$$

from which the result of (4.37) is obvious. $\qquad\square$

The following theorem not only shows the limits of Lotka's approach but also provides an extension to his theory.

Theorem 4.18 (Feller). In order that the solution $B(t)$ of the non-homogeneous renewal equation of (4.16) be representable in the series expansion of the form (4.36), where the series converges absolutely for $t>0$ and where the r_k denote the roots of the characteristic equation

$$*\phi(s) = \int_0^\infty \exp(-st)\phi(t)dt = 1 \qquad (4.40)$$

it is necessary that $*B(s)$ be a single-valued function, and in addition it is necessary and sufficient that the Laplace transform $*B(s)$ admit an expansion

$$*B(s) = \frac{*G(s)}{1 - *\phi(s)} = \sum \frac{A_k}{s - r_k} \qquad (4.41)$$

and that $\sum |A_k|$ converges absolutely. Furthermore, the coefficients are determined by

$$A_k = -*G(s)/*\phi'(s). \qquad (4.42)$$

Proof: For a detailed development and proof of this theorem, consult the article by Feller [13]. □

Theorem 4.18 is then generalized to accommodate the possibility of multiple roots of the characteristic equation whose total number of roots may be finite or infinite. This is formally presented as follows.

Theorem 4.19 (Feller). Given the hypotheses of Theorem 4.18, and let r_k be a root of the characteristic equation (4.40) having multiplicity σ_k. A necessary and sufficient condition that the fundamental equation (4.16) admit a solution of the form

$$B(t) = \sum_k \sum_{j=1}^{\sigma_k} (A_{kj}/(j-1)!)t^{j-1} \exp(r_k t) \qquad (4.43)$$

is that the Laplace transform $*B(s)$ have the expansion

$$*B(s) = \sum_k \sum_{j=1}^{\sigma_k} \frac{A_{kj}}{(s-r_k)^j} \qquad (4.44)$$

and that $\sum |A_{kj}|$ converges.

Proof: For a discussion on this theorem, consult Feller [14]. □

In Lemma 4.17 and in Theorems 4.18 and 4.19 it is easily seen that a unique inverse Laplace transform of $*\phi$ and $*G$ indeed exist. In the case of $*B$,

89

it can be shown [15] that a unique inverse Laplace transform also exists. Demographic considerations ensure that the functions B, G, and ϕ are well-behaved and satisfy the conditions set forth in Theorem 4.18 by Feller [16] even so far as the calculation of the A_k as [17]

$$A_k = \int_0^\beta \exp(-r_k t)G(t)dt \bigg/ \int_0^\beta x\exp(-r_k x)\phi(x)dx. \qquad (4.45)$$

This expression can be reduced to

$$A_k = -B_0/\Psi'(r_k) \qquad (4.46)$$

as shown by Keyfitz [18], where B_0 represents the initial births, Ψ the characteristic function, and r_k a root of the characteristic equation (4.21). In particular, when the multiplicities of the characteristic roots are all unity, Feller's result of (4.43) reduces to that proposed by Lotka, save the assumption that the number of distinct roots must be infinite.

Lotka's guess that the solution to the homogeneous population renewal equation (4.23) is a series of exponentials, and that this series can be made to satisfy the non-homogeneous population renewal equation (4.16), has turned out to be correct provided that the conditions set forth by Feller are satisfied. Assuming that these conditions hold, a solution to the fundamental equation of (4.16) is

$$B(t) = a_1 \exp(r't) + \sum_{i=2}^{m} \sum_{j=1}^{\sigma_i} a_{ij} t^{j-1} \exp(r_i t) \qquad (4.47)$$

where for characteristic equation (4.40) there are m roots (finite or infinite) r_i with multiplicity σ_i and where r' is its principal characteristic root. In the event all the multiplicities of the characteristic roots are unity, then (4.47) reduces to

$$B(t) = a_1 \exp(r't) + \sum_{i=2}^{m} a_i \exp(r_i t) \qquad (4.48)$$

which is similar to the solution conjectured by Lotka. Lotka's work has now been made mathematically sound and his method justified.

4.5 Asymptotic Considerations

The characteristic equation, whether viewed from the standpoint of Lotka or Feller, results in a principal characteristic root r' which is real, unique, and by Theorem 4.15 dominates the real part of all other characteristic values. These properties result in the following:

Theorem 4.20. Let the birth function of the non-homogeneous population renewal equation (4.16) be described as in equation (4.43). In the limit as $t \to \infty$,

90

$B(t)$ becomes asymptotic to its leading term. That is, as time t approaches infinity,

$$B(t) \sim a_1 \exp(r't) \qquad (4.49)$$

where the coefficient a_1 is real and positive.

Proof: The fact that a_1 is real and positive can be deduced immediately from (4.46). Multiplying (4.47) by $\exp(-r't)$ results in

$$\exp(-r't)B(t) = a_1 + \sum_{i=2}^{m} \sum_{j=1}^{\sigma_i} a_{ij} t^{j-1} \exp(-(r'-r_i)t).$$

Since $r' > \mathrm{Re}(r_i)$, for sufficiently large values of t the exponential will force all terms in the double summation to approach 0 as $t \to \infty$, from which the assertion of the theorem is immediate. $\qquad\qquad\square$

The discussion in this chapter thus far has been based on the premises of the stable theory of population – specifically, for a population closed to migration, and where $\phi(x) = m(x)p(x)$ was time invariant. The *number of females* whose age is on the interval $[x, x+dx)$ at time t is $F(x, t)dx$. The *total number of females at time t*, denoted $F_T(t)$, is just

$$F_T(t) = \int_0^\omega F(x, t)dx \qquad (4.50)$$

which leads to the following:

Definition 4.21. The fraction of the population, defined by the ratio of the number of females aged x to the total number of females at time t, is

$$c(x, t) = F(x, t)/F_T(t) \qquad (4.51)$$

where $F_T(t)$ is defined by (4.50).

This leads to the following important result in the stable theory of population.

Theorem 4.22. Let c be defined according to (4.51), and let F describe the number of females aged x at time t in a stable population. As time becomes unbounded, c becomes a function of age alone and is described by

$$c(x) = \exp(-r'x)p(x) \bigg/ \int_0^\omega \exp(-r'x)p(x)dx \qquad (4.52)$$

where r' is the principal characteristic root, and where p is the survivorship probability function.

91

Proof: From expressions (4.14) and (4.51) the portion of females who are aged x at time t, recalling $dt = dx$, is

$$c(x, t) = B(t - x)p(x) \Big/ \int_0^\omega B(t - x)p(x)dx.$$

But by Theorem 4.23 for $t \to \infty$ this can be written as

$$c(x, t) \sim a_1 \exp(r'(t - x)p(x)) \Big/ \int_0^\omega a_1 \exp(r'(t - x)p(x))dx$$

which reduces to

$$c(x, t) \sim a_1 \exp(r't) \exp(-r'x)p(x) \Big/ a_1 \exp(r't) \int_0 \exp(-r'x)p(x)dx.$$

Since the $a_1 \exp(r't)$ cancel, clearly $c(x, t) \to c(x)$ and the assertion of the theorem is demonstrated. $\qquad\qquad\qquad\qquad\qquad\qquad\qquad\qquad\qquad\qquad\qquad\qquad\quad$ □

The interpretation of this theorem is that the age distribution of females described by function c becomes a function of age alone, independent of time, as $t \to \infty$. It is in this sense that a population is said to 'stabilize' in that the percentage of females at any age x will be asymptotically the same for all values of increasing time.

4.6 Conclusion

The continuous time stable population model is attributed to Lotka, and rightly so. While there may have been some mathematical flaws in his thinking, these defects were considered by Feller and resulted in a justification of Lotka's beliefs. Furthermore, because of its ability to utilize the tools of analysis, the continuous time model has received much exposure, as will be seen in Chapters Six and Seven, and has become the dominant model in the study of stable population theory.

It would be unfair to attribute sole credit to Lotka for the continuous time model. In 1926 A.C. McKendrick [19] developed a different approach to the continuous time model. His effort resulted in a partial differential equation of the form

$$\frac{\partial F(x, t)}{\partial x} + \frac{\partial F(x, t)}{\partial t} + \mu(x)F(x, t) = 0$$

where x and t represent age and time, μ represents the force of mortality, and F the population density. McKendrick's work received little attention until 1959 when the model was again presented by H. von Foerster [20]. A more detailed description of this model is given as an Appendix.

4.7 Notes for Chapter Four

[1] Sharpe, F.R. and Lotka, A.J. (1911), A problem in age-distribution. Philosophical Magazine, Ser. 6, vol. 21, p. 435.

[2] Ibid., p. 435.

[3] Lotka, A.J. (1907), Relation between birth rates and death rates. Science, N.S., vol. 26, p. 21 ff.

[4] Sharpe and Lotka (1911), op. cit., p. 435 ff.

[5] Davis, H.T. (1962), Introduction to nonlinear differential and integral equations. p. 414.

[6] Sharpe and Lotka (1911), op. cit., pp. 435-438. Note that the article totals four pages only.

[7] Feller, W. (1941), On the integral equation of renewal theory. Annals of Mathematical Statistics, vol. 12, pp. 243-267.

[8] Ibid.

[9] Feller (1941), op. cit., p. 258.

[10] Ibid., p. 260.

[11] Ibid.

[12] Ross, S.L. (1974), Differential equations. Second Ed., p. 380.

[13] Feller (1941), op. cit., p. 263.

[14] Ibid., p. 264.

[15] Hoppenstead, F. (1975), Mathematical theories of populations: Demographics, genetics and epidemics. pp. 7-8.

[16] Feller (1941), op. cit., p. 263.

[17] Ibid.

[18] Keyfitz, N. (1968 (1977)), Introduction to the mathematics of population with revisions. p. 106.

[19] McKendrick, A.C. (1926), Applications of mathematics to medical problems. Proceedings Edinburgh Mathematical Society, vol. 44, pp. 98-130.

[20] von Foerster, H. (1959), Some remarks on changing populations, in the kinetics of cellular proliferation, Grune and Stratton, New York.

5. The Discrete Time Matrix Model

5.1 Introduction

The discrete time recurrence model and the continuous time model which were discussed in Chapters Three and Four focused on the births that occurred at a particular time and their relationship to the births that occurred prior to this time. In each case the age distribution of the population was discussed almost as an adjunct to the model and not as an integral part of it. Perhaps this was unfortunate since it was the asymptotic age distribution of the model that gave meaning to the concept of a 'stable' population.

In the discrete time matrix model, the age structure of the population will be treated as the primary ingredient of the model. Unlike the discrete time recurrence model, the focus will be on the total age distribution where births constitute but one part of this distribution. Furthermore, the matrix model will be developed from a projection viewpoint rather than from a 'historical' one. Since the discrete time recurrence model and the discrete time matrix model are basically equivalent, much of the notation that will be used in this chapter will have been previously defined in prior chapters.

5.2 Development of the Discrete Time Matrix Model

As in Sect. 2.3 of Chapter Two, let the age structure of a population at time t' be stratified in $w+1$ strata, each having an age width of h years. The age intervals are

$$[0, h), [h, 2h), \dots, [ih, (i+1)h), \dots, [wh, (w+1)h)$$

where $i = 0, 1, 2, \dots, w$. The number of females in the age interval $[ih, (i+1)h)$ at time t' is denoted $F_i'(t')$. If g_{i+1}' is the probability at time t' that a female in age interval $[ih, (i+1)h)$ survives to age interval $[(i+1)h, (i+2)h)$ at time $t'+h$ then

$$F_{i+1}'(t'+h) = g_{i+1}' F_i'(t') \qquad (5.1)$$

for $0 \le i \le w$. Furthermore, the females in each age category at time t' may provide a female birth contribution to the first female age category at time t'

$+h$. If $m_i'h$ represents the ratio of the number of female births resulting from the females in the ith age category to the total number of females in that category, then the total number of births in the time interval $(t', t'+h]$ is

$$\sum_{i=0}^{w} m_i' F_i'(t') h. \tag{5.2}$$

But not all these female births may survive to the first $[0, h)$ age category. If g_0' is the probability of surviving birth to the first age category then it is true that

$$F_0'(t'+h) = \sum_{i=0}^{w} g_0' m_i' F_i'(t') h. \tag{5.3}$$

Figure 5.1 illustrates the meaning of equations (5.1) and (5.3). Notice how this parallels the development of the discrete time recursive model in Chapters Two and Three.

The usual interpretation of time t' is in annual units or years. However, as was demonstrated in Sect. 3.3, Lemma 3.10, it is very convenient to normalize equations (5.1) and (5.3) so that time is expressed in units of h years. Letting $t = t'/h$, $k = i+1$, $m_k = m_{i+1}'h$, $g_k = g_{i+1}'$ and $F_k(t) = F_i'(t')$, equations (5.3) and (5.1) become respectively,

$$F_1(t+1) = \sum_{k=1}^{n'} g_0 m_k F_k(t) \tag{5.4}$$

and

$$F_{k+1}(t+1) = g_k(t) F_k(t) \tag{5.5}$$

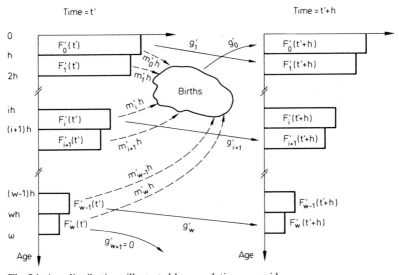

Fig. 5.1. Age distributions illustrated by population pyramids

for the $n'=w+1$ strata where $k=1,2,\ldots,n'$. In expanded form equations (5.4) and (5.5) become

$$
\begin{bmatrix}
F_1(t+1) \\
F_2(t+1) \\
F_3(t+1) \\
\vdots \\
F_{n'}(t+1)
\end{bmatrix}
=
\begin{bmatrix}
g_0 m_1 & g_0 m_2 & g_0 m_3 & \cdots & g_0 m_{n'-1} & g_0 m_{n'} \\
g_1 & 0 & 0 & \cdots & 0 & 0 \\
0 & g_2 & 0 & \cdots & 0 & 0 \\
\vdots & \vdots & \vdots & & \vdots & \vdots \\
0 & 0 & 0 & \cdots & g_{n'-1} & 0
\end{bmatrix}
\begin{bmatrix}
F_1(t) \\
F_2(t) \\
F_3(t) \\
\vdots \\
F_{n'}(t)
\end{bmatrix}.
\tag{5.6}
$$

In matrix notation, with obvious equivalences, this system of equations becomes

$$
\overline{\mathbb{F}}_{t+1} = \overline{\mathbb{Z}}\,\overline{\mathbb{F}}_t
\tag{5.7}
$$

which is a recursive matrix equation. The $n' \times n'$ matrix $\overline{\mathbb{Z}}$ is called the *projection matrix* of the population; the elements of $\overline{\mathbb{Z}}$ are all time invariant since by the premises of stable theory, m_k and g_k are not time dependent. Vectors $\overline{\mathbb{F}}_t$ are called *population distribution vectors*.

Some historical notes are worth mentioning at this point. The first evidence of the use of matrices in the stable theory of population is credited to Harro Bernardelli who, in an appendix to his 1941 publication [1], formulated a population projection matrix and derives characteristic values relating to it. One year later, E.G. Lewis [2] showed, via matrices, that population age distributions display some periodicity before settling down to a stable distribution. In addition, Lewis showed circumstances where these oscillations do not dampen out but continue indefinitely. In 1945 P.H. Leslie wrote a comprehensive article [3] on the use of matrices in stable population theory. Because of this work, the projection matrix $\overline{\mathbb{Z}}$ is often called a *Leslie matrix*.

The reproductive capability of the females of a population usually ends at age β which is often less than ω the ultimate age of life. For human populations this is definitely the case. In this respect, if n is the age index corresponding to age β, then

$$
m_{n+1} = m_{n+2} = \ldots = m_{n'} = 0.
$$

This enables one to represent the population projection matrix $\overline{\mathbb{Z}}$ as

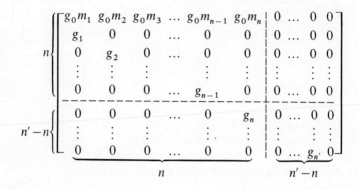

98

Again, with obvious equivalences

$$\overline{\mathbb{Z}} = \begin{bmatrix} \mathbb{Z} & \mathbb{O} \\ \text{ic} & \text{dl} \end{bmatrix} \qquad (5.8)$$

where $\mathbb{Z}$ is a $n \times n$ submatrix which partitions $\overline{\mathbb{Z}}$ into four parts the others being $\mathbb{O}$, ic and dl. In a similar manner the column vector $\overline{\mathbb{F}}_t$ can be partitioned into conformable parts $\mathbb{F}_t$ and lb_t whereby (5.7) can be rewritten as [4]

$$\begin{bmatrix} \mathbb{F}_{t+1} \\ \text{lb}_{t+1} \end{bmatrix} = \begin{bmatrix} \mathbb{Z} & \mathbb{O} \\ \text{ic} & \text{dl} \end{bmatrix} \begin{bmatrix} \mathbb{F}_t \\ \text{lb}_t \end{bmatrix} \qquad (5.9)$$

where $\mathbb{F}_t$ is a $n \times 1$ submatrix of vector $\overline{\mathbb{F}}_t$. The significance of representing (5.7) in the form of (5.9) will be seen after demonstrating the following:

Theorem 5.1. Let $\overline{\mathbb{F}}_t$ and $\overline{\mathbb{Z}}$ be defined as per (5.6). If k is a positive integer, then

$$\overline{\mathbb{F}}_{t+k} = \overline{\mathbb{Z}}^k \overline{\mathbb{F}}_t. \qquad (5.10)$$

Proof: From the discussion leading to (5.7), matrix $\overline{\mathbb{Z}}$ represents the projection of a population age structure between two consecutive time intervals. Thus,

$$\begin{aligned} \overline{\mathbb{F}}_{t+k} &= \overline{\mathbb{Z}}\, \overline{\mathbb{F}}_{t+k-1} \\ &= \overline{\mathbb{Z}}\,\overline{\mathbb{Z}}\, \overline{\mathbb{F}}_{t+k-2} \\ &= \overline{\mathbb{Z}}\,\overline{\mathbb{Z}}\,\overline{\mathbb{Z}} \dots \overline{\mathbb{Z}}\,\overline{\mathbb{Z}}\, \overline{\mathbb{F}}_t \end{aligned}$$

for k factors of $\overline{\mathbb{Z}}$ from which the result is immediate. $\qquad \square$

Lemma 5.2 (Leslie). Let $\overline{\mathbb{Z}}$ be represented as in (5.8). Then

(a)
$$\overline{\mathbb{Z}}^k = \begin{bmatrix} \mathbb{Z}^k & \mathbb{O} \\ \text{ir} & \text{dl}^k \end{bmatrix} \qquad (5.11)$$

where ir is a function of $\mathbb{Z}$, ic and dl.
  (b) Moreover, for $k \geq n' - n$

$$\text{dl} = \mathbb{O}. \qquad (5.12)$$

Proof: Straightforward matrix multiplication will produce these results. For a more in-depth discussion, consult Leslie [5]. $\qquad \square$

Part (b) of Lemma 5.2 expresses the obvious fact that females who are alive in the post-reproductive ages make no contribution to the female population after they themselves are dead. This leads to the following:

Theorem 5.3. Let a population at time t be projected to time $t+k$ according to (5.10) of Theorem 5.1. Then

$$\mathbb{F}_{t+k} = \mathbf{Z}^k \mathbb{F}_t. \tag{5.13}$$

Proof: Combining Theorem 5.1 with Lemma 5.2 and expression (5.9) results in a partitioned matrix expression

$$\begin{bmatrix} \mathbb{F}_{t+k} \\ \mathbb{b}_{t+k} \end{bmatrix} = \begin{bmatrix} \mathbf{Z}^k & \mathbb{O} \\ \mathbb{r} & \mathbb{d}^k \end{bmatrix} \begin{bmatrix} \mathbb{F}_t \\ \mathbb{b}_t \end{bmatrix}.$$

Then by ordinary matrix multiplication the assertion of the theorem is demonstrated. $\square$

The significance of Theorem 5.3 is that for any discrete time interval k, the age distribution vector through the reproductive years for females at time t, when multiplied by the projection matrix to the kth power, gives the age distribution vector for females through the reproductive years at time $t+k$.

For the remaining discussion of this chapter it will be assumed that the assertion of Theorem 5.3 holds. The matrix $\mathbf{Z}$ will be referred to as the *projection matrix* of the population and is defined as

$$\mathbf{Z} = \begin{bmatrix} g_0 m_1 & g_0 m_2 & g_0 m_3 & \cdots & g_0 m_{n-1} & g_0 m_n \\ g_1 & 0 & 0 & \cdots & 0 & 0 \\ 0 & g_2 & 0 & \cdots & 0 & 0 \\ 0 & 0 & g_3 & \cdots & 0 & 0 \\ \vdots & \vdots & \vdots & & \vdots & \vdots \\ 0 & 0 & 0 & \cdots & g_{n-1} & 0 \end{bmatrix} \tag{5.14}$$

where n is the index of the last age interval which contains β, the last age of reproduction. The age distribution vector $\mathbb{F}_t$ at time t will contain the first n age intervals and defined as

$$\mathbb{F}_t = \begin{bmatrix} F_1(t) \\ F_2(t) \\ F_3(t) \\ \vdots \\ F_n(t) \end{bmatrix}. \tag{5.15}$$

These n intervals are the only ones necessary for population renewal.

5.3 Population Stability and the Matrix Model

In previous chapters it was demonstrated that the concept of stability in mathematical demography implied that the ratio of females at a particular age or age category compared to the total number of females was asymptotically a constant, independent of time. From the standpoint of matrices this implies that the age distribution vector $\mathbb{F}$ at time $t+1$ is proportional to the age distribution vector at time t. Symbolically, if s is a complex constant, then for sufficiently large t,

$$\mathbb{F}_{t+1} = s\mathbb{F}_t. \tag{5.16}$$

This results in the following:

Theorem 5.4. Given a population that has achieved stability. Then

$$[\mathbb{Z} - s\mathbb{I}]\mathbb{F}_t = \mathbb{O} \tag{5.17}$$

where $\mathbb{Z}$ is the $n \times n$ projection matrix that is defined by (5.14), $\mathbb{F}_t$ is the age distribution matrix defined by (5.15), $\mathbb{I}$ is the identity matrix of order n, and s is a complex scalar.

Proof: For any time t it is true that

$$\mathbb{F}_{t+1} = \mathbb{Z}\mathbb{F}_t. \tag{5.18}$$

Substituting (5.18) into (5.16) yields

$$\mathbb{Z}\mathbb{F}_t = s\mathbb{F}_t$$

from which (5.17) is an immediate consequence. $\qquad\square$

Since $\mathbb{F}_t$ cannot be a null vector, the system of equations represented by (5.17) is consistent if and only if

$$\det(\mathbb{Z} - s\mathbb{I}) = 0. \tag{5.19}$$

This equation is called the *characteristic equation* of the projection matrix $\mathbb{Z}$ which can be written as

$$\begin{vmatrix} g_0 m_1 - s & g_0 m_2 & g_0 m_3 & \cdots & g_0 m_{n-1} & g_0 m_n \\ g_1 & -s & 0 & \cdots & 0 & 0 \\ 0 & g_2 & -s & \cdots & 0 & 0 \\ \vdots & \vdots & \vdots & & \vdots & \vdots \\ 0 & 0 & 0 & \cdots & g_{n-1} & -s \end{vmatrix} = 0. \tag{5.20}$$

Expansion of (5.20) results in

$$s^n - m_1 g_0 s^{n-1} - m_2 g_0 g_1 s^{n-2} - m_3 g_0 g_1 g_2 s^{n-3} - \cdots$$
$$- m_{n-1} g_0 g_1 g_2 \cdots g_{n-2} s - m_n g_0 g_1 \cdots g_{n-1} = 0 \tag{5.21}$$

which is a polynomial equation in variable s of degree n. Letting

$$\phi_i = m_i \left(\prod_{j=0}^{i-1} g_j \right) \qquad (5.22)$$

results in a similar polynomial of the form

$$s^n - \phi_1 s^{n-1} - \phi_2 s^{n-2} - \ldots - \phi_n = 0. \qquad (5.23)$$

The coefficients ϕ_i represent the net maternity function in dicrete form. All the ϕ_i are non-negative. The characteristic equation (5.23) has been encountered several times before. Hence, the deductions from this equation are similar to those that were previously derived in the discussions of the discrete time recurrence model and the continuous time model. Namely, there is a unique positive real root s' which dominates the magnitude of all other roots; there are exactly n roots to this equation, and complex roots must appear in conjugate pairs.

The aforementioned conclusions can be derived from the standpoint of matrices. This will require the following [6]:

Definition 5.5. A matrix $\mathbb{C} = [c_{ij}]$ is a *non-negative matrix* if all its elements are non-negative. Moreover, if $\mathbb{C}$ is a square matrix such that a permutation of the indices reduces $\mathbb{C}$ to the form

$$\mathbb{C}' = \begin{bmatrix} \mathbb{C}_1 & \mathbb{O} \\ \mathbb{C}_2 & \mathbb{C}_3 \end{bmatrix} \qquad (5.24)$$

where $\mathbb{C}_1$ and $\mathbb{C}_3$ are square matrices, then $\mathbb{C}$ is called *reducible*. Otherwise $\mathbb{C}$ is called *irreducible*.

Theorem 5.6. The projection matrix $\mathbb{Z}$ is non-negative and irreducible.

Proof: Since the values if m_i and g_i are all non-negative, and the product $g_0 m_i$ is non-negative, it is clear that $\mathbb{Z}$ is a non-negative matrix.

To show that $\mathbb{Z}$ is irreducible, first let $\mathbb{Z} = [a_{ij}]$ be an $n \times n$ matrix such that the elements $a_{1n}, a_{2,1}, a_{3,2}, \ldots, a_{n,n-1}$ are positive, a necessary requirement for a projection matrix. Suppose there were a permutation q on the indices such that the new rearranged matrix were reducible and thus would take the form of (5.24). Let the "south-west" most 0 entry of the block be the $(k, k+1)$ entry of such a matrix. Then in order for the square submatrices $\mathbb{C}_1$ and $\mathbb{C}_3$ of (5.24) to exist, it is necessary that $1 < k < n$. The condition for a pair of indices (i, j) to be in the zero block is:

$$i \leq k \quad \text{and} \quad j \geq k+1. \qquad (5.25)$$

Since $a_{21} > 0$, it follows that $a_{q(2), q(1)}$ cannot be in the zero block, and by (5.25) this means that for an element to be out of the zero block the following

102

disjunctive conditions are required on the indices (i, j):

$$
\begin{array}{llll}
q(2) > k & \text{or} \quad q(1) < k+1 & q(3) > k & \text{or} \quad q(2) < k+1 \\
q(4) > k & \text{or} \quad q(3) < k+1 & q(5) > k & \text{or} \quad q(4) < k+1 \\
\vdots & \qquad \vdots & \vdots & \qquad \vdots \\
q(n) > k & \text{or} \quad q(n-1) < k+1 & q(1) > k & \text{or} \quad q(n) < k+1.
\end{array}
\tag{5.26}
$$

But there must be some i such that $q(i) = k$ since a permutation is a one-to-one, onto mapping. Then looking at the $(i-1)^{\text{th}}$ in the disjunctive list of (5.26) one obtains

$$
q(i) > k \quad \text{or} \quad q(i-1) < k+1 \quad \text{or both.}
$$

Since $q(i) = k$ it is impossible for $q(i) > k$ and so the disjunction implies $q(i-1) < k+1$. Applying this to the previous line gives $q(i-2) < k+1$. Then continuing in a reverse manner, one reaches the first line to obtain the condition $q(1) < k+1$. Now the last line implies $q(n) < k+1$. Continuing to work downward, one eventually obtains $q(i) < k+1$ for all values of i. But since $k < n$ this is impossible for at least one $q(i) = n$, in which case $\mathbb{C}_1$ does not exist, which is a contradiction. Hence, $\mathbf{Z}$ is not reducible. $\qquad \square$

Theorem 5.7. Because it is non-negative and irreducible, the projection matrix $\mathbf{Z}$ always has a characteristic number s' which is a simple positive real root of its characteristic equation. Moreover, the moduli of the other characteristic numbers are at most s'.

Proof: This is a direct result of the Perron-Frobenius theory on non-negative matrices [7, 8]. Consult also Gantmacher [9]. $\qquad \square$

While Theorem 5.7 guarantees the existence of a simple positive characteristic root s', it does not preclude the possibility that the moduli of other characteristic roots may equal s'. To investigate this further, the following is required.

Definition 5.8. Let a non-negative irreducible matrix have a characteristic equation with principal root $s' = s_1$. Suppose there are exactly h characteristic numbers of modulus

$$
s' = s_1 = |s_2| = \ldots = |s_h|.
$$

If $h > 1$ the matrix is called *imprimitive of index h*.
If $h = 1$, then the matrix is *primitive*.

The index of imprimitivity can be calculated if one considers only the nonzero coefficients of the characteristic equation written in the form

$$
s^n + \sum_{i=1}^{k} a_i s^{n_i} = 0
$$

103

where $a_i \neq 0$ and where $n > n_{i-1} > n_i$. The index of imprimitivity h is the greatest common divisor of the difference between adjacent exponents [10]. That is,

$$h = \text{GCD} \{n - n_1, n_1 - n_2, \ldots, n_{k-1} - n_k\}.$$

This leads to the following:

Theorem 5.9. The projection matrix $\mathbb{Z}$ is primitive. Moreover, the principal root s' dominates all other characteristic roots in magnitude.

Proof: A population can be stratified such that two fertility periods have indices that are relatively prime. For the case of human reproduction, between the age of α and β there is continuous fertility. By ensuring that there are at least two consecutive age categories during this period, that is, for some i, $m_i \neq 0$ and $m_{i+1} \neq 0$, the indices are relatively prime and therefore, $\mathbb{Z}$ is primitive. That s' dominates all other roots in magnitude is obvious from Definition 5.8. □

The characteristic equation (5.23) in theory may have characteristic roots, or eigenvalues, that are of algebraic multiplicity greater than one. In practice, however, such a situation has yet to occur. For the case when all eigenvalues are of unit multiplicity, the characteristic polynomial equation of degree n when taken over the field of complex numbers will exhibit exactly n distinct roots. The distinctness of the eigenvalues guarantees the diagonalizability of the projection matrix $\mathbb{Z}$. Again, that $\mathbb{Z}$ is indeed diagonalizable is based solely on empirical demographic evidence. The case of distinct eigenvalues is the subject of the following section. Section 5.5 investigates the case when eigenvalues have algebraic multiplicities greater than or equal to unity.

5.4 Stable Theory when the Eigenvalues are Distinct

The ramifications of stable theory of population will now be investigated when the projection matrix has distinct eigenvalues. Specifically, the $n \times n$ projection matrix $\mathbb{Z}$ defined by (5.14) has n eigenvalues s_j which are all distinct. Each eigenvalue, therefore, will generate a set of left and right eigenvectors denoted $\mathbb{X}_i$ and $\mathbb{Y}_j$ respectively, where

$$\mathbb{X}_i = [x_{i1} x_{i2} x_{i3} \ldots x_{in}] \tag{5.27}$$

and

$$\mathbb{Y}_j = \begin{bmatrix} y_{1j} \\ y_{2j} \\ y_{3j} \\ \vdots \\ y_{nj} \end{bmatrix} \tag{5.28}$$

whereby the left eigenvector satisfies

$$\mathbf{X}_i \mathbf{Z} = s_i \mathbf{X}_i \tag{5.29}$$

and the right eigenvector satisfies

$$\mathbf{Z} \mathbf{Y}_j = s_j \mathbf{Y}_j. \tag{5.30}$$

For the case of the right eigenvector $\mathbf{Y}_j$ the following is true.

Theorem 5.10. Let s_j be an eigenvalue of the projection matrix $\mathbf{Z}$. A right eigenvector $\mathbf{Y}_j$ corresponding to this eigenvalue has entries which are generated by

$$y_{k+1,j} = \prod_{i=1}^{k} g_i / s_j^k \tag{5.31}$$

for $k = 1, 2, 3, \ldots, n-1$ and where $y_{1,j} = 1$.

Proof: Equation (5.30) can be written as

$$
\begin{bmatrix}
g_0 m_1 & g_0 m_2 & g_0 m_3 & \cdots & g_0 m_{n-1} & g_0 m_n \\
g_1 & 0 & 0 & \cdots & 0 & 0 \\
0 & g_2 & 0 & \cdots & 0 & 0 \\
\vdots & \vdots & \vdots & & \vdots & \vdots \\
0 & 0 & 0 & \cdots & g_{n-1} & 0
\end{bmatrix}
\begin{bmatrix}
y_{1j} \\ y_{2j} \\ y_{3j} \\ \vdots \\ y_{nj}
\end{bmatrix}
= s_j
\begin{bmatrix}
y_{1j} \\ y_{2j} \\ y_{3j} \\ \vdots \\ y_{nj}
\end{bmatrix}.
$$

Since any non-zero scalar multiple of an eigenvector is also en eigenvector, any entry y_{ij} can be set to a non-zero arbitrary value; set $y_{1j} = 1$. Ordinary matrix multiplication shows that

$$g_{i-1} y_{i-1,j} = s_j y_{ij}$$

for $i = 2, 3, \ldots, n$.
  Recursively,

$$y_{2j} = g_1 / s_j, \quad y_{3j} = g_1 g_2 / s_j^2, \quad y_{4j} = g_1 g_2 g_3 / s_j^3,$$

and so forth, whereby the result of (5.31) is obtained. $\qquad\Box$

Theorem 5.11. Let s_i be a distinct eigenvalue of the projection matrix $\mathbf{Z}$. A left eigenvector $\mathbf{X}_i$ corresponding to this eigenvalue has entries which are generated by

$$x_{ij} = \left[s_i^{j-1} - \sum_{k=1}^{j-1} s_i^{j-1-k} m_k \left(\prod_{h=0}^{k-1} g_h \right) \right] \Bigg/ \left(\prod_{h=1}^{j-1} g_h \right) \tag{5.32}$$

for $j = 2, 3, \ldots, n$ and where $x_{i1} = 1$.

Proof: The expansion by multiplication of equation (5.29) generates an expression of the form, for $k = 1, 2, 3, \ldots, n-1$,

$$g_0 m_k x_{i1} + g_k x_{i,k+1} = s_i x_{ik}.$$

Since a scalar multiple of an eigenvector is also an eigenvector, it is possible to arbitrarily set $x_{i1} = 1$ from which the recursive expression

$$x_{i,k+1} = [s_i x_{ik} - g_0 m_k]/g_k$$

is obtained. By recursive substitution beginning with

$$x_{i,k+1} = (s_i [(s_i x_{i,k-1} - g_0 m_{k-1})/g_{k-1}] - g_0 m_k)/g_k$$

and after letting $j = k+1$, result (5.32) is obtained. $\qquad\square$

The assumption of distinct eigenvalues is sufficient to guarantee that the set of left eigenvectors $\mathbb{X}_i$ are linearly independent, and that the set of right eigenvectors $\mathbb{Y}_j$ are linearly independent. In each of these sets there are n such eigenvectors. Hence, the n eigenvectors form a basis for the n-dimensional vector space that they create. Thus, any vector in this space can be written as a linear combination of these eigenvectors. In particular, the age distribution vector $\mathbb{F}_t$ can be expressed as

$$\mathbb{F}_t = \sum_{j=1}^{n} a_j \mathbb{Y}_j \tag{5.33}$$

or as

$$\mathbb{F}_t = \sum_{i=1}^{n} a_i' \mathbb{X}_i \tag{5.34}$$

for some discrete time $t = 0, 1, 2, \ldots$.

The important feature of the two aforementioned sets of eigenvectors is they can be used to construct $n \times n$ transition matrices of the form

$$\mathbb{Y} = [\mathbb{Y}_1 \, \mathbb{Y}_2 \ldots \mathbb{Y}_n] = \begin{bmatrix} y_{11} & y_{12} & \cdots & y_{1n} \\ y_{21} & y_{22} & \cdots & y_{2n} \\ \vdots & \vdots & & \vdots \\ y_{n1} & y_{n2} & \cdots & y_{nn} \end{bmatrix} \tag{5.35}$$

and

$$\mathbb{X} = \begin{bmatrix} \mathbb{X}_1 \\ \mathbb{X}_2 \\ \vdots \\ \mathbb{X}_n \end{bmatrix} = \begin{bmatrix} x_{11} & x_{12} & \cdots & x_{1n} \\ x_{21} & x_{22} & \cdots & x_{2n} \\ \vdots & \vdots & & \vdots \\ x_{n1} & x_{n2} & \cdots & x_{nn} \end{bmatrix} \tag{5.36}$$

where $\mathbb{X}$ and $\mathbb{Y}$ are both non-singular. This leads to the following:

106

Theorem 5.12. Given a population projection matrix $\mathbb{Z}$ having n distinct eigenvalues. Then $\mathbb{Z}$ is diagonalizable and

$$\mathbb{Z}=\mathbb{Y}\mathbb{D}\mathbb{Y}^{-1}=\mathbb{X}^{-1}\mathbb{D}\mathbb{X} \tag{5.37}$$

where $\mathbb{Y}$ and $\mathbb{X}$ are transition matrices defined by equations (5.35) and (5.36), and where $\mathbb{D}$ is a diagonal matrix whose entries are the n distinct eigenvalues.

Proof: Since $\mathbb{Z}$ is an $n \times n$ matrix, the n distinct eigenvalues ensure that it is diagonalizable where the diagonal matrix $\mathbb{D}$ is expressed as

$$\mathbb{D}=\begin{bmatrix} s_1 & 0 & 0 & \dots & 0 \\ 0 & s_2 & 0 & \dots & 0 \\ 0 & 0 & s_3 & \dots & 0 \\ \vdots & \vdots & \vdots & & \vdots \\ 0 & 0 & 0 & \dots & s_n \end{bmatrix} \tag{5.38}$$

for eigenvalues $s_1, s_2, s_3, \dots, s_n$. Then by the definition of eigenvalues and eigenvectors, similar matrices $\mathbb{Z}$ and $\mathbb{D}$ are related by

$$\mathbb{Z}\mathbb{Y}=\mathbb{Y}\mathbb{D}$$

and

$$\mathbb{X}\mathbb{Z}=\mathbb{D}\mathbb{X}.$$

Since $\mathbb{X}$ and $\mathbb{Y}$ are invertible, (5.37) follows immediately. $\qquad\square$

Lemma 5.13. Let k be a positive integer. Then

$$\mathbb{D}^k=\begin{bmatrix} s_1^k & 0 & 0 & \dots & 0 \\ 0 & s_2^k & 0 & \dots & 0 \\ 0 & 0 & s_3^k & \dots & 0 \\ \vdots & \vdots & \vdots & & \vdots \\ 0 & 0 & 0 & \dots & s_n^k \end{bmatrix}. \tag{5.39}$$

Proof: By straightforward calculation, this result is true for any diagonal matrix. $\qquad\square$

Lemma 5.14. For projection matrix $\mathbb{Z}$, diagonal matrix $\mathbb{D}$, and transition matrices $\mathbb{X}$ and $\mathbb{Y}$,

$$\mathbb{Z}^k=\mathbb{Y}\mathbb{D}^k\mathbb{Y}^{-1} \tag{5.40}$$

and

$$\mathbb{Z}^k=\mathbb{X}^{-1}\mathbb{D}^k\mathbb{X}. \tag{5.41}$$

Proof: Using induction on k, Theorem 5.12 ensures that the assertion is correct for $k=1$ since

$$\mathbb{Z}=\mathbb{Y}\mathbb{D}\mathbb{Y}^{-1}$$

107

for the transition matrix $\mathbb{Y}$. Assume (5.40) is true. Then

$$\mathbb{Z}^{k+1}=\mathbb{Z}\mathbb{Z}^k=\mathbb{Y}\mathbb{D}\mathbb{Y}^{-1}\mathbb{Y}\mathbb{D}^k\mathbb{Y}^{-1}$$

which becomes

$$\mathbb{Z}^{k+1}=\mathbb{Y}\mathbb{D}\mathbb{D}^k\mathbb{Y}^{-1}$$

from which the result (5.40) is immediate. By similar reasoning, the result (5.41) can also be shown to be true. $\qquad\square$

There is an interesting property relating the left and right eigenvectors $\mathbb{X}_i$ and $\mathbb{Y}_j$, as shown in the following:

Lemma 5.15. Let $\mathbb{X}=[\mathbb{X}_i]$ and $\mathbb{Y}=[\mathbb{Y}_j]$ as defined by the expressions (5.36) and (5.35) respectively. Then
  (a) For $i \neq j$

$$\mathbb{X}_i\mathbb{Y}_j=0. \tag{5.42}$$

  (b) The product of the transition matrices $\mathbb{X}$ and $\mathbb{Y}$ is a diagonal matrix.

Proof: From equation (5.29) multiplying on the right by $\mathbb{Y}_j$ gives

$$\mathbb{X}_i\mathbb{Z}\mathbb{Y}_j=s_i\mathbb{X}_i\mathbb{Y}_j. \tag{5.43}$$

From equation (5.30) multiplying on the left by $\mathbb{X}_i$ gives

$$\mathbb{X}_i\mathbb{Z}\mathbb{Y}_j=s_j\mathbb{X}_i\mathbb{Y}_j. \tag{5.44}$$

Equating (5.43) and (5.44) results in

$$(s_i-s_j)\mathbb{X}_i\mathbb{Y}_j=0.$$

Since the eigenvalues are distinct, then $s_i \neq s_j$ and the assertion of (5.42) is demonstrated.
  The product of the transition matrices is easily seen to be diagonal by virtue of (5.42). That is,

$$\mathbb{X}\mathbb{Y}=\begin{bmatrix}\mathbb{X}_1\\\mathbb{X}_2\\\vdots\\\mathbb{X}_n\end{bmatrix}[\mathbb{Y}_1\ \mathbb{Y}_2\ ...\ \mathbb{Y}_n]=\begin{bmatrix}c_1 & 0 & ... & 0\\0 & c_2 & ... & 0\\\vdots & \vdots & & \vdots\\0 & 0 & ... & c_n\end{bmatrix}$$

where

$$c_i=\mathbb{X}_i\mathbb{Y}_i \tag{5.45}$$

for $i=1, 2, ..., n$. $\qquad\square$

The left and right eigenvectors are known only to within a multiplicative constant. If these vectors are normalized by the magnitude of (5.45), then the following results.

Theorem 5.16. Let the left eigenvector be normalized such that

$$\overline{\mathbb{X}}_i = \mathbb{X}_i / \mathbb{X}_i \mathbb{Y}_i \tag{5.46}$$

for $i = 1, 2, \ldots, n$. Then the product of the normalized left transition matrix and the right transition matrix is the identity matrix. That is,

$$\overline{\mathbb{X}} \mathbb{Y} = \mathbb{I}. \tag{5.47}$$

Proof: Since $c_i = \mathbb{X}_i \mathbb{Y}_i$ then

$$\overline{\mathbb{X}} = \begin{bmatrix} \mathbb{X}_1/c_1 \\ \mathbb{X}_2/c_2 \\ \vdots \\ \mathbb{X}_n/c_n \end{bmatrix} = \begin{bmatrix} \overline{\mathbb{X}}_1 \\ \overline{\mathbb{X}}_2 \\ \vdots \\ \overline{\mathbb{X}}_n \end{bmatrix}. \tag{5.48}$$

Then for each $i = 1, 2, \ldots, n$ and $j = 1, 2, \ldots, n$

$$\overline{\mathbb{X}}_i \mathbb{Y}_j = \begin{cases} 0 & \text{for } i \neq j \\ 1 & \text{for } i = j \end{cases} \tag{5.49}$$

from which the assertion of the theorem is demonstrated. $\square$

Corollary 5.17. Let $\mathbb{Z}$ be the projection matrix defined by (5.14), let $\mathbb{D}$ be the diagonal matrix of the distinct eigenvalues of $\mathbb{Z}$ defined by (5.38), let $\mathbb{Y}$ be the transition matrix defined by (5.35) and let $\overline{\mathbb{X}}$ be the normalized transition matrix of (5.48). Then

$$\mathbb{Z}^k = \mathbb{Y} \mathbb{D}^k \overline{\mathbb{X}}. \tag{5.50}$$

Proof: From Theorem 5.16, $\mathbb{Y}^{-1} = \overline{\mathbb{X}}$. Substitution of this fact into expression (5.40) gives the result immediately. $\square$

The usefulness of Theorem 5.16 and Corollary 5.17 will be seen momentarily.

The age distribution vector $\mathbb{F}_t$ gives the female population for the first n age categories at a particular time t. In practice, the time is measured from some reference time t^*. Then the population projection from (5.13) of Theorem 5.3 can be expressed as

$$\mathbb{F}_{t^* + k} = \mathbb{Z}^k \mathbb{F}_{t^*} \tag{5.51}$$

which describes the age distribution k time units after t^*. Since this is a relative comparison between $\mathbb{F}_{t^* + k}$ and $\mathbb{F}_{t^*}$, it is customary to set $t^* = 0$, thereby obtaining

$$\mathbb{F}_k = \mathbf{Z}^k \mathbb{F}_0. \tag{5.52}$$

The vector $\mathbb{F}_0$ is called the *initial age distribution vector*. But the value of k now represents the discrete time laps from time zero. For purposes of convenience a change in variable is in order, replacing k by the variable t in which case

$$\mathbb{F}_t = \mathbf{Z}^t \mathbb{F}_0 \tag{5.53}$$

for discrete time $t = 0, 1, 2, \ldots$. Note that $\mathbb{F}_t$ still retains its definition of (5.15) with the understanding that t is relative to an initial time of zero. This leads to the following important theorem for the discrete time matrix model in the stable theory of population.

Theorem 5.18. Let a population have a projection matrix $\mathbf{Z}$ with distinct eigenvalues s_j and having corresponding eigenvectors $\mathbb{Y}_j$. Then

$$\mathbb{F}_t = \sum_{j=1}^{n} a_j s_j^t \mathbb{Y}_j \tag{5.54}$$

where the constant coefficients a_j are determined by

$$a_j = \overline{\mathbb{X}}_j \mathbb{F}_0 \tag{5.55}$$

for initial age distribution vector $\mathbb{F}_0$.

Proof: From (5.33), the n-dimensional vector $\mathbb{F}_t$ for $t = 0$ is expressed as

$$\mathbb{F}_0 = \sum_{j=1}^{n} a_j \mathbb{Y}_j. \tag{5.56}$$

Multiplying both sides by $\overline{\mathbb{X}}_i$, and using (5.49) results in

$$\overline{\mathbb{X}}_i \mathbb{F}_0 = \sum_{j=1}^{n} a_j \overline{\mathbb{X}}_i \mathbb{Y}_j$$

from which (5.55) is established. Furthermore, using (5.53) as well as (5.50) results in

$$\mathbb{F}_t = \mathbb{Y} \mathbb{D}^t \overline{\mathbb{X}} \mathbb{F}_0. \tag{5.57}$$

Combining (5.56) with (5.57) yields

$$\mathbb{F}_t = \sum_{j=1}^{n} a_j \mathbb{Y} \mathbb{D}^t \overline{\mathbb{X}} \mathbb{Y}_j. \tag{5.58}$$

But $\bar{\mathbb{X}}\,\mathbb{Y}_j$ is just a column vector in n-space whose j^{th} entry is 1, while all other entries are zero; that is,

$$\bar{\mathbb{X}}\,\mathbb{Y}_j = \begin{bmatrix} \bar{\mathbb{X}}_1 \\ \bar{\mathbb{X}}_2 \\ \vdots \\ \bar{\mathbb{X}}_n \end{bmatrix} \mathbb{Y}_j = \begin{bmatrix} 0 \\ 0 \\ \vdots \\ 1 \\ \vdots \\ 0 \end{bmatrix}. \tag{5.59}$$

The $n \times n$ matrix $\mathbb{Y}\,\mathbb{D}^t$ is just

$$[\mathbb{Y}_1\,\mathbb{Y}_2 \,\ldots\, \mathbb{Y}_n] \begin{bmatrix} s_1^t & 0 & \ldots & 0 \\ 0 & s_2^t & \ldots & 0 \\ \vdots & \vdots & & \vdots \\ 0 & 0 & \ldots & s_n^t \end{bmatrix}$$

or

$$\mathbb{Y}\,\mathbb{D}^t = [s_1^t\,\mathbb{Y}_1 \quad s_2^t\,\mathbb{Y}_2 \quad \ldots \quad s_n^t\,\mathbb{Y}_n]. \tag{5.60}$$

Combining (5.60) with (5.59) yields

$$\mathbb{Y}\,\mathbb{D}^t\bar{\mathbb{X}}\,\mathbb{Y}_j = s_j^t\,\mathbb{Y}_j.$$

Using this in conjunction with (5.58) gives the required result. □

It has already been shown, especially from the standpoint of non-negative, irreducible, primitive matrices, that the unique, positive eigenvalue $s' = s_1$ dominates in magnitude all other eigenvalues of the projection matrix $\mathbb{Z}$. This results in the following:

Theorem 5.19. Let $\mathbb{F}_t$ be described as in (5.54). As time becomes unbounded,

$$\mathbb{F}_t \sim a_1 s_1^t\,\mathbb{Y}_1. \tag{5.61}$$

Proof: Rewrite (5.54) in the form

$$s_1^{-t}\mathbb{F}_t = \sum_{j=1}^{n} a_j(s_j/s_1)^t\,\mathbb{Y}_j. \tag{5.62}$$

Since s_1 dominates all other eigenvalues, it is clear that as $t \to \infty$,

$$(s_j/s_1)^t \to 0$$

for $j = 2, 3, \ldots, n$. Asymptotically, therefore, (5.62) reduces to the required result. □

Corollary 5.20

$$\mathbb{Y}_1 \sim \mathbb{Z}^t \mathbb{F}_0 / (s_1^t a_1). \tag{5.63}$$

Proof: Combining (5.61) and (5.53), the result is immediate. $\qquad\square$

Because of its important role in Theorem 5.19, $\mathbb{Y}_1$ is called the *principal stable eigenvector*. Its importance is magnified in that it represents the t-fold projection of the initial age distribution vector $\mathbb{F}_0$. That is, regardless of the initial age distribution, a population under the premises of stable theory will converge to a scalar multiple of the principal eigenvector $\mathbb{Y}_1$. This is the true meaning of stability for a population, that any age distribution will converge to a stable age distribution; this is the *ergodic property* in mathematical demography.

Some aspects of the previous discussion are worth noting. The equation (5.62) reduces to

$$s_1^{-t} \mathbb{F}_t \sim a_1 \mathbb{Y}_1 \tag{5.64}$$

as $t \to \infty$. It has been mentioned that the coefficient a_1 is real and positive [11]. Also, from (5.61) it is clear that the elements of $\mathbb{F}_t$, which are the number of females in an age category at time t, are proportional to the exponential s_1^t. Specifically, for $i = 1, 2, \ldots, n$,

$$F_i(t) \sim a_1 y_{i1} s_1^t \tag{5.65}$$

for sufficiently large t. This indicates that the ith age category at time t is asymptotically approximated by the product of a_1, the eigenvector element y_{i1}, and the t power of the principal eigenvalue. In particular, the births that survive to the first age category, $F_1(t)$, are represented exponentially as

$$F_1(t) \sim a_1 y_{11} s_1^t. \tag{5.66}$$

Since $y_{11} = 1$ from Theorem 5.10, then with $s' = s_1$,

$$F_1(t) \sim a_1 s'^t. \tag{5.67}$$

This is a conclusion reminiscent of the conclusions obtained in the discrete time recurrence model as well as the continuous time model.

5.5 Stable Theory with Eigenvalues Not all Distinct [12]

Thus far the discussion has centered on the characteristic equation of (5.23) and the projection matrix $\mathbb{Z}$ having n distinct roots or eigenvalues. It is reasonable to concentrate on this case since demographic examples all seem to have this property. But suppose the eigenvalues are not distinct. The conclusions of the previous section are no longer valid. The literature has not yet addressed itself to this question other than by casual mention. This problem is now investigated.

Consider the characteristic equation of (5.23) which is a polynomial of degree n where the coefficients ϕ_i are non-negative real numbers. Suppose this equation has p distinct roots s_i with respective multiplicities σ_i such that $p \le n$. By the Perron-Frobenius theory of non-negative matrices $s' = s_1$ is a simple root and therefore, equation (5.23) can be factored over the complex field as

$$(s-s_1)^{\sigma_1}(s-s_2)^{\sigma_2}(s-s_3)^{\sigma_3} \dots (s-s_p)^{\sigma_p} = 0 \qquad (5.68)$$

where

$$1 + \sum_{i=2}^{p} \sigma_i = n \qquad (5.69)$$

with the understanding that $\sigma_1 = 1$. The multiplicities σ_i of the p eigenvalues s_i of the $n \times n$ projection matrix $\mathbf{Z}$ suggest the use of a Jordan canonical form representation for $\mathbf{Z}$. The theorem is now presented for convenience.

Theorem 5.21 (Jordan). Let $\mathbf{Z}$ represent a linear operator T on an n-dimensional vector space V over the complex numbers. Let (5.68) be the characteristic polynomial of T. Then there exists a basis of V such that the related matrix of T is

$$\mathbb{J} = \text{diag}\,\{\mathbb{J}_1, \mathbb{J}_2, \mathbb{J}_3, \dots, \mathbb{J}_p\} \qquad (5.70)$$

where $\mathbb{J}_i$ is a square matrix of order σ_i for $i = 1, 2, \dots, p$ which is of the form

$$\mathbb{J}_i = \text{diag}\,\{\mathbb{J}_{i1}, \mathbb{J}_{i2}, \dots, \mathbb{J}_{iq(i)}\} \qquad (5.71)$$

such that $\mathbb{J}_{ij}$ is a square matrix of order k_{ij} defined by

$$\mathbb{J}_{ij} = \begin{bmatrix} s_i & 0 & 0 & \dots & 0 & 0 \\ 1 & s_i & 0 & \dots & 0 & 0 \\ 0 & 1 & s_i & \dots & 0 & 0 \\ \vdots & \vdots & \vdots & & \vdots & \vdots \\ 0 & 0 & 0 & \dots & s_i & 0 \\ 0 & 0 & 0 & \dots & 1 & s_i \end{bmatrix} \qquad (5.72)$$

and where

$$k_{i1} \ge k_{i2} \ge k_{i3} \ge \dots \ge k_{iq(i)} \qquad (5.73)$$

with

$$\sum_{j=1}^{q(i)} k_{ij} = \sigma_i. \qquad (5.74)$$

Proof: For a development and proof of this theorem, consult Moore [13]. ☐

113

The matrix of (5.72) is called a *little Jordan block*, or *elementary Jordan block*. The matrix of (5.71) is called a *big Jordan block*, while the matrix of (5.70) is the *Jordan Canonical form*. Theorem 5.21 basically states that any matrix of order n is similar to a Jordan matrix $\mathbb{J}$ [14]. This leads to the following:

Lemma 5.22. Let $\mathbb{Z}$ be a projection matrix of order n and let $\mathbb{J}$ be the Jordan matrix defined by Theorem 5.21. Then there exists a non-singular matrix $\mathbb{Q}$ such that

$$\mathbb{Q}^{-1}\mathbb{Z}\mathbb{Q}=\mathbb{J} \tag{5.75}$$

and

$$\mathbb{Z}^t=\mathbb{Q}\mathbb{J}^t\mathbb{Q}^{-1}. \tag{5.76}$$

Proof: Statement (5.75) is a mathematical statement showing that matrices $\mathbb{Z}$ and $\mathbb{J}$ are similar, which is the assertion of Jordan's theorem. Since $\mathbb{Q}$ is non-singular, pre-multiplying (5.75) by $\mathbb{Q}$ and post-multiplying by $\mathbb{Q}^{-1}$ yields

$$\mathbb{Z}=\mathbb{Q}\mathbb{J}\mathbb{Q}^{-1}$$

whereby using the argument described in Lemma 5.14, the result of statement (5.76) is obtained. ☐

5.5.1 *The case of 2 distinct eigenvalues*

In order to demonstrate the case of non-distinct eigenvalues, consider a population matrix $\mathbb{Z}$ whose corresponding characteristic polynomial is of the form

$$(s-s')(s-\bar{c})^{\sigma_2}=0 \tag{5.77}$$

where s' is the principal eigenvalue, and $\bar{c}$ is the only other eigenvalue having multiplicity $\sigma_2=n-1$ with n the order of $\mathbb{Z}$. Since s' is simple, the big Jordan block is a 1×1 matrix, and by necessity there is but one 1×1 little Jordan block, thereby

$$\mathbb{J}_1=\mathbb{J}_{11}=[s'].$$

Since $\bar{c}$ is the only other eigenvalue of multiplicity σ_2, then the second big Jordan block is of order $(n-1)\times(n-1)$. While there may be as many as $q(2)$ little Jordan blocks according to Theorem 5.21, for simplicity consider the case when $q(2)=1$. Then

$$\mathbb{J}_2=\mathbb{J}_{21}=\begin{bmatrix} \bar{c} & 0 & 0 & \dots & 0 & 0 \\ 1 & \bar{c} & 0 & \dots & 0 & 0 \\ 0 & 1 & \bar{c} & \dots & 0 & 0 \\ \vdots & \vdots & \vdots & & \vdots & \vdots \\ 0 & 0 & 0 & \dots & 1 & \bar{c} \end{bmatrix}. \tag{5.78}$$

114

Hence, the Jordan canonical matrix $\mathbb{J}$ which is similar to $\mathbb{Z}$ is

$$\mathbb{J} = \begin{bmatrix} \mathbb{J}_1 & \mathbb{O} \\ \mathbb{O} & \mathbb{J}_2 \end{bmatrix} = \begin{bmatrix} s' & \mathbb{O} \\ \mathbb{O} & \mathbb{J}_2 \end{bmatrix} \tag{5.79}$$

where $\mathbb{J}_2$ is defined by (5.78), and s' is the principal eigenvalue.

A t-fold projection of a population requires powers of $\mathbb{J}$ by virtue of Lemma 5.22. Before investigating this the following is useful.

Lemma 5.23. Let $\mathbb{J}$ be defined as in (5.79). Then

(a)
$$\mathbb{J} = \begin{bmatrix} s' & \mathbb{O} \\ \mathbb{O} & \mathbb{O} \end{bmatrix} + \begin{bmatrix} 0 & \mathbb{O} \\ \mathbb{O} & \mathbb{J}_2 \end{bmatrix} \tag{5.80}$$

(b)
$$\begin{bmatrix} s' & \mathbb{O} \\ \mathbb{O} & \mathbb{O} \end{bmatrix}^t = \begin{bmatrix} s'^t & \mathbb{O} \\ \mathbb{O} & \mathbb{O} \end{bmatrix} \tag{5.81}$$

(c)
$$\begin{bmatrix} 0 & \mathbb{O} \\ \mathbb{O} & \mathbb{J}_2 \end{bmatrix}^t = \begin{bmatrix} 0 & \mathbb{O} \\ \mathbb{O} & \mathbb{J}_2^t \end{bmatrix}. \tag{5.82}$$

(d) For non-negative integers a and b,

$$\begin{bmatrix} s' & \mathbb{O} \\ \mathbb{O} & \mathbb{O} \end{bmatrix}^a \begin{bmatrix} 0 & \mathbb{O} \\ \mathbb{O} & \mathbb{J}_2 \end{bmatrix}^b = \mathbb{O}. \tag{5.83}$$

Proof: (a) By definition of addition of partitioned matrices.

(b), (c) By matrix multiplication.

(d) After using (5.81) and (5.82) with ordinary matrix multiplication. □

Lemma 5.24.

$$\mathbb{J}^t = \begin{bmatrix} s'^t & \mathbb{O} \\ \mathbb{O} & \mathbb{O} \end{bmatrix} + \begin{bmatrix} \mathbb{O} & \mathbb{O} \\ \mathbb{O} & \mathbb{J}_2^t \end{bmatrix}. \tag{5.84}$$

Proof: Using (5.80) and a binomial expansion yields

$$\mathbb{J}^t = \left(\begin{bmatrix} s' & \mathbb{O} \\ \mathbb{O} & \mathbb{O} \end{bmatrix} + \begin{bmatrix} 0 & \mathbb{O} \\ \mathbb{O} & \mathbb{J}_2 \end{bmatrix} \right)^t = \sum_{i=0}^{t} \binom{t}{i} \begin{bmatrix} s' & \mathbb{O} \\ \mathbb{O} & \mathbb{O} \end{bmatrix}^{t-i} \begin{bmatrix} 0 & \mathbb{O} \\ \mathbb{O} & \mathbb{J}_2 \end{bmatrix}^i.$$

Except when $i=0$ or $i=t$, the product of the two matrices is $\mathbb{O}$ by Lemma 5.23. By the same lemma the result of (5.84) is shown. □

The form of the little Jordan blocks of Theorem 5.21 results in some interesting properties concerning the entries of powers of these blocks, as expressed in the following theorem. (Also, see Pollard [15].)

Theorem 5.25. Let $\mathbb{H}$ be a square matrix of order k where $\mathbb{H}$ is expressed in the form of (5.78). Then for $t>k$,

(a)
$$\mathbb{H}^t = [h_{ij}] \tag{5.85}$$

115

where the entries of this lower triangular matrix are

$$h_{ij} = \begin{cases} \binom{t}{i-j} \bar{c}^{t-(i-j)} & \text{for } j \le i \\ 0 & \text{for } j > i. \end{cases}$$

(5.86)

(b) The elements h_{ij} are bounded such that

$$|h_{ij}| \le [|\bar{c}|^{j-i}/p!] t^p |\bar{c}|^t$$

(5.87)

for $p = i - j$.

Proof: (a) Let $\mathbb{I}$ be an $n \times n$ identity matrix and let $\mathbb{S}$ be the subdiagonal matrix defined as

$$\mathbb{S} = \begin{bmatrix} 0 & 0 & 0 & 0 & \dots & 0 & 0 \\ 1 & 0 & 0 & 0 & \dots & 0 & 0 \\ 0 & 1 & 0 & 0 & \dots & 0 & 0 \\ 0 & 0 & 1 & 0 & \dots & 0 & 0 \\ \vdots & \vdots & \vdots & \vdots & & \vdots & \vdots \\ 0 & 0 & 0 & 0 & \dots & 1 & 0 \end{bmatrix}.$$

Then $\mathbb{H}$ can be written as

$$\mathbb{H} = \bar{c}\,\mathbb{I} + \mathbb{S}.$$

Since it is clear that $\mathbb{I}\mathbb{S} = \mathbb{S}\mathbb{I} = \mathbb{S}$, then with this commutativity the binomial theorem applies and

$$\mathbb{H}^t = (\bar{c}\,\mathbb{I} + \mathbb{S})^t = \bar{c}^t\,\mathbb{I} + \binom{t}{1}\bar{c}^{t-1}\mathbb{S}\,\mathbb{I}^{t-1} + \binom{t}{2}\bar{c}^{t-2}\mathbb{S}^2\,\mathbb{I}^{t-2} + \dots.$$

It is easy to verify that

$\mathbb{S}^2$ = has a subdiagonal of 1's two steps from the main diagonal;
$\mathbb{S}^3$ = has a subdiagonal of 2's three steps from the main diagonal;

$\vdots$

$\mathbb{S}^{n-1}$ = has just a single 1 at the $(n, 1)$ position.

and that

$$\mathbb{S}^n = \mathbb{S}^{n+1} = \dots = \mathbb{O}.$$

Thus,

$$\mathbb{H}^t = \bar{c}^t\,\mathbb{I} \qquad\qquad \text{main diagonal entries}$$

$$+ \binom{t}{1}\bar{c}^{t-1}\mathbb{S} \qquad\qquad \text{first subdiagonal entries}$$

$$+ \binom{t}{2}\bar{c}^{t-2}\mathbb{S}^2 \qquad\qquad \text{second subdiagonal entries}$$

$\vdots \qquad\qquad\qquad\qquad\qquad \vdots$

$$+ \binom{t}{n-1}\bar{c}^{t-n+1}\mathbb{S}^{n-1} \qquad \text{lower left entry.}$$

This shows that the entries p "steps" down from the main diagonal are all $\binom{t}{p} \bar{c}^{t-p}$ while those above the main diagonal are all zero. Therefore, the expression of (5.86) is demonstrated.

(b) In (5.86) let $p = i - j$ whereby for $p = 0, 1, 2, \ldots, k-1$

$$h_{ij} = \binom{t}{p} \bar{c}^{t-p}$$

while $h_{ij} = 0$ for $p < 0$. Expanding this expression and rearrangings, results in

$$h_{ij} = \left[\frac{\bar{c}^{-p}}{p!} \right] t(t-1)(t-2) \ldots (t-p+1) \bar{c}^t. \tag{5.88}$$

But each of the factors $(t-1), (t-2), \ldots, (t-p+1)$ of (5.88) is less than the value of t, and since $t > k > p$, this results in

$$h_{ij} \le [\bar{c}^{-p}/p!] t^p \bar{c}^t.$$

Taking the magnitude of both sides of this expression demonstrates the conclusion of the theorem. $\qquad\square$

Corollary 5.26. Let a projection matrix have a principal eigenvalue s' and let $\bar{c}$ be another eigenvalue of the matrix with multiplicity greater than or equal to unity. If $\mathbb{J}_{i'j'}$ is any little Jordan block corresponding to $\bar{c}$ of the form (5.78), and if $\mathbb{K} = \mathbb{H}/s'$, then

$$\mathbb{K}^t = [h'_{ij}] = [\mathbb{J}_{i'j'}/s']^t \tag{5.89}$$

then

$$h'_{ij} \le [|\bar{c}|^{-p}/p!] t^p |\bar{c}/s'|^t \tag{5.90}$$

and

$$\lim_{t \to \infty} \mathbb{K}^t = \mathbb{0}. \tag{5.91}$$

Proof: Statement (5.90) is obvious by reason of Theorem 5.25 and statement (5.87) where $h'_{ij} = h_{ij}/s'$. Again by Theorem 5.25, since $\mathbb{K}^t$ is lower triangular, all of its entries are either zero or bounded by (5.90). But since s' dominates the magnitude of all other eigenvalues, then as $t \to \infty$, $|\bar{c}/s'|^t \to 0$. Furthermore, it can be shown that $t^p |\bar{c}/s'|^t \to 0$ as $t \to \infty$ from which the result of (5.91) is immediate. $\qquad\square$

While Corollary 5.26 is true for any little Jordan block, in particular $\mathbb{J}_2 = \mathbb{J}_{21}$ as defined by (5.78) for the characteristic equation of (5.77). Hence, from an initial population $\mathbb{F}_0$ it is possible to obtain the population $\mathbb{F}_t$ at time t, as is shown in the following using Jordan canonical form.

117

Theorem 5.27. Let a population have a projection matrix $\mathbb{Z}$ whose characteristic equation is given by (5.77) where $\mathbb{F}_0$ is its initial age distribution. Then for discrete time $t = 0, 1, 2, 3, \ldots$.

(a) The age structure at time t is

$$\mathbb{F}_t = \mathbb{Q} \begin{bmatrix} s'^t & \mathbb{O} \\ \mathbb{O} & \mathbb{O} \end{bmatrix} \mathbb{Q}^{-1} \mathbb{F}_0 + \mathbb{Q} \begin{bmatrix} \mathbb{O} & \mathbb{O} \\ \mathbb{O} & \mathbb{J}_2^t \end{bmatrix} \mathbb{Q}^{-1} \mathbb{F}_0 \tag{5.92}$$

where $\mathbb{Q}$ is an invertible matrix generated by the eigenvectors corresponding to the eigenvalues of the characteristic equation, where s' is the principal eigenvalue, and where $\mathbb{J}_2$ is the Jordan block formed by eigenvalue $\bar{c}$.

(b) As t becomes unbounded, then asymptotically

$$\mathbb{F}_t \sim a_1 s'^t \mathbb{Y}_1 \tag{5.93}$$

where $\mathbb{Y}_1$ is the principal eigenvector corresponding to s'.

Proof: (a) Substituting (5.76) into (5.53) results in

$$\mathbb{F}_t = \mathbb{Q} \mathbb{J}^t \mathbb{Q}^{-1} \mathbb{F}_0.$$

By use of (5.84) of Lemma 5.24, the result of (5.92) follows immediately.

(b) The matrix $\mathbb{Z}$ has two eigenvalues: s' with unit multiplicity, and $\bar{c}$ with multiplicity of $n-1$. Since $\mathbb{J} = \mathrm{diag}\{\mathbb{J}_1, \mathbb{J}_2\}$ is similar to $\mathbb{Z}$, $\mathbb{J}$ has the same eigenvalues of $\mathbb{Z}$. For eigenvalues s' there corresponds exactly one eigenvector; call it $\mathbb{Y}_1$. Since the geometric multiplicity is less than or equal to the algebraic multiplicity of an eigenvalue, then for $m \le n$, let $\mathbb{Y}_2, \mathbb{Y}_3, \mathbb{Y}_4, \ldots, \mathbb{Y}_m$ be the linearly independent eigenvectors corresponding to eigenvalue $\bar{c}$ with geometric multiplicity of $m-1$. It is possible to construct an additional $n-m$ linearly independent vectors [16], called *generalized eigenvectors*, $\mathbb{Y}_{m+1}, \mathbb{Y}_{m+2}, \mathbb{Y}_{m+3}, \ldots, \mathbb{Y}_n$ which can be used to construct the $n \times n$ transition matrix $\mathbb{Q}$ such that

$$\mathbb{Q} = [\mathbb{Y}_1 \, \mathbb{Y}_2 \, \cdots \, \mathbb{Y}_m \, \mathbb{Y}_{m+1} \, \cdots \, \mathbb{Y}_n]$$

where $\mathbb{Q}$ is non-singular. Factor s'^t from the right side of (5.92). This results in

$$s'^{-t} \mathbb{F}_t = \mathbb{Q} \begin{bmatrix} 1 & \mathbb{O} \\ \mathbb{O} & \mathbb{O} \end{bmatrix} \mathbb{Q}^{-1} \mathbb{F}_0 + \mathbb{Q} \begin{bmatrix} \mathbb{O} & \mathbb{O} \\ \mathbb{O} & (\mathbb{J}_2/s')^t \end{bmatrix} \mathbb{Q}^{-1} \mathbb{F}_0 \tag{5.94}$$

It is easily verifiable that

$$\mathbb{Q} \begin{bmatrix} 1 & \mathbb{O} \\ \mathbb{O} & \mathbb{O} \end{bmatrix} = [\mathbb{Y}_1 \, \mathbb{O}]$$

which is a $n \times n$ matrix. The matrix $\mathbb{Q}^{-1} \mathbb{F}_0$ is an $n \times 1$ column matrix. Suppose its entries are $a_1, a_2, a_3, \ldots, a_n$. Then it is clear that

118

$$[\mathbb{Y}_1 \; \mathbb{O}] \begin{bmatrix} a_1 \\ a_2 \\ \vdots \\ a_n \end{bmatrix} = a_1 \mathbb{Y}_1.$$

Hence, (5.94) becomes

$$s'^{-t}\mathbb{F}_t = a_1 \mathbb{Y}_1 + \mathbb{Q} \begin{bmatrix} \mathbb{O} & \mathbb{O} \\ \mathbb{O} & (\mathbb{J}_2/s')^t \end{bmatrix} \begin{bmatrix} a_1 \\ a_2 \\ a_n \end{bmatrix}. \qquad (5.95)$$

But by Corollary 5.26, $(\mathbb{J}_2/s')^t \to 0$ as $t \to \infty$. Thus, (5.95) reduces to

$$s'^{-1}\mathbb{F}_t = a_1 \mathbb{Y}_1 + \mathbb{O}$$

from which the assertion of the theorem is demonstrated. $\qquad\square$

Equation (5.92) of Theorem 5.27 is the analog of the special case where all the eigenvalues are distinct, as described previously in Theorem 5.18. Statement (5.93) of Theorem 5.27 is identical to the conclusion of Theorem 5.19 which shows that irrespective of the nature (distinct or not distinct) of the eigenvalues, the asymptotic behavior of a population is the same; that is, it will converge to the same age structure. The results of Theorem 5.27 were based on the assumption that the projection matrix had only two distinct eigenvalues s' and $\bar{c}$, with the multiplicity of $\bar{c}$ greater than or equal to one. It is also of interest to investigate the more general case – the case where the projection matrix is of order n where there are p distinct eigenvalues s_i for $p \leq n$, having multiplicities σ_i, and where its characteristic equation is of the form (5.68). This case is now discussed.

5.5.2 The case of p distinct eigenvalues

When the characteristic equation of (5.23) of degree n has p distinct eigenvalues where $p \leq n$, then it has a factorization as described by (5.68). In this case, the projection matrix $\mathbb{Z}$ would be similar to a Jordan matrix as defined by Theorem 5.21. This results in the following:

Lemma 5.28. Let $\mathbb{J}$ be a Jordan matrix as defined in Theorem 5.21. Then

$$\mathbb{J}^t = \text{diag} \{s'^t, \mathbb{J}_{2\,1}^t, \ldots, \mathbb{J}_{2\,q(2)}^t, \ldots, \mathbb{J}_{p\,1}^t, \ldots, \mathbb{J}_{p\,q(p)}^t\}. \qquad (5.96)$$

Proof: For big Jordan block $\mathbb{J}_i$ it is easily verifiable that for diagonal matrix $\mathbb{J}$,

$$\mathbb{J}^t = \text{diag} \{\mathbb{J}_1^t, \mathbb{J}_2^t, \ldots, \mathbb{J}_p^t\}$$

and since each big Jordan block is a diagonal matrix of little Jordan blocks, by the same argument it can easily be seen that the assertion of the Lemma is demonstrated. $\square$

Corollary 5.29. Let $\mathbb{J}_{ij}$ be the jth little Jordan block associated with the ith eigenvalue of the characteristic equation (5.23). For principal eigenvalue s' let

$$\mathbb{J}'_{ij} = \mathbb{J}_{ij}/s'. \tag{5.97}$$

Then an $n \times n$ matrix representation of $(\mathbb{J}/s')^t$ is

$$(\mathbb{J}/s')^t = \begin{bmatrix} 1 & 0 & \dots & 0 \\ 0 & \mathbb{O} & \dots & \mathbb{O} \\ \vdots & \vdots & & \vdots \\ 0 & \mathbb{O} & \dots & \mathbb{O} \end{bmatrix} + \begin{bmatrix} 0 & \mathbb{O} & \dots & \mathbb{O} \\ \mathbb{O} & \mathbb{J}''^t_{2\ 1} & \dots & \mathbb{O} \\ \vdots & \vdots & & \vdots \\ \mathbb{O} & \mathbb{O} & \dots & \mathbb{O} \end{bmatrix}$$

$$+ \dots + \begin{bmatrix} 0 & \mathbb{O} & \dots & \mathbb{O} \\ \mathbb{O} & \mathbb{O} & \dots & \mathbb{O} \\ \vdots & \vdots & & \vdots \\ \mathbb{O} & \mathbb{O} & \dots & \mathbb{J}''^t_{p\ q(p)} \end{bmatrix}. \tag{5.98}$$

Proof: From statement (5.96) divide each side by s'^t. Then by definition of matrix addition the result is immediate. $\square$

Corollary 5.30. For all $t \geq 0$ the elements of each $\mathbb{J}''^t_{ij}$ are bounded.

Proof: The right side of expression (5.87) can be divided by s'^t from which a calculation will show that $\mathbb{J}''^t_{ij}$ is bounded by a constant as substantiated by Corollary 5.26. $\square$

Theorem 5.31. Let $\mathbb{F}_0$ and $\mathbb{F}_t$ be the familiar age distribution vectors and let $\mathbb{Q}$ be the transition matrix for similar matrices $\mathbb{J}$ and projection matrix $\mathbb{Z}$. Then for little Jordan block $\mathbb{J}_{ij}$, the age distribution at time t is

$$\mathbb{F}_t = s'^t \mathbb{Q} \begin{bmatrix} 1 & \mathbb{O} & \dots & \mathbb{O} & \dots & \mathbb{O} \\ \vdots & \vdots & & \vdots & & \vdots \\ \mathbb{O} & \mathbb{O} & \dots & \mathbb{O} & \dots & \mathbb{O} \\ \vdots & \vdots & & \vdots & & \vdots \\ \mathbb{O} & \mathbb{O} & \dots & \mathbb{O} & \dots & \mathbb{O} \end{bmatrix} \mathbb{Q}^{-1} \mathbb{F}_0$$

$$+ \sum_{i=2}^{p} \sum_{j=1}^{q(i)} \mathbb{Q} \begin{bmatrix} 0 & \mathbb{O} & \dots & \mathbb{O} & \dots & \mathbb{O} \\ \vdots & \vdots & & \vdots & & \vdots \\ \mathbb{O} & \mathbb{O} & \dots & \mathbb{J}^t_{ij} & \dots & \mathbb{O} \\ \vdots & \vdots & & \vdots & & \vdots \\ \mathbb{O} & \mathbb{O} & \dots & \mathbb{O} & \dots & \mathbb{O} \end{bmatrix} \mathbb{Q}^{-1} \mathbb{F}_0 \tag{5.99}$$

where $\mathbb{J}^t_{ij}$ assumes a new diagonal position for each i, j.

Proof: By Lemma 5.22 $\mathbb{Z}^t = \mathbb{Q}\mathbb{J}^t\mathbb{Q}^{-1}$, and since $\mathbb{F}_t = \mathbb{Z}^t\mathbb{F}_0$ then use of Corollary 5.29 after multiplying (5.98) by s''^t gives the required result. Note that the expanded matrices of (5.99) are square of order n, and that each of the n diagonal positions contain either a 1 or a diagonal element of a little Jordan block. □

The columns of the transition matrix $\mathbb{Q}$ include the generalized eigenvectors with the principal eigenvector $\mathbb{Y}_1$ in the first column. The product $\mathbb{Q}^{-1}\mathbb{F}_0$ is a column vector with entries a_i. This leads to the following:

Lemma 5.32.

$$\mathbb{Q}\begin{bmatrix} 1 & \mathbb{O} & \mathbb{O} & \dots & \mathbb{O} \\ \mathbb{O} & \mathbb{O} & \mathbb{O} & \dots & \mathbb{O} \\ \mathbb{O} & \mathbb{O} & \mathbb{O} & \dots & \mathbb{O} \\ \vdots & \vdots & \vdots & & \vdots \\ \mathbb{O} & \mathbb{O} & \mathbb{O} & \dots & \mathbb{O} \end{bmatrix} \mathbb{Q}^{-1}\mathbb{F}_0 = a_1\,\mathbb{Y}_1. \qquad (5.100)$$

Proof: Since the first column of $\mathbb{Q}$ is $\mathbb{Y}_1$, the product of $\mathbb{Q}$ with the expanded matrix of (5.100) results in an $n \times n$ matrix with zeros everywhere except for the first column which is $\mathbb{Y}_1$. Since $\mathbb{Q}^{-1}\mathbb{F}_0$ is a column matrix with entries a_i then

$$[\mathbb{Y}_1 \mathbb{O}\mathbb{O} \dots \mathbb{O}]\begin{bmatrix} a_1 \\ \vdots \\ a_n \end{bmatrix} = a_1\,\mathbb{Y}_1$$

which proves the lemma. □

It has already been shown by Theorem 5.25 that the tth power of a little Jordan block will result in a lower triangular matrix. Let this matrix start at the rth column of $\mathbb{J}$. Then the product

$$\mathbb{Q} \times \begin{bmatrix} \mathbb{O} & \mathbb{O} & \mathbb{O} \\ \hline \mathbb{O} & \mathbb{J}^t_{ij} & \mathbb{O} \\ \hline \mathbb{O} & \mathbb{O} & \mathbb{O} \end{bmatrix}$$

can be expressed, with s'' representing one of the s_i, as

$$[\mathbb{Y}_1 \dots \mathbb{Y}_r \dots \mathbb{Y}_{r+k-1} \dots \mathbb{Y}_n]$$

$$\times \begin{bmatrix} \mathbb{O} & & \mathbb{O} & \dots & \mathbb{O} \\ \hline & s''^t & 0 & \dots & 0 \\ \mathbb{O} & c_{r+1,r} & s''^t & \dots & 0 & \mathbb{O} \\ & \vdots & \vdots & & \vdots \\ & c_{r+k-1,r} & c_{r+k-1,r+1} & \dots & s''^t \\ \hline \mathbb{O} & & \mathbb{O} & & \mathbb{O} \end{bmatrix} \qquad (5.101)$$

where c_{ij} is a function of t; that is, c_{ij} is of the form $\binom{t}{p} s''^{t-p}$, and where $\mathbb{Y}_r$ through $\mathbb{Y}_{r+k-1}$ are the eigenvectors corresponding to the eigenvalue s'' of the little Jordan block $\mathbb{J}^t_{ij}$ of order k. Then for each little Jordan block, multiplication of (5.101) results in an expression which is an $n \times n$ matrix whose columns are:

Col. 1: $\qquad \mathbb{O}$

$\quad \vdots \qquad\qquad \vdots$

Col. $r-1$: $\qquad \mathbb{O}$

Col. r: $\qquad s''^t \mathbb{Y}_r + c_{r+1,r} \mathbb{Y}_{r+1} + \ldots + c_{r+k-1,r} \mathbb{Y}_{r+k-1}$

Col. $r+1$: $\qquad s''^t \mathbb{Y}_{r+1} + c_{r+2,r+1} \mathbb{Y}_{r+2} + \ldots + c_{r+k-1,r+1} \mathbb{Y}_{r+k-1}$

Col. $r+2$: $\qquad s''^t \mathbb{Y}_{r+2} + c_{r+3,r+2} \mathbb{Y}_{r+3} + \ldots + c_{r+k-1,r+2} \mathbb{Y}_{r+k-1}$

$\quad \vdots \qquad\qquad \vdots$

Col. $r+k-1$: $\qquad s''^t \mathbb{Y}_{r+k-1}$

Col. $r+k$: $\qquad \mathbb{O}$

$\quad \vdots \qquad\qquad \vdots$

Col. n: $\qquad \mathbb{O}.$ $\qquad\qquad\qquad\qquad\qquad\qquad$ (5.102)

This matrix can be rearranged as a sum of matrices whereby each addend matrix is such that all its entries are zero except for the jth column, where $r \le j \le r+k-1$. Thus, the matrix expressed in (5.102) can be written as

$$
s''^t
\begin{cases}
[\mathbb{O} \ldots \mathbb{O} \;\; \mathbb{Y}_r \quad \mathbb{O} \quad\;\; \mathbb{O} \;\ldots\; \mathbb{O} \quad \mathbb{O} \ldots \mathbb{O}] \\
+[\mathbb{O} \ldots \mathbb{O} \quad \mathbb{O} \;\; \mathbb{Y}_{r+1} \quad \mathbb{O} \;\ldots\; \mathbb{O} \quad \mathbb{O} \ldots \mathbb{O}] \\
+[\mathbb{O} \ldots \mathbb{O} \quad \mathbb{O} \quad \mathbb{O} \quad \mathbb{Y}_{r+2} \ldots \;\; \mathbb{O} \quad \mathbb{O} \ldots \mathbb{O}] \\
\quad \vdots \qquad \vdots \quad \vdots \quad \vdots \quad\;\; \vdots \qquad \vdots \quad \vdots \qquad \vdots \\
+[\mathbb{O} \ldots \mathbb{O} \quad \mathbb{O} \quad \mathbb{O} \quad \mathbb{O} \;\;\ldots\; \mathbb{Y}_{r+k-1} \; \mathbb{O} \ldots \mathbb{O}]
\end{cases}
$$

$$
+ \sum_{u=r+1}^{r+k-1} c_{u,r} \qquad [\mathbb{O} \ldots \mathbb{O} \;\; \mathbb{Y}_u \;\; \mathbb{O} \quad \mathbb{O} \ldots \mathbb{O} \quad \mathbb{O} \quad \mathbb{O} \ldots \mathbb{O}]
$$

$$
+ \sum_{u=r+2}^{r+k-1} c_{u,r+1} \qquad [\mathbb{O} \ldots \mathbb{O} \quad \mathbb{O} \;\; \mathbb{Y}_u \;\; \mathbb{O} \ldots \mathbb{O} \quad \mathbb{O} \quad \mathbb{O} \ldots \mathbb{O}]
$$

$$
+ \sum_{u=r+3}^{r+k-1} c_{u,r+2} \qquad [\mathbb{O} \ldots \mathbb{O} \quad \mathbb{O} \quad \mathbb{O} \;\; \mathbb{Y}_u \ldots \mathbb{O} \quad \mathbb{O} \quad \mathbb{O} \ldots \mathbb{O}]
$$

$$
\quad \vdots \qquad\qquad \vdots \quad \vdots \quad \vdots \quad \vdots \quad \vdots \quad \vdots \quad \vdots \quad \vdots \quad \vdots
$$

$$
+ \sum_{u=r+k-1}^{r+k-1} c_{u,r+k-2} [\underbrace{\mathbb{O} \ldots \mathbb{O} \quad \mathbb{O} \quad \mathbb{O} \quad \mathbb{O} \ldots \;\; \mathbb{Y}_u \;\; \mathbb{O} \quad \mathbb{O} \ldots \mathbb{O}}_{k \text{ columns}}].
$$

$\qquad\qquad\qquad\qquad\qquad\qquad\qquad\qquad\qquad\qquad\qquad\qquad$ (5.103)

The significance of (5.103) is that when each of the matrices multiplies the column matrix $\mathbb{Q}^{-1} \mathbb{F}_0$, the result is the column $\mathbb{Y}_u$ multiplied by the scalar a_u, the uth entry of $\mathbb{Q}^{-1} \mathbb{F}_0$. In this case the double summation of (5.99) reduces to the form

$$a_r s''^t \mathbf{Y}_r + a_{r-1} s''^t \quad \mathbf{Y}_{r+1} + a_{r+2} s''^t \quad \mathbf{Y}_{r+2} + \dots + a_{r+k-1} s''^t \quad \mathbf{Y}_{r+k-1}$$
$$+ a_{r+1} c_{r+1,r} \mathbf{Y}_{r+1} + a_{r+2} c_{r+2,r} \mathbf{Y}_{r+2} + \dots + a_{r+k-1} c_{r+k-1,r} \mathbf{Y}_{r+k-1}$$
$$+ \cdot \quad \cdot \quad \cdot \quad \cdot \quad \cdot \quad \cdot \quad \cdot \quad \cdot \quad \cdot \quad \cdot \quad \cdot \quad \cdot \quad \cdot \quad \cdot \quad \cdot$$
$$+ \dots + a_{r+k-1} c_{r+k-1,\; r+k-2} \mathbf{Y}_{r+k-1}$$

$$(5.104)$$

Regrouping terms of (5.104) shows that the contribution of each little Jordan block of the double summation of (5.99) has the form

$$s''^t \sum_{u=r}^{r+k-1} a_u \mathbf{Y}_u + \sum_{u=r+1}^{r+k-1} \left(\sum_{v=r}^{u-1} c_{u,v} \right) a_u \mathbf{Y}_u \qquad (5.105)$$

with the understanding that the double summation equals zero if $k=1$. The previous discussion proves the following:

Lemma 5.33. Let $\mathbf{J}_{ij}$ be a little Jordan block of order k whose initial diagonal entry is at the (r, r) position of the Jordan matrix $\mathbf{J}$. Let $\mathbf{Y}_r, \mathbf{Y}_{r+1}, \dots, \mathbf{Y}_{r+k-1}$ be the eigenvectors of $\mathbf{Q}$ corresponding to the eigenvalue s'' of this little Jordan block. Then

$$\mathbf{Q} \begin{bmatrix} \mathbf{0} & \mathbf{0} & \mathbf{0} \\ \mathbf{0} & \mathbf{J}'_{ij} & \mathbf{0} \\ \mathbf{0} & \mathbf{0} & \mathbf{0} \end{bmatrix} \mathbf{Q}^{-1} \mathbf{F}_0 \qquad (5.106)$$

is a column vector expressible in the form (5.105).

Corollary 5.34. In the expression (5.105), let d_u be a function of t defined by

$$d_u =: \sum_{v=r}^{u-1} c_{u,v}. \qquad (5.107)$$

Then the magnitude of d_u is a lower order of s''^t.

Proof: From expression (5.87) each $c_{u,v}$, which is a function of t, is of lower order of s''^t. Since the sum is also of lower order, then $d_u = o(s''^t)$. $\square$

Expression (5.105) can be rewritten as

$$a_r s''^t \mathbf{Y}_r + \sum_{u=r+1}^{r+k-1} a_u (s''^t + d_u) \mathbf{Y}_u \qquad (5.108)$$

which leads to the salient result of this section.

123

Theorem 5.35. Let a population have a projection matrix $\mathbb{Z}$ whose characteristic equation is given by (5.68). Let $\mathbb{Q}$ be the transition matrix for $\mathbb{Z}$ and the Jordan matrix $\mathbb{J}$ where the columns of $\mathbb{Q}$ are the eigenvectors and generalized eigenvectors generated by the eigenvalues s_i, $s' = s_1$ being the principal eigenvalue, and are denoted $\mathbb{Y}_1, \mathbb{Y}_2, \ldots, \mathbb{Y}_n$ where n is the order of $\mathbb{Z}$. If $\mathbb{F}_t$ is the age distribution at time $t = 0, 1, 2, \ldots$ then for little Jordan blocks of order k

$$\mathbb{F}_t = a_1 s'^t \mathbb{Y}_1 + \sum_{i=2}^{p} \sum_{j=1}^{q(i)} \left[a_r s_i^t \mathbb{Y}_r + \sum_{u=r+1}^{r+k-1} a_u (s_i^t + d_u) \mathbb{Y}_u \right] \tag{5.109}$$

where r and k are functions of both i and j denoting the appropriate diagonal location of the little Jordan block, where a_u is a constant, and where d_u is a function of t of order lower than s_i^t.

Proof: The age distribution at time t is given by (5.99) of Theorem 5.31. By use of Lemma 5.32 the principal term $a_1 s'^t \mathbb{Y}_1$ is obtained. The use of Lemma 5.33 and Corollary 5.34 with expression (5.108) gives the required result. $\qquad\square$

Theorem 5.36. Let $\mathbb{F}_t$ be defined by (5.109) of Theorem 5.35. As time t becomes unbounded, then asymptotically

$$\mathbb{F}_t \sim a_1 s'^t \mathbb{Y}_1. \tag{5.110}$$

Proof: The argument is similar to that posed in Theorem 5.27. It has previously been established that s' dominates in magnitude all other eigenvalues, and since d_u is of order lower than s_i^t, s' also dominates in magnitude d_u. Therefore, by virtue of Corollary 5.30

$$s'^{-t} \mathbb{F}_t = a_1 \mathbb{Y}_1 + \text{terms of order zero}$$

and the assertion of the theorem is established. $\qquad\square$

As a special case when $p = n$, statement (5.109) of Theorem 5.35 reduces to statement (5.54) of Theorem 5.18 (the case for distinct eigenvalues). In this situation by necessity $k = 1$ for each little Jordan block and furthermore, $q(i) = 1$ for all i, and r is equal to i. In this case (5.109) becomes

$$\mathbb{F}_t = a_1 s'^t \mathbb{Y}_1 + \sum_{i=2}^{n} \sum_{j=1}^{1} \left[a_i s_i^t \mathbb{Y}_i + \sum_{u=i+1}^{i} a_u (s_i^t + d_u) \mathbb{Y}_u \right]. \tag{5.111}$$

The summation indexed by u is understood to be zero whereby the result reduces to that of statement (5.54).

5.6 Conclusion

In this chapter a rather complete and detailed discussion on the use of matrices in the stable theory of population has been presented. The discussion focused on the generalized eigenvalue situation involving both distinct and non-distinct eigenvalues to the characteristic equation. The literature assumes, at least from the practical viewpoint, that the eigenvalues are distinct and it has in effect ignored the possibility of eigenvalues having multiplicities greater than unity. Section 5.5 of this chapter has addressed this problem, and shows that the general case reduces to the case of distinct eigenvalues when the eigenvalues are all simple.

Extensions to the aforementioned are possible. In the model that was presented, the population was divided into age groups of uniform width, where the size of each age group at time t corresponded to the respective component of the population distribution vector $\mathbb{F}_0$. An extension to such an age distribution is given by Lefkovitch [17], where the population is divided into unequal "stage" groups. The consequences of this extension are similar to the classical stable model.

5.7 Notes for Chapter Five

[1] Bernardelli, H. (1941), Population waves. Journal of the Burma Research Society, vol. 31, part 1, pp. 1–18.
[2] Lewis, E.G. (1942), On the generation and growth of a population. Sankhya, vol. 6, pp. 93–96.
[3] Leslie, P.H. (1945), On the use of matrices in certain population mathematics. Biometrika, vol. 33, pp. 183–212.
[4] Ibid., p. 187.
[5] Ibid., p. 187.
[6] Gantmacher, F.R. (1959), Applications of the theory of matrices. p. 61.
[7] Perron, O. (1907), Zur Theorie der Matrizen. Mathematische Annalen, vol. 64, p. 248 ff.
[8] Frobenius, G. (1912), Über Matrizen aus nicht negativen Elementen. Sitzungsberichte der Königlich Preussischen Akademie der Wissenschaften, Berlin, p. 456 ff.
[9] Gantmacher, op. cit., p. 64 ff.
[10] Ibid., p.
[11] Meyer, W. (1982), Asymptotic birth trajectories in the discrete form of stable population theory. Theoretical Population Biology, vol. 21, no. 2, pp. 167–170.
[12] The development of this section is primarily due to the invention of the author.
[13] Moore, John T. (1968), Elements of linear algebra and matrix theory. p. 327 ff.
[14] Noble, Ben (1969), Applied linear algebra. p. 361 ff.
[15] Pollard, J.H. (1973), Mathematical models for the growth of human populations. pp. 44–45.
[16] Noble, Ben, op. cit., pp. 363–366.
[17] Lefkovitch, L.P. (1965), The study of population growth in organisms grouped by stages. Biometrics, vol. 21, pp. 1–18.

6. Comparative Aspects of Stable Population Models

6.1 Introduction

In Chapter Two the fundamental premises of stable population theory, as well as the other foundations for respective stable models, were introduced. The models were of two basic types: discrete time models, and the continuous model. The two discrete time models illustrated were the recursive or finite difference model as discussed in Chapter Three, and the matrix model as discussed in Chapter Five. The continuous model was discussed in Chapter Four, and an alternate approach to this model is given as an appendix. It is now the intent to consolidate these models by highlighting their similarities and their differences.

6.2 Similarities Among the Stable Models

There are certain similarities which exist among the three stable models. For purposes of comparison the three models will be treated in the following order:
1. Discrete Time Recursive, DTR;
2. Discrete Time Matrix, DTM;
3. Continuous Time, CT.

Wherever possible, reference will be made to the place of discussion in previous chapters.

Consider the initial age distribution. In the DTR model and the DTM model this was the female population at exact time t for each age interval $[ih, (i+1)h)$, and was first introduced in Chapter Two under population pyramids. In the CT model the number of females in the age interval $[x, x+h)$ at exact time t was considered. Then by (2.3), (5.15) and Definition 4.1, respectively

DTR: $\qquad\qquad\qquad$ $F_i(t), \qquad 0 \leq i \leq w$ $\qquad\qquad$ (6.1)

DTM: $\qquad\qquad\qquad$ $\mathbb{F}_t$ $\qquad\qquad\qquad\qquad\qquad\qquad$ (6.2)

CT: $\qquad\qquad\qquad\quad$ $F(x,t), \qquad 0 \leq x \leq \omega$ $\qquad\quad$ (6.3)

represent the age distributions for the three models.

The models display a similarity with respect to mortality. In Chapter Two the survivorship ratio was defined by (2.4) of Definition 2.2. The probability of surviving birth to the age indexed by i, given by (2.19), is

DTR: $$p_i = \prod_{j=0}^{i} g_j \qquad (6.4)$$

for survivorship ratio g_i. The DTM model exhibits the same definition by virtue of (5.5) and (5.22). For the CT model from (4.5)

CT: $$p(x) = F(x, t)/B(t - x). \qquad (6.5)$$

Note that the expansion of (6.4) results in an expression

$$p_i = F_i(t)/B_h(t - ih) \qquad (6.6)$$

as demonstrated by (2.34). The survivorship ratios can be obtained from a standard life table at time t via the $_h l_x$ or $_h L_x$ values.

Fertility is another important aspect present in each of the models. In the DTR model by equation (2.10) the annual maternity rate per female for the age category indexed by i at time t is

$$m_i = B_{h,i}(t)/F_i(t - h)h \qquad (6.7)$$

and by (2.13)

DTR: $$B_h(t) = \sum_{i=0}^{w} m_i F_i(t - h)h \qquad (6.8)$$

where $B_h(t)$ is the number of female births on the time interval $(t - h, t]$. In the DTM model by equation (5.3),

DTM: $$F_0'(t' + h) = \sum_{i=0}^{w} g_0' m_i' F_i'(t')h \qquad (6.9)$$

is an expression of fertility represented by the first row of the projection matrix. In the CT model equation (4.10) gives

CT: $$B(t) = \int_0^{\omega} F(x, t)m(x)dx \qquad (6.10)$$

which is similar to (6.8) and (6.9). Unlike mortality rates, fertility rates cannot be derived from a life table but must be obtained by a census or vital statistics register.

Another similarity exhibited by the three deterministic models is their population renewal formulations. Here the net maternity function ϕ plays an important role. In the DTR model by equation (3.25)

DTR: $$B(t) = \sum_{k=1}^{n} \phi_k B(t - k). \qquad (6.11)$$

In the DTM model equation (5.13) gives

DTM: $$\mathbb{F}_{t+k} = \mathbb{Z}^k \mathbb{F}_t. \tag{6.12}$$

The notational form of (6.12) may not seem to correspond to the form of (6.11). However, the births at time $t+k$ is related to the first entry of $\mathbb{F}_{t+k}$ while the births at time t is the first entry of $\mathbb{F}_t$. By ordinary matrix multiplication, the scalar $F_1(t+k)$ is the product of the first row of projection matrix $\mathbb{Z}^k$ by the column $\mathbb{F}_t$. This dot product is exactly analogous to equation (6.11). For the CT model the renewal process is manifested by equation (4.22) as

CT: $$B(t) = \int_0^t B(t-x)\phi(x)dx \tag{6.13}$$

where $\phi(x) = m(x)p(x)$.

Each of the three deterministic models exhibits a characteristic equation. For the DTR model from equations (3.27) and (3.37) the characteristic equation is

DTR: $$\sum_{k=1}^{n} \phi_k s^{-k} = 1. \tag{6.14}$$

The characteristic equation for the DTM model is given by (5.19) as

DTM: $$\det(\mathbb{Z} - s\mathbb{I}) = 0. \tag{6.15}$$

Expansion of (6.15) demonstrates that it is identical to (6.14). It has been shown that under the condition that fertility is non-zero in two relatively prime indices, these equations will exhibit a unique, positive real root which dominates the magnitude of the remaining characteristic roots. The CT model equation (4.25) gives

CT: $$\int_\alpha^\beta \exp(-rx)\phi(x)dx = 1. \tag{6.16}$$

As in the discrete case, the continuous model also exhibits a unique, dominant root. For comparative purposes, recall that $s = \exp(r)$ which enables the dominant root of the continuous model to be any real number. The dominance of the principal root is the salient feature which leads to the stable theory of population.

Another striking feature in the three stable deterministic models is that their analyses unfold solutions that are similar in form. The solution to the DTR model is given by (3.30) as

DTR: $$B(t) = a_1 s_1^t + \sum_{i=2}^{n'} \sum_{j=1}^{\sigma_i} a_{ij} t^{j-1} s_i^t \tag{6.17}$$

130

and for the DTM from equation (5.109) as

DTM:
$$\mathbb{F}_t = a_1 s'^t \mathbb{Y}_1 + \sum_{i=2}^{p} \sum_{j=1}^{q(i)} \left[a_r s_i^t \mathbb{Y}_r + \sum_{u=r+1}^{r+k-1} a_u (s_i^t + d_u) \mathbb{Y}_u \right] \tag{6.18}$$

where r is a function of both i and j, and d_u of lower order of s_i^t. For the CT model equation (4.47) with m finite or infinite gives

CT:
$$B(t) = a_1 \exp(r't) + \sum_{i=2}^{m} \sum_{j=1}^{\sigma_i} a_{ij} t^{j-1} \exp(r_i t). \tag{6.19}$$

Equations (6.17), (6.18) and (6.19) are in a form which can accommodate characteristic values with multiplicities greater than unity. In practice, however, the characteristic values are usually distinct. In this case these equations reduce to

DTR:
$$B(t) = a_1 s_1^t + \sum_{i=2}^{n'} a_i s_i^t \tag{6.20}$$

DTM:
$$\mathbb{F}_t = a_1 s'^t \mathbb{Y}_1 + \sum_{i=2}^{n} a_i s_i^t \mathbb{Y}_i \tag{6.21}$$

CT:
$$B(t) = a_1 \exp(r't) + \sum_{k=2}^{m} a_k \exp(r_k t) \tag{6.22}$$

respectively, where m of (6.22) may be finite or infinite.

Asymptotic similarities are self evident due to the dominance of the principal characteristic root. As time t becomes unbounded, the aforementioned solutions to the three models reduce to

DTR:
$$B(t) \sim a_1 s_1^t \tag{6.23}$$

DTM:
$$\mathbb{F}_t \sim a_1 s'^t \mathbb{Y}_1 \tag{6.24}$$

CT:
$$B(t) \sim a_1 \exp(r't) \tag{6.25}$$

respectively. In addition, the coefficient a_1 is always positive.

Other than notation, it is clear that the three stable deterministic models display strong similarities. The similarities have been highlighted from the viewpoint of mortality, fertility, renewal formulations and their attendant characteristic equations, solution formulations and their reduced asymptotic forms. Of particular note is that the first entry of the age distribution vector $\mathbb{F}_t$ represents the survivors of birth to the first age interval. Thus, the DTR model is just a particular version of the DTM model thereby making these models equivalent.

6.3 Differences Among the Stable Models

Other than obvious notational differences, the major difference between the two discrete models and the continuous model is that their development and resulting solution formulations are respectively discrete and continuous functions. In particular, in the DTR model the exponential expression

$$a_1 s_1^t \tag{6.26}$$

is not a continuous function. For the DTM model this was obvious since powers of the projection matrix were formed by whole number exponents. That is, $\mathbf{Z}^t$ had meaning for t a non-negative integer.

Another difference is that in the discrete models the characteristic equation always generated a finite number of characteristic values. In the continuous model it is possible to have an infinite number characteristic values, as demonstrated by Feller [1] and assumed by Lotka [2]. It has been noted by Feller that the representation of the birth function by an infinite series of exponentials is not always possible [3]. Empirical demographic situations, however, show that such an exponential series is a correct representation [4], [5].

6.4 Conclusion

In retrospect, it is clear that the models of Malthus, Gompertz, Makeham and Verhulst, as discussed in Chapter One, were oversimplifications of the theory of population when compared to the models of the stable theory of population. These earlier models, however, are not obsolete and can be utilized effectively where applicable. Furthermore, the stable models themselves are not to be construed as perfect models; they are valid models provided that the premises of stable theory (closure to migration, age-specific birth rates and death rates are independent of time) are satisfied. In reality, this is not always true.

However, the stable theory of population does present and develop strong mathematical machinery which can be used to provides an analysis of the long-term behavior of a population. The discussion of stable theory usually focuses on human population because of the availability of data. Nothing, however, precludes its use to other biological populations of to other fields of interest.

6.5 Notes for Chapter Six

[1] Feller, W. (1941), On the integral equation of renewal theory. Annals of Mathematical Statistics, vol. 12, p. 263.
[2] Sharpe, F.R. and Lotka, A.J. (1911), A problem in age-Distribution. Philosophical Magazine, Ser. 6, vol 21, p. 435.
[3] Feller, W., op. cit.
[4] Pollard, J.H. (1973), Mathematical models for the growth of human populations. p. 26.
[5] Keyfitz, N. (1968), Introduction to the mathematics of population. p. 51.

7. Extensions of Stable Population Theory

7.1 Introduction

The developments and results of the previous chapters can be summarized by the following statement:

Given a population
(a) that is closed to migration,
(b) that has time invariant age-specific birth rates, and
(c) that has time invariant age-specific death rates.

Then regardless of the initial age distribution, the population will converge to a proportional age distribution that depends solely on the age-specific rates of birth and death as time increases without bound. In addition, the size of each age group grows exponentially, and each age group has the same growth rate.

This statement does focus on the heart of stable population theory, namely, that a population converges asymptotically to an ultimate age distribution called the *stable age distribution*. A population having this property is referred to as being *strongly ergodic* in that it 'forgets' any previous age distribution [1]. This is explicitly shown in statement (6.24) which is repeated here as

$$\mathbb{F}_t \sim a_1 s'^t \mathbb{Y}_1. \tag{7.1}$$

The age distribution at time t, $\mathbb{F}_t$, is proportional not to the initial age distribution $\mathbb{F}_0$, but to $\mathbb{Y}_1$, the eigenvector corresponding to the principal eigenvalue s'.

The discussion which follows demonstrates some of the mathematical extensions of the stable theory of population. Because of its convenience from the standpoint of analysis, the continuous time model functions and definitions will be used as the basic vehicle of discussion. Wherever appropriate, however, discrete model terminology will also be used.

7.2 Some Parameters of Stable Population Theory

For time t and $n > 0$, consider the time interval $[t - n, t + n)$ of length $2n$. Let P_t be the total number of individuals of a population alive at time t. If B_t

134

represents the total number of live births on this time interval, and D_t represents the total number of deaths on this time interval, then the ratios

$$b_c = B_t/P_t \qquad (7.2)$$

and

$$d_c = D_t/P_t \qquad (7.3)$$

are respectively the *crude birth rate* and the *crude death rate* of the population at time t. In practice the time interval is usually a calendar year, causing P_t to be the mid-year population, and both b_c and d_c are calculated as annual rates. The difference between these two rates is the *crude rate of increase*, denoted r_c, written simply as

$$r_c = b_c - d_c \qquad (7.4)$$

for crude birth and death rates b_c and d_c [2].

Before investigating the implications of stable theory on these definitions, recall from Chapter Four some basic ideas. The number of females whose age was exactly x at time t was given by $F(x, t)$, and the number of females whose age lies in the interval $[x, x+dx)$ at time t is $F(x, t)dx$. Then from (4.50) the *total number of females* alive at time t, denoted $F_T(t)$, is

$$F_T(t) = \int_0^\omega F(x, t)dx. \qquad (7.5)$$

By Lemma 4.5 the *number of females born* to women of any age at time t is given by

$$B_t = \int_0^\omega F(x, t)m(x)dx \qquad (7.6)$$

where m is the age-specific birth function. By definition the *portion of the female population* between ages x and $x+dx$ at time t is given by (4.51) as

$$c(x, t)dx = F(x, t)dx/F_T(t). \qquad (7.7)$$

This results in the following:

Lemma 7.1. The crude birth rate at time t is

$$b_c = \int_0^\omega c(x, t)m(x)dx. \qquad (7.8)$$

Proof: From (7.7)

$$F(x, t)dx = F_T(t)c(x, t)dx$$

where F_T is independent of age x. From (7.2) and (7.6)

$$b_c = \int_0^\omega c(x, t)m(x)dx \bigg/ \int_0^\omega c(x, t)dx \qquad (7.9)$$

135

after cancelling $F_T(t)$. But out of necessity over the whole of life, the second integral of (7.9) must be unity, from which the required result is obtained. □

The lemma makes intuitive sense since it is a weighted average of the age-specific annual maternity rates, the weights being the fractions of the whole female population at the various ages.

From the viewpoint of mortality, the index which expresses the annual rate of mortality at the precise moment of attaining age x is the *force of mortality function* expressed according to (1.30) as

$$\mu(x) = \frac{-1}{p(x)} \frac{d}{dx} [p(x)] = \frac{-d}{dx} [\ln p(x)] \tag{7.10}$$

where $p(x)$ is proportional to the survivorship function $l(x)$. The number of female deaths between the ages x and $x+dx$ for the female population at time t is $F(x,t)\mu(x)dx$, whereby the total number of deaths for all ages is

$$D_t = \int_0^\omega F(x,t)\mu(x)dx. \tag{7.11}$$

This leads to the following:

Lemma 7.2. The crude death rate at time t is

$$d_c = \int_0^\omega c(x,t)\mu(x)dx. \tag{7.12}$$

Proof: From (7.3) with (7.5) and (7.11)

$$d_c = \int_0^\omega F(x,t)\mu(x)dx/F_T(t)$$

and after using (7.7) and cancelling $F_T(t)$

$$d_c = \int_0^\omega c(x,t)\mu(x)dx \Big/ \int_0^\omega c(x,t)dx. \tag{7.13}$$

Again, since the second integral of (7.13) is necessarily unity, the required result is immediate. □

As in the case with the crude birth rate, this lemma makes intuitive sense in that the crude death rate is a weighted average of the instantaneous mortality function. Combining Lemmas 7.1 and 7.2 leads to the following:

Theorem 7.3. Let b_c and d_c respectively equal the crude birth rate and the crude death rate. The crude rate of increase at time t is

$$r_c = \int_0^\omega c(x,t)[m(x) - \mu(x)]dx \tag{7.14}$$

136

where m is the continuous maternity function at exact age x, and μ is the instantaneous force of mortality function.

Proof: Substitution of (7.8) and (7.12) into (7.4) gives the required result immediately. □

The previous results of this section are true for any population that is closed to migration. When a population is stable, however, some further interesting facts are true. The first fact is contained in the following:

Lemma 7.4. Let a population be stable and let b_c be the crude birth rate at time t. If

$$b = 1 \left/ \int_0^\omega \exp(-rx)p(x)dx \right. \tag{7.15}$$

where r is the principal root of the characteristic equation of the continuous stable model, and $p(x)$ is the probability of surviving birth to age x, then

$$\lim_{t \to \infty} b_c = b. \tag{7.16}$$

Proof: From Theorem 4.22, as $t \to \infty$

$$c(x, t) \to \exp(-rx)p(x) \left/ \int_0^\omega \exp(-rx)p(x)dx = c(x) \right. \tag{7.17}$$

a function of x alone. Substituting into (7.8) and taking the limit gives

$$\lim_{t \to \infty} b_c = \int_0^\omega \exp(-rx)m(x)p(x)dx \left/ \int_0^\omega \exp(-rx)p(x)dx. \right. \tag{7.18}$$

Recalling that the first integral of (7.18) is just the characteristic function, which equals unity by (4.25), then by (7.15) the result is immediate. □

Definition 7.5. The value b as defined by (7.15) is called the *intrinsic birth rate* of a stable population.

By similar reasoning, another property of stable theory can be developed as shown in the following:

Lemma 7.6. Given a stable population with d_c the crude death rate at time t. Let b, r and p be defined as in Lemma 7.4. Then

$$\lim_{t \to \infty} d_c = -b \int_0^\omega \exp(-rx)d(p(x)). \tag{7.19}$$

Proof: As $t \to \infty$ with the use of (7.10) and (7.17) in (7.12)

$$\lim_{t \to \infty} d_c = - \int_0^\omega \exp(-rx)d(p(x)) \left/ \int_0^\omega \exp(-rx)p(x)dx \right. .$$

Then by use of (7.15) the result is immediate. □

Definition 7.7. Let d equal the limit of the crude death rate as $t \to \infty$. Then

$$d = -b \int_0^\omega \exp(-rx)d(p(x)) \tag{7.20}$$

is called the *intrinsic death rate* of a stable population.

The literature assumes without verification that the difference between the intrinsic birth rate and the intrinsic death rate is the value r. The following supports and justifies this belief.

Theorem 7.8. Given a stable population where the intrinsic rates of birth and death are defined by (7.15) and (7.20) respectively. Let r denote the principal characteristic root of the characteristic equation (4.25) of the continuous stable model. Then

$$r = b - d. \tag{7.21}$$

Proof: Using the definitions of the intrinsic birth rate b and the intrinsic death rate d gives

$$b - d = b\left[1 + \int_0^\omega \exp(-rx)d(p(x))\right].$$

Using integration by parts,

$$b - d = b\left[1 + \exp(-r\omega)p(\omega) - p(0) + r\int_0^\omega \exp(-rx)p(x)dx\right].$$

Since $p(\omega) = 0$ and $p(0) = 1$, then by (7.15)

$$b - d = b[1 - 1 + r/b] = r$$

which was to be demonstrated. □

Definition 7.9. The value $r = b - d$, which is the principal characteristic value, is called the *intrinsic rate of growth*.

The intrinsic rates r, b and d coupled with the age-specific functions of maternity m and mortality μ, and the age distribution function c, form the fundamental parameters or functions of stable population theory. Recalling

138

that $p(x)=l(x)/l_0$ and the expression for the force of mortality, the following interrelationships are hereby summarized:

1. $p(x)=\exp(-\int \mu(x)dx)$ (7.22)

2. $\int_{\alpha}^{\beta} \exp(-rx)m(x)p(x)dx=1$ (7.23)

3. $r=b-d$ (7.24)

4. $c(x)=b\exp(-rx)p(x)$ (7.25)

5. $b=1\left/\int_{0}^{\omega} \exp(-rx)p(x)dx\right.$ (7.26)

6. $d=-b\int_{0}^{\omega} \exp(-rx)d(p(x))$.   (7.27)

Note that from (7.25) $c(0)=b$. Also note that it is not possible to obtain the maternity function m from these equations by use of one or more of the other parameters, implying that m must be given independently. In addition, μ and p are explicitly related by (7.22) so even though there are seven parameters (p, μ, m, c, r, b, d) in the above relations, only six are fundamental. For a more in-depth discussion of these interrelationships, the reader is advised to consult Keyfitz [3]. As a final note, if the intrinsic rate of growth r is zero, then the stable model conforms to Definition 1.13 and the population is stationary. That is $b=d$.

7.3 Some Fertility Measures in Stable Population Theory

By previous definition, the crude birth rate is the ratio of the total births to the total population when taken over a particular time interval. The ratio of the total number of births, both sexes, compared to the female population alive between α and β, the first and last age of reproduction, is called the *general fertility rate*. If this ratio is available for females at each age or age category between α and β, then the ratio is called the *age-specific fertility rate* for both sexes. The sum over all ages or age categories between α and β is called the *total fertility rate* [4].

If one considers only female births from a female population, then the maternity function m is used to describe the probability of a woman whose age falls on the interval $[x, x+dx)$ giving birth to a female child. This probability is given as

$$m(x)dx$$

and leads to the following [5]:

Definition 7.10. The number of female children that a female just born may expect to bear during her reproductive life, ignoring the possibility of mor-

139

tality, is called the *gross reproduction rate* and is defined as

$$\text{GRR} = \int_\alpha^\beta m(x)\,dx. \tag{7.28}$$

The GRR assumes that the female survives to age β; clearly, this is not the case in real life. What is of interest is the probability that a female birth survives to age interval $[x, x+dx)$ and herself gives birth to a female child. This is precisely the *net maternity function* ϕ defined as

$$\phi(x)\,dx = p(x)m(x)\,dx$$

which leads to the following [6]:

Definition 7.11. The number of female children that a female just born may expect to bear during her reproductive life is called the *net reproduction rate* and is defined as

$$\text{NRR} = R_0 = \int_\alpha^\beta p(x)m(x)\,dx. \tag{7.29}$$

Effectively, the NRR is a replacement ratio based on a given regime of mortality and fertility.

The NRR has interesting properties. When NRR is unity, the females are replacing themselves exactly. Also, recalling the characteristic function of the continuous model described as

$$\Psi(r) = \int_\alpha^\beta \exp(-rx)p(x)m(x)\,dx \tag{7.30}$$

the function Ψ becomes the NRR when $r=0$; that is,

$$\text{NRR} = R_0 = \Psi(0) \tag{7.31}$$

which is the vertical axis intercept for the characteristic function Ψ. In addition, the NRR has a direct bearing on the intrinsic growth rate of a population as shown in the following:

Lemma 7.12. Given a stable population with intrinsic growth rate r, and let NRR be defined by (7.29). The following is true:

$$\text{NRR} < 1 \quad \text{iff} \quad r < 0 \tag{7.32}$$

$$\text{NRR} = 1 \quad \text{iff} \quad r = 0 \tag{7.33}$$

$$\text{NRR} > 1 \quad \text{iff} \quad r > 0. \tag{7.34}$$

Proof: Recalling that the characteristic function equals unity for all values of its argument, then for net maternity function ϕ

140

$$1=\int_\alpha^\beta \exp(-rx)\phi(x)dx \lessgtr \int_\alpha^\beta \exp(0)\phi(x)dx = NRR$$

as r is negative, zero, or positive, which was to be shown. □

As previously mentioned, the NRR is a measure by which a female birth will be replaced. The *length of a generation*, denoted T, is the time in which this replacement takes place. In this respect, the number of births at time t is proportional to the number of births at time $t-T$. The constant of proportionality is just the net reproduction rate, R_0. This leads to the following:

Lemma 7.13. Given a stable population with intrinsic growth rate r and net reproduction rate R_0. The length of a generation, T, is

$$T = \ln(R_0)/r \tag{7.35}$$

provided $r \neq 0$.

Proof: Since the birth at times t and $t-T$ are proportional, then

$$B(t) = R_0 B(t-T). \tag{7.36}$$

Since r is a solution to the characteristic equation of the continuous model, a solution for $B(t)$ is $a_1 \exp(rt)$ which, when substituted into (7.36), gives

$$1 = R_0 \exp(-rT)$$

from which the assertion of the lemma is demonstrated. □

For a stationary population when $r=0$, $R_0=1$ and (7.35) is an indeterminate. Before investigating this situation further, the following is required [7].

Definition 7.14. Let the net maternity function ϕ be a function of age x defined over the interval of reproduction $[\alpha, \beta]$. The *mean length of a generation*, denoted T_0, is defined as

$$T_0 = \int_\alpha^\beta x\phi(x)dx \bigg/ \int_\alpha^\beta \phi(x)dx. \tag{7.37}$$

Corollary 7.15. In a stationary population, the length of a generation equals the mean length of a generation. That is,

$$T = T_0. \tag{7.38}$$

Proof: In a deleted neighborhood of $r=0$, expression (7.35) holds. Noting that $\Psi(r)=1$ and $\Psi(0)=R_0$, a Taylor expansion of $\Psi(r)$ about $r=0$ yields

$$\lim_{r \to 0} T = -\lim_{r \to 0}(1/r)[\ln(\Psi(r)) - \ln R_0]$$

$$= -\lim_{r \to 0}(1/r)\left[\ln \Psi(0) + \frac{\Psi'(0)}{\Psi(0)}r + \frac{\Psi(0)\Psi''(0) - (\Psi'(0))^2}{2!\,\Psi(0)\Psi(0)}r^2 + \ldots - \ln R_0\right].$$

Cancelling $\ln \Psi(0)$ with $\ln R_0$, distributing $(1/r)$, and noting that

$$T_0 = -\Psi'(0)/\Psi(0)$$

the required result is obtained. $\qquad\qquad\qquad\qquad\qquad\qquad\qquad\qquad$ □

The previous discussion leads to the following [8]:

Definition 7.16. Given a stable population with the intrinsic rate of increase as r and with α, β, ϕ and x previously defined. The *mean age of childbearing* is defined as

$$\bar{A} = \int_{\alpha}^{\beta} x \exp(-rx)\phi(x)dx \bigg/ \int_{\alpha}^{\beta} \exp(-rx)\phi(x)dx. \qquad (7.39)$$

It can be shown [9] that an approximation to the length of a generation is the arithmetic mean of the average length of a generation and the mean age of childbearing. That is,

$$T \doteq (\bar{A} + T_0)/2. \qquad (7.40)$$

In particular, the mean age of childbearing in a stationary population is trivially the mean length of a generation.

As a final notion relating to fertility, the concept of *reproductive value* is considered. In 1930 Fisher [10] proposed that when a child is born, it owes society a new life or lives repayable by that child's own offspring. The rate of interest at which the debt to society is to be repaid is the intrinsic rate of growth, r. In terms of the female population, the chance that a newborn female survives to age x and gives birth to another female between the ages x and $x + dx$ is as before, $p(x)m(x)dx$. If the value of this birth is discounted back through x years at an annual rate of r compounded continuously, then the value of this child is

$$\exp(-rx)p(x)m(x)dx. \qquad (7.41)$$

Fisher points out that the aggregate of all these values when taken over the ages of fertility, α to β, is the *unit birth*. This also gives meaning to the characteristic equation of the continuous model, being the integral of expression (7.41) equal to unity.

It is now possible to calculate the amount of "debt" that is outstanding at the time when a female has reached the age of y where $0 \le y \le \beta$. The expected number of births during the age interval $[x, x+dx)$ by those females already reaching age y is

$$[l(x)/l(y)]m(x)dx$$

as shown from Fig. 7.1. When discounted back by $x-y$ years, the expected number of births is

$$\exp(-r(x-y))[l(x)/l(y)]m(x)dx.$$

142

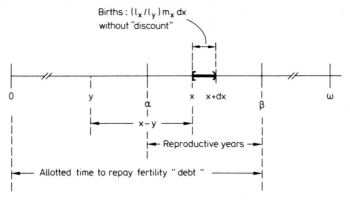

Fig. 7.1. Illustration on the concept of reproductive value

The limiting sum of these values from age y to age β, the age by which the 'debt' must be repaid, leads to the following [11] for $l(x) = l_0 p(x)$.

Definition 7.17. Let r, p, m, x, and y have their usual meaning. Then

$$v(y) = \frac{\exp(ry)}{p(y)} \int_y^\beta \exp(-rx) p(x) m(x) dx \qquad (7.42)$$

is called the *reproductive value* at age y for $[0 \le y \le \beta]$.

Note that $v(0) = 1$, and for $y > \beta$, $v(y) = 0$ as expected. In addition, if at age y the reproductive value is multiplied by the population at that age and summed over all ages, the following results [12].

Definition 7.18. Let $F(y) dy$ be the number of females on the age interval $[y, y + dy)$. Then

$$V = \int_0^\beta F(y) v(y) dy \qquad (7.43)$$

is called the *total reproductive value* of the female population.

The value V can be interpreted as the number of female children to be born in the future by those females in the present population under the influence of the intrinsic rate of growth. Other interesting aspects of reproductive value are possible and the interested reader may consult Keyfitz [13] or Fisher [14].

7.4 Some Applications of Stable Population Theory

It is the purpose of this section to illustrate a few applications derived from stable population theory. The interested reader may wish to consult other sources such as Keyfitz [15] for a broader discussion on this topic.

Mean of a Population Substructure

It has previously been shown that the fraction of the population between ages a and $a+da$ at time t for a stable population is

$$c(a)da = b\exp(-ra)p(a)da \qquad (7.44)$$

where p is the probability of surviving to age a from birth, and b is the intrinsic birth rate. This leads to the following:

Lemma 7.19. Let x and y be any two ages between 0 and ω such that $x \leq y$. The *fraction of people* between ages x and y, denoted $C(x, y)$, is

$$C(x, y) = \int_x^y c(a)da = b\int_x^y \exp(-ra)p(a)da \qquad (7.45)$$

where $c(a)\,da$ is given by (7.44).

Proof: The result is immediate after integration of (7.44). □

Theorem 7.20. Let the fraction of people between ages x and y be given as in (7.45). The *mean age of the population* between ages x and y is

$$\bar{a}_{x,y} = \int_x^y a\exp(-ra)p(a)da \Big/ \int_x^y \exp(-ra)p(a)da. \qquad (7.46)$$

Proof: For each age $a \in [x, y]$, its value is scaled by $c(a)$, the proportion of people at age a. Taking the limiting sum over all ages between x and y, and dividing by the fraction of the population between x and y, $C(x, y)$, gives the first moment, which is the desired result. □

Corollary 7.21. Let $\bar{a}$ denote the *mean age of a stable population*. Then

$$\bar{a} = \int_0^\omega ac(a)da \qquad (7.47)$$

where $c(a)da$ is given by (7.44).

Proof: From (7.46)

$$\bar{a} = \bar{a}_{0,\omega} = \int_0^\omega a\exp(-ra)p(a)da \Big/ \int_0^\omega \exp(-ra)p(a)da. \qquad (7.48)$$

Since the second integral of (7.48) is $1/b$, combining it with the first of these integrals gives the result immediately. □

It is possible to estimate $\bar{a}$ if $c(a)$ is a step function with constant values over age intervals of width equal to n. Using (7.47) with w the index of the last

144

age interval results in

$$\bar{a} = \int_0^\omega ac(a)da = \sum_{k=0}^{w-1} \int_{kn}^{(k+1)n} ac(a)da. \tag{7.49}$$

Letting a be the average of the limits of integration results in the approximation

$$\bar{a} \doteq \sum_{k=0}^{w-1} (2k+1)n/2 \int_{kn}^{(k+1)n} c(a)da \tag{7.50}$$

or from (7.45),

$$\bar{a} \doteq n \sum_{k=0}^{w-1} (k+0.5) C(kn, (k+1)n). \tag{7.51}$$

Therefore, given the fraction of the population on the age interval $[kn, (k+1)n)$ for $k=0, 1, \ldots, w-1$, an approximation to the mean age of a population can be obtained as shown in (7.51).

An interesting property concerning the mean of a population between two ages is shown in the following:

Theorem 7.22. Let $c(a)$ be the age distribution function of a stable population. Let $\bar{a}_{x,y}$ be the mean of the population between ages x and y as given in (7.46), which is a function of r, the intrinsic rate of growth. Then

$$\frac{d}{dr} [\bar{a}_{x,y}] = -\sigma_{x,y}^2 \tag{7.52}$$

where $\sigma_{x,y}^2$, a function of r, is the *variance of the age* distribution between ages x and y.

Proof: The derivative of (7.46) with respect to r by the quotient rule and Leibnitz' rule gives, after rearranging,

$$\frac{d}{dr} [\bar{a}_{x,y}] = -\left[\frac{\int_x^y a^2 \exp(-ra)p(a)da}{\int_x^y \exp(-ra)p(a)da} - \left\{ \frac{\int_x^y a \exp(-ra)p(a)da}{\int_x^y \exp(-ra)p(a)da} \right\}^2 \right]$$

which is recognized as the expression for variance, and the theorem is demonstrated. ☐

Corollary 7.23. Let $\bar{a}$ be the mean of the population as described from (7.48). Then

$$\frac{d}{dr} [\bar{a}] = -\sigma^2 \tag{7.53}$$

where σ^2 is the variance of the entire population between ages 0 and ω, and is a function of r.

145

Proof: Let $x=0$ and $y=\omega$ in Theorem 7.22 and the result is immediate. $\square$

The literature sometimes assumes that the difference between two population means for two different age intervals of the same population is independent of the intrinsic rate of growth [16]. The following refutes that claim.

Theorem 7.24. Let $\bar{a}'$ and $\bar{a}''$ be two means on the same population as given by (7.46). Then

$$\frac{d}{dr}[\bar{a}'-\bar{a}'']=-[\sigma'^2-\sigma''^2] \tag{7.54}$$

where the variances, as described by Theorem 7.22 relating to means $\bar{a}'$ and $\bar{a}''$, are σ'^2 and σ''^2 respectively.

Proof: This is an immediate consequence from Theorem 7.22. $\square$

The significance of Theorem 7.24 is that the difference between two means of the same population is not independent of r unless $\sigma'^2-\sigma''^2=0$ for all values of r.

Estimating the Intrinsic Rate of Growth

The salient parameter of any stable population in terms of stable theory is the value r, the intrinsic rate of growth. This intrinsic rate will be estimated from the assumption that a life table exists for the population, and the possible presence of a census.

Suppose r is to be estimated for a population where only a single census is available, which provides a count by age of all individuals of the population at time t. Let $F(x,t)$ represent the number of individuals aged x at time t, which are the survivors of those born x years ago under the influence of the average survivor function L_x. Then for two different cohorts at time t

$$F(x,t) \doteq L_x B(t-x)$$

and

$$F(y,t) \doteq L_y B(t-y)$$

where the births are not known. If the population is in a stable state, then

$$\frac{F(x,t)/F(y,t)}{L_x/L_y} \doteq \frac{B(t-x)}{B(t-y)} = \frac{\exp(r(t-x))}{\exp(r(t-y))} = \exp(r(y-x))$$

where $B(t)=a_1 \exp(rt)$ from stable population theory. Solving for r yields

$$r \doteq \frac{1}{y-x} \ln\left[\frac{F(x,t)/F(y,t)}{L_x/L_y}\right] \tag{7.55}$$

146

as an estimate for r, where the values of F are obtained from a census and the values of L from a lifetable. A procedure such as this may be useful in the study of a developing country where only one census is available and where a lifetable is available from a neighboring country.

When two census years are available in a stable population, a lifetable is not required and the guesswork of L_x/L_y is eliminated. In this case the estimate of r is much easier. Suppose a census in available for years t' and t''. Then for a given age x, the population at time t' is

$$F(x, t') \doteq L_x B(t' - x)$$

while the population at time t'' is

$$F(x, t'') \doteq L_x B(t'' - x).$$

The stability assumption of the population ensures that L_x is the same at times t' and t'', Then

$$F(x, t')/F(x, t'') \doteq B(t' - x)/B(t'' - x) = \exp(r(t' - t''))$$

whereby

$$r \doteq \frac{1}{t' - t''} \ln [F(x, t')/F(x, t'')] \tag{7.56}$$

as an estimate for the intrinsic rate of growth.

Estimating the Intrinsic Rate of Birth

An extension of the previous discussion is the estimation of the intrinsic birth rate b of a stable population. From (7.45) with $y = x + n$

$$C(x, x+n) = b \int_{x}^{x+n} \exp(-ra)p(a)da. \tag{7.57}$$

If the interval from x to $x + n$ is small enough, a constant approximation to the exponential function is appropriate with an evaluation at the midpoint of the interval. This results in

$$C(x, x+n) \doteq b \exp(-r(x+n/2)) \int_{x}^{x+n} p(a)da. \tag{7.58}$$

Interpreting the integral of (7.58) as ${}_nL_x$ within a radix of l_0, enables one to write

$$\exp(r(x+n/2)) \doteq b \, {}_nL_x/C(x, x+n).$$

When considered at two different ages x and y, this becomes

$$r \doteq (1/(x+n/2)) \ln \left[\frac{b \, {}_nL_x}{C(x, x+n)} \right] \doteq (1/(y+n/2)) \ln \left[\frac{b \, {}_nL_y}{C(y, y+n)} \right].$$

147

After rearrangement and cancellation this becomes

$$b^{(y-x)} \doteq [C(x, x+n)/_nL_x]^{y+n/2}/[C(y, y+n)/_nL_y]^{x+n/2}$$

from which

$$b \doteq \left[\frac{[C(x, x+n)/_nL_x]^{y+n/2}}{[C(y, y+n)/_nL_y]^{x+n/2}} \right]^{1/(y-x)}. \qquad (7.59)$$

Thus, the intrinsic birth rate can be obtained by a census and a life table on the assumption that the population is stable.

Pensions-Their Cost and Response to Population Change

Consider a stable population where a portion of the population is on a pension while another portion of the population makes contributions to the pensions. At a particular point in time let P be the size of the entire population whose contributors are aged between u and v with salaries that are all equal and of value S. Let the pensioners of this population be aged between v and ω such that all receive the same pension of value R. For economic balance, excluding administrative cost, the total contributions to the pension system must equal the total receipts by the pensioners. If g is the fraction of the salary of a contributor that is required to maintain the pension system, then

$$g S P C(u, v) = R P C(v, \omega) \qquad (7.60)$$

where $C(u, v)$ and $C(v, \omega)$ are defined by Definition 7.19. Clearly,

$$g = (R/S)[C(v, \omega)/C(u, v)] \qquad (7.61)$$

enabling the determination of what portion of salary is required by those contributors whose age is on the interval $[u, v)$ to receive a pension upon reaching age v, which is the fraction R/S of their previous salary.

An interesting aspect to this pension application is to show how a change in r, the intrinsic rate of growth, affects the value of g. Upon taking the natural logarithm of (7.61) and taking the derivative with respect to r, one obtains

$$\frac{d}{dr}[\ln g] = (1/C(v, \omega)) \frac{d}{dr}[C(v, \omega)] - (1/C(u, v)) \frac{d}{dr}[C(u, v)]. \qquad (7.62)$$

This leads to the following:

Lemma 7.25. Let $C(x, y)$ be defined according to (7.45). Then

$$\frac{d}{dr} C(x, y) = (\bar{a} - \bar{a}_{x, y}) C(x, y) \qquad (7.63)$$

148

where $\bar{a}$ is the population mean over all ages 0 to ω, and where $\bar{a}_{x,y}$ is the mean of the population between ages x and y.

Proof: By (7.45) and (7.15), use of the quotient rule and Leibnitz' rule gives

$$\frac{d}{dr}[C(x, y)] = \left[-\int_0^\omega E\,da \int_x^y aE\,da + \int_x^y E\,da \int_0^\omega aE\,da\right] \bigg/ \left[\int_0^\omega E\,da\right]^2$$

where $E = \exp(-ra)p(a)$. Combining and rearranging gives the required result. $\square$

Using Lemma 7.25 for the expressions in (7.62) gives

$$(1/C(v, \omega))\frac{d}{dr}[C(v, \omega)] = \bar{a} - \bar{a}_p \qquad (7.64)$$

where $\bar{a}_p$ is the mean age of the pensioners, and

$$(1/C(u, v))\frac{d}{dr}[C(u, v)] = \bar{a} - \bar{a}_c \qquad (7.65)$$

where $\bar{a}_c$ is the mean age of the contributors. Substituting (7.64) and (7.65) into (7.62) yields

$$\frac{d}{dr}[\ln g] = -(\bar{a}_p - \bar{a}_c). \qquad (7.66)$$

If it is assumed that $\bar{a}_p - \bar{a}_c$ is a constant, the solution is

$$g = k\exp(-(\bar{a}_p - \bar{a}_c)r). \qquad (7.67)$$

Note that $\bar{a}_p - \bar{a}_c$ is in general a function of r (see Theorem 7.24) and is positive, approximately 25 years. This shows that an increase in r generates a decrease in g, while a decrease in r generates an increase in g.

Other Applications

There are many applications of stable population theory, too numerous to list here. It may be worth while, however to mention a few examples of a biological nature that may interest the reader. For instance, in a comprehensive article by Cole [17], a study is made on the manner in which the first age of reproduction, α, affects the intrinsic rate of growth, r. As another example, in the study of spawning, stock and recruitment of fish in fisheries, an interesting study is made by Levin [18] and Levin and Goodyear [19] on the manner in which the age structure of the fishery affects the stability of the model. In the field of genetics, there is a growing interest in the mathematical modelling of such structures as demonstrated by recent literature; a work by Jacquard [20] is an example of this. In the area of epidemiology, a study of the works of Anderson [21], May [22] and Getz [23] should provide a good mathematical perspective on the subject. Even in the non-stable biological models, such as the competition of species as described by Volterra [24], or the competition of nutrients as demonstrated by Hale and Somolinos [25], there is an abundance of mathematical applications. Interestingly, many of the biological applications to mathematics have yet to be investigated.

7.5 Perturbations of Stable Population Theory

With the advance of civilization and medicine, the twentieth century has experienced a sharp decline in the death rate for most nations. Also, economic, social and political considerations has caused the birth rate of many nations to decline and fluctuate. Thus, the age-specific rates of birth and death can no longer be assumed to be independent of time, and the premises of stable population theory as applied to human populations are greatly weakened. This as well as other factors, has led demographers to remould the classical stable models without eliminating their underlying features.

In 1957 Coale [26] conjectured the concept of *weak ergodicity* as applied to stable theory. Briefly stated, Coale believed that even though fertility and mortality rates were functions of time, a population would still tend to 'forget' its past, that is, its initial age structure. In 1961 Lopez [27] proved that two populations closed to migration and experiencing the same age-specific fertility and mortality rates that were not necessarily independent of time would, with the passing of time, adopt age distributions that were proportional to each other. That is, the age distribution of a closed population tends to 'forget' its past shape, and is determined exclusively by the history of fertility and mortality. In symbolic form, if $\mathbb{E}(t)$ and $\mathbb{F}(t)$ are two population vectors at time t, and $\mathbb{Z}(t)$ is the projection matrix for each of these populations whose elements of fertility and mortality are functions of time, then

$$\mathbb{E}(t+n) = \left[\prod_{i=0}^{n-1} \mathbb{Z}(t+i) \right] \mathbb{E}(t)$$

and

$$\mathbb{F}(t+n) = \left[\prod_{i=0}^{n-1} \mathbb{Z}(t+i) \right] \mathbb{F}(t).$$

Lopez then proves that as $n \to \infty$

$$\mathbb{E}(t+n) = k \mathbb{F}(t+n) \tag{7.68}$$

for some constant k.

In 1963 Coale [28] proposed a situation in which a population would experience birth rates that are independent of time, while the death rates would vary uniformly with time. A closed population having these characteristics is called *quasi-stable*. The following is a generalization of Coale's thinking.

150

Theorem 7.26. Let a population at time t' have a force of mortality function μ with a survivorship function l that are functions of age alone. For $t \geq 0$ let $l^*(a, t)$ be the survivorship function at age a and at a time t years after time t', and let $\mu^*(a, t)$ be the force of mortality function with corresponding interpretation. If

$$\mu^*(a, t) = \mu(a) + G(a, t) \tag{7.69}$$

such that $G(a, 0) = 0$, then

$$l^*(a, t) = k\,l(a) \exp\left(-\int G(a, t)\,da\right) \tag{7.70}$$

where k is an arbitrary constant.

Proof: By the definition of the force of mortality, $\mu(a) = -[\ln l(a)]'$ so at time t for μ^* described in (7.69)

$$l^*(a, t) = k \exp\left[-\int [\mu(a) + G(a, t)]\,da\right]$$

whereby from ordinary calculus the result is obtained. $\qquad\qquad\square$

For example, if $G(a, t) = k'(t - t')$ then

$$l^*(a, t) = k\,l(a) \exp(-k'(t - t')a) \tag{7.71}$$

which is similar to that proposed by Coale. If instead, $G(a, t) = \mu(a)f(t)$, which describes a change in the force of mortality that is proportional to the original force of mortality by a factor that depends on the time beyond t', then

$$l^*(a, t) = k\,l(a)[l(a)]^{f(t)}. \tag{7.72}$$

Both equations (7.71) and (7.72) illustrate that a situation of decreasing mortality results in an increase in survivorship, as expected. That is,

$$\mu^*(a, t) < \mu(a) \Leftrightarrow l^*(a, t) > l(a). \tag{7.73}$$

Results such as these are useful to demographers since they can be used to construct life tables at some future time. When coupled with an estimate for the intrinsic rate of growth, for example, the structure of a population at a future time can be determined.

It is possible to construct a myriad of non-stable theory situations as extensions or perturbations of stable population theory in the classical sense. In one such extension, Frauenthal [29] represents the age-specific maternity function as a function of both age and time by

$$m(x, t) = m(x)[1 + \gamma(B_0 - B(t - x))/B(t - x)]$$

for constants γ and B_0 and birth function B. This model is founded on a conjecture by Easterlin [30, 31] which states that women born in large cohorts have fewer children than those born in small cohorts. In another extension, Espenshade [32] discusses the effects of immigration on the stable model showing that a constant influx of immigrants having a fixed age distribution with a net reproductive rate less than unity results in a stationary population. For further extensions on the stable theory of population, the reader is directed to Coale [33], Keyfitz [34], Zuev [35], and McFarland [36].

7.6 Conclusion

The extensions of the stable theory of population presented herein were developed as continuous representations because of the obvious advantages of the calculus. Analogous counterparts are possible for the discrete time versions. It should be noted that due to the fact data is received in discrete form, demographic calculations are usually performed in the setting of a discrete model. Thus, given a schedule of mortality and fertility, the values by age for p (or l) and m are obtained, from which the other stable parameters r, b, d, and c can be calculated. Clearly, the stable theory of population offers more than global projections as manifested by early population models. Even though the theory may not be directly applicable to all demographic cases, it does provide a strong analytical tool for the determination of population behavior.

7.7 Notes for Chapter Seven

[1] Coale, A. (1972), The growth and structure of human populations – A mathematical investigation. p. 3.
[2] Keyfitz, N. and Flieger, W. (1971), Population, facts and methods of demography. p. 50.
[3] Keyfitz, N. (1968), Introduction to mathematics of population, with revisions. pp. 170–183.
[4] Spiegelman, M. (1976). Introduction to demography. Revised Edition. p. 254 ff.
[5] Coale, A., op. cit., p. 18.
[6] Ibid., p. 18.
[7] Ibid., p. 120.
[8] Ibid., p. 19.
[9] Keyfitz, N. (1968), op. cit., p. 126.
[10] Fisher, R.A. (1930), The genetical theory of natural selection. pp. 25–30.
[11] Ibid., p. 27.
[12] Keyfitz, N. (1977), Applied mathematical demography. p. 145.
[13] Ibid., p. 142 ff.
[14] Fisher, R.A. (1930), op. cit.
[15] Keyfitz, N. (1977), op. cit., chap. 4.
[16] Ibid., p. 88.

[17] Cole, L.C. (1954), The population consequences of life history phenomena. The Quarterly Review of Biology, vol. 29, no. 2, pp. 103–137.

[18] Levin, S.A. (1981), Age structure and stability in multiple-age spawning populations. Renewable Resource Management, T.L. Vincent and J.M. Skowronski, eds., Lecture Notes in Biomathematics, Springer-Verlag, vol. 39, pp. 21–45.

[19] Levin, S.A. and Goodyear, C.P. (1980), Analyis of an age-structured fishery model. J. Mathematical Biology, vol. 9, pp. 245–274.

[20] Jacquard, A. (1970), The genetic structure of population. Biomathematics, vol. 5, Springer-Verlag.

[21] Anderson, R.M. and May, R.M. (1979), Population biology of infectious diseases, Part I. Nature, vol. 280, pp. 361–367.

[22] May, R.M. (1979), Population biology of infectious diseases, Part II. Nature, vol. 280, pp. 455–461.

[23] Getz, W.M. and Pickering, J. (1983), Epidemic models: Thresholds and population regulation. American Naturalist, vol. 121, pp. 892–898.

[24] Volterra, Vito (1926), Variazioni e fluttuazioni del numero d'individui in specie animali conventi. Memorie della R. Accademia Nazionale dei Lincei.

[25] Hale, J. and Somolinos, A. (1983), Competition for fluctuating nutrients. Journal of Mathematical Biology, vol. 18, pp. 255–280.

[26] Coale, A. (1957), How the age distribution of a human population is determined. Cold Spring Harbor Symposia on Quantitative Biology, vol. 22, pp. 83–89.

[27] Lopez, A. (1961), Problems in stable population theory, pp. 42–63.

[28] Coale, A. (1963), Estimates of various demographic measures through the quasi-stable age distribution. Emerging techniques in Population Research, pp. 175–193.

[29] Frauenthal, J.C. (1975), A dynamic model for human population growth. Theoretical Population Biology, vol. 8, pp. 64–73.

[30] Easterlin, R.A. (1961), The american baby boom in historical perspective. American economic Review, vol. 51, pp. 869–911.

[31] Easterlin, R.A. (1968), The current fertility decline and projected fertility changes. Population, Labor Force and Long Swings in Economic Growth: The American Experience, chap. 5.

[32] Espenshade, T.J., Bouvier, L.F. and Arthur, W.B. (1982), Immigration and the stable population model. Demography, vol. 19, no. 1, pp. 125–133.

[33] Coale, A. (1972), op. cit.

[34] Keyfitz, N. (1977), op. cit.

[35] Zuev, G.M. and Soroko, E.L. (1978), Mathematical description of migration processes. Avtomatika i Telemekhanika (Moscow), no. 7, pp. 94–101.

[36] McFarland, D.D. (1969), On the theory of stable populations: A new and elementary proof of the theorems under weaker assumptions. Demography, vol. 6, pp. 301–322.

8. The Kingdom of Denmark – A Demographic Example

8.1 Introduction

The three premises of classical stable theory of population (closure to migration, time independent age-specific birth and death rates), if staunchly upheld, would eliminate virtually every existing biological population as a subject for its use. One must concede, for example, that human population is exposed to migration, and that birth rates and death rates are not constant over time. In this light, one may erroneously conclude that stable theory, even in its classical sense, serves little or no purpose. This is far from true. It must be remembered that stable theory serves as a model for study of a given population, and not as an impeccable image of it. Viewed in this manner, the concepts and formulations of stable theory do have much to offer, both as a mathematical entity as well as an applicable tool to be used in population study.

In certain areas of the world it may be possible to find regions that satisfy the premises of stable theory, at least in an approximate way. However, even if such regions did exist, the data that would be necessary to form a mathematical study may be very incomplete or even non-existent. An example of this situation would be a developing nation, whose long-time customs and traditions would make it an excellent candidate for satisfying the premises of stable theory, but whose record keeping on vital statistics would probably be non-existent.

There do exist, however, certain areas of the world that have maintained population records on migration, mortality and fertility over long periods of time. This is particularly true in the Scandinavian countries which have been leaders in the development of a modern society and have kept population records from as far back as the eighteenth century. The Kingdom of Denmark, one of the most progressive countries in today's world, is an excellent example of a country that has experienced the pains and benefits of a growing society over two centuries and, at the same time, has strived to obtain and maintain accurate data on its population. It is the intent of the author at this time, to present a panoramic overview of the population of Denmark and the implications it may have to the stable theory of population.

8.2 A Chronological Summary of Demographic Data Retrieval in Denmark

Denmark is one of the few countries in the world with a long history of interest and manifestation in the collection of demographic information. It is the purpose of this section to highlight events in a chronological manner in order to illustrate the demographic development of Denmark. For more detail and background, the interested reader may wish to refer to Andersen [1] or Matthiessen [2]. An asterisk (*) following a date indicates a significant event as viewed by the author.

1645*:   parish registers become compulsory whereby rescripts showing births, deaths and marriages were maintained by the clergy.

1735:   summaries of parish registers become available through the General-Extract on an annual basis.

1769, 15 August*:   the first census of Denmark; government officials interview each household; municipalities make summary tables of the population by sex, age (six age categories for people under age 48), maritial status and occupation.

1775:   clergy issued prescribed schedules to indicate births by sex and legitimacy, and deaths by sex and 10-year age categories.

1783:   marriages included in prescribed schedules of 1775.

1787, 1 July*:   second Danish census; same as 1769, with the inclusion of names of individuals.

1796*:   founding of the Tabelkontoret, the first statistical office which was to conduct the census of 1801.

1800:   births also documented as live-births or stillborn.

1801, 1 February*:   third census of Denmark as conducted by the Tabelkontoret; population distribution measured in 10-year age categories; results completed in 1819 and published with results of the 1834 census.

1829:   death certificate introduced in Copenhagen.

1834*:   Tabelkommissionen established to conduct 1834 census and the publication of Danish Population Statistics.

1834, 18 February: fourth census of Denmar, similar to that of 1801.

1835:   marriages recorded to include age of each partner; deaths recorded in smaller age categories.

1840, 1 February*:   fifth census of Denmark; death and population categories in five-year intervals (e.g., 0, 1–2, 3–4, 5–9, 10–14, ... years).

1845, 1 February: sixth census of Denmark.

1847:   death certificates required in provincial towns.

1850, 1 February: seventh census of Denmark.

1850*:   national statistics office, which is known today as Danmarks Statistik, is founded.

1850's: death certificates required in rural towns.

1855, 1 February: eighth census of Denmark.

1860, 1 February*:   ninth census of Denmark; schedules include births by age of mother in 5-year age categories.

1870, 1 February*:   tenth census of Denmark; use of a questionnaire in towns which was filled by individuals, delivered to municipal offices, and tabulated at the national statistics office.

1877:   birth certificates required in Copenhagen and held by clergymen.

1880, 1 February: eleventh census of Denmark.

1890, 1 February: twelfth census of Denmark.

1896:   statistics on divorces more detailed.

1900:   birth certificates required in all of Denmark.

1901, 1 February: thirteenth census of Denmark.

1906, 1 February: fourteenth census of Denmark.

1911, 1 February: fifteenth census of Denmark.

1911*:   annual schedule of vital statistics replaced by immediate reporting of individual information on births, deaths and marriages.

1916, 1 February: sixteenth census of Denmark.

1920, 15 June*:   Sønderjylland transferred to Denmark from Germany; Danish population increases by more than 163,000 people.

1921, 1 February: seventeenth census of Denmark.

1922:   civil marriages reported directly to secular authorities rather than to the clergy.

1924*:   compulsory use of continuous population registers established for all municipalities of Denmark.

1925, 5 November: eighteenth census of Denmark.

1930, 5 November: nineteenth census of Denmark.

1935*:   census questionnaire distributed to all individuals in Denmark including those in rural regions.

1935, 5 November: twentieth census of Denmark.

1930's late: legal abortion permitted by reason of social circumstances.

1940, 5 November: twenty-first census of Denmark.

1945, 15 June: twenty-second census of Denmark.

1950, 7 November: twenty-third census of Denmark.

1955, 1 October: twenty-fourth census of Denmark.

1960, 26 September: twenty-fifth census of Denmark.

1960's*:   wide-spread social acceptance of the use of contraceptives; legal abortions permitted in special circumstances.

1965, 27 September: twenty-sixth census of Denmark.

1968*:   Central Population Register (CPR) established in Denmark; automated process of continuous registration of statistical data.

1970:   abortion legalized for all women over the age of 38.

1970, 9 November*:   twenty-seventh census of Denmark – the last census of Denmark using questionnaires.

1973, 1 October: all Danish women have right to legal abortion.

1975:   scheduled census cancelled due to the success of the CPR.

1976, 1 January*:   first Danish census based on registers only.

1981, 1 January: second Danish census based on registers only.

1982, 1 January*:   total population of Denmark declines after 152 years of growth.

The Central Population Register (CPR) is worthy of comment. The CPR is administered by the Danish government through its Danish Ministry of Interior. The register contains information about all people who now reside, or who have resided in Denmark since 1968, or in Greenland since 1972, as well as all other persons who have certain relations with the Kingdom of Denmark. Each person is assigned a ten-digit CPR number according to the format

Day of birth	Month of birth	Year of birth		Century of birth	Code numbers	Sex
X X	X X	X X		X	X X	X

Date of birth	Reference number

which acts as a personal identification number for each person. The CPR contains, among other information: name, residence, citizenship, place of birth, migration information, marital status, occupation, employment status, employer, cross-referencing (eg. parents, children), significant date registrations (eg. marriage, divorce), and living status. In addition, further registers are maintained such as taxation, pensions, unemployment, social, hospital, medical, educational, real property, commercial enterprises and housing. Interbranching between these registers, such as a correlation between occupation and cause of death, is utilized. The interested reader may wish to consult two publications from Danmarks Statistik [3, 4] or a United States government publication [5] for further information on this topic.

8.3 Migration, Mortality and Fertility in Denmark

It was previously mentioned that the fundamental premises of stable population theory are closure to migration, and time independent age-specific birth rates and death rates. In this section, an overview of certain demographic aspects of Denmark, relative to these premises of stable theory, will be investigated. The Kingdom of Denmark is one of the unique countries in the world that has a long history of demographic data which can provide sufficient information for the study of its population.

The most important premise of stable theory is that the population be closed to migration. The migration pattern of Denmark can be classified in three phases: (a) a long period of negligible international migration prior to the year 1860; (b) a period from 1860 to 1929 where migration was primarily emigratory; (c) a period of small net migration from 1930 to the present. Unfortunately, the weakest documentation of Danish population is its migration patterns before the year 1929. However, there is sufficient evidence to suggest that the period before 1860 was such, that during this time the Danish population was closed to migration [6]. From 1860 to 1929, there is some

159

information on Danish emigration, but only little information on Danish immigration. Table 8.1 shows the net migration for Danish males for the period 1855 to 1929, as compiled by Matthiessen [7], together with the ratio between the number of net emigrants among males and females.

Table 8.1. Net male migration, Denmark, 1855–1934, by Matthiessen

Calendar years	Male migrants −emigrants +immigrants	Ratio M/F
1855–1859	+ 3400	
1860–1869	−13000	
1870–1879	−30200	3.1
1880–1889	−51800	2.4
1890–1899	−26500	3.1
1900–1904	−25600	2.2
1905–1909	−20000	3.0
1910–1914	−21700	6.4
1915–1919	+ 5200	
1921–1924	− 9400	
1925–1929	−17900	2.4
1930–1934	+17000	

From this table, the highest period of emigration occurred between 1880 and 1889 when 51,800 males emigrated from Denmark on a net basis. For this worst case of population closure, an annual average of 5,180 net males emigrated and an annual average of 2,158 net females emigrated. Since the female population over this ten-year interval was approximately 1,057,500, the percent female net emigration for this period is 0.203. Thus, during the period 1860 to 1929, there did exist noticeable female migration but not to be extent where it was disruptive to the Danish population. From the pragmatic point of view, therefore, the population of Denmark, particularly the female population, can be considered relatively closed during this period. From 1929 to the present, accurate data exists on migration, indicating an oscillatory pattern of net migration. This phase of migration, as well as the previous two phases of migration, are shown in Fig. 8.1. It can therefore be concluded, within practical limitations, that the population of Denmark is closed to migration over the time period ending with the present, and for as far back as at least two centuries.

Information on the fertility and mortality aspects of Denmark is much more substantial than that of migration. Figure 8.2 shows a graph of both the crude death rate and the crude birth rate from 1735 to 1976, as compiled by Andersen [8]. A more detailed profile of these crude rates is shown in Fig. 8.3 [9]. During this 240-year period mortality has decreased on the average. From 1735 to 1780, mortality remained, on the average, a constant. From 1780 to 1890, mortality exhibits a marked decrease due primarily to the Danish agric-

Immigration

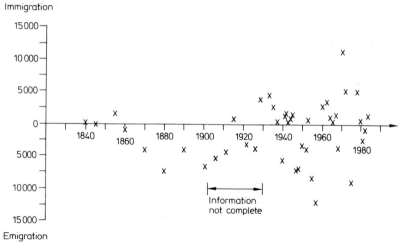

Fig. 8.1. Net Migration, Denmark, 1840 to 1983

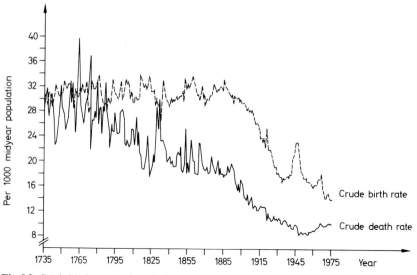

Fig. 8.2. Crude birth rate and crude death rate, Denmark, 1735 to 1976 (Credit to O. Andersen)

ultural reforms of the late 1700's when more than 65 % of Danish land workers became land owners. From 1890 to 1955, a greater decrease in mortality is manifested by the strong advances of medical science in the second half of the nineteenth century and the first half of the twentieth century. The gradual increase in the crude death rate after 1955 is due to the changing age structure of the Danish population

161

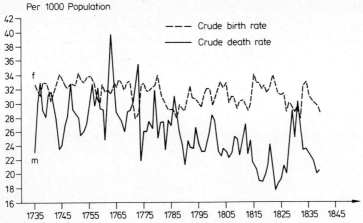

Fig. 8.3. Crude birth rate and crude death rate. Denmark, 1735 to 1839 (Credit to O. Andersen)

Considering fertility aspects, the crude birth rate can be interpreted as being relatively constant from 1735 to 1890. The sharp decrease in fertility from 1890 to 1935 is attributed to the transition of Denmark from a society that was primarily agricultural, to one that was emerging industrial. The birth booms of World War I and World War II are clearly shown. The birth peak of the 1960's is due to the offspring of the birth boom of the 1940's, as well as to the anticipated economic security among married couples. Clearly, investigation of just the crude death rate and the crude birth rate suggests the possibility that the corresponding age-specific rates of death and birth are not time independent, and as a result, the population would not be stable.

Age-specific fertility rates have been published by the Danish government [10, 11] from the year 1901 to the present. These rates are in five-year age categories starting with age 15 and ending with the age of 49. The Danish government did collect age-specific fertility information during the period from 1860 to 1900; unfortunately, it is not complete and little has been published [12. 13].

There does exist, however, a publication by Matthiessen [14] in which age-specific fertility rates are given by the birth cohort of females for generations 1815/19 to 1940/44. This is shown in Table 8.2. While this information is very useful, what is required is age-specific fertility rates according to time. That is, cohort information must be converted to information over intervals of time. One means of doing this is by an analysis using a Lexis grid. This is shown in Chart 8.1. The chart shows Age versus Time for ages from 0 to 50 over time from the year 1860 to the year 1930. Entries written horizontally are extracted from Table 8.2; entries written diagonally have been computed by the author. On the assumption that there is a uniform distribution of females in each parallelogram representing the birth cohort of females, the computation of value for each rectangle is taken as the arithmetic mean of the values of adjacent parallelograms. For example, consider the rectangle corresponding to the age category 20 to 24 over the time period 1905 to 1909. The females

162

contributing to the births, both male and female, in this age-time category, are the members of both the 1880/84 as well as the 1885/89 cohorts whose parallelogram values are respectively 145.4 and 143.0, the average being 144.2. These average values represent the 'raw' age-specific fertility rates over the five-year time periods as indicated. Their sum over the seven, five-year age categories from ages 15 to 49, gives the total fertility rate for the indicated time period. Call this the 'raw' total fertility rate. Comparing the 'raw' total fertility rates from 1901 to 1929 with the actual published total fertility rates over the same time period, shows a discrepency of less than 2 percent. This implies that the 'raw' age-specific fertility rates from 1860 to 1900 are accurate, and the method by which they were compiled is sound.

Table 8.2. Age-specific fertility rates per 1000 females for generations of females 1815/19–1940/44, Denmark, compiled by Matthiessen

Generation	15, 20	20, 25	25, 30	30, 35	35, 40	40, 45	45, 50
1815/19							12.6
1820/24						102.4	11.6
1825/29					187.0	96.4	10.7
1830/34				234.0	187.4	94.6	10.6
1835/39			226.6	235.3	193.9	96.1	10.3
1840/44	10.0*	117.4	222.0	236.7	191.0	92.6	9.1
1845/49	11.0	119.9	226.6	240.6	186.5	88.3	8.3
1850/54	11.5	126.0	238.1	237.4	183.8	82.7	7.8
1855/59	13.1	133.0	243.7	227.8	176.9	74.8	6.8
1860/64	14.1	134.6	233.0	215.4	163.5	65.8	5.9
1865/69	14.7	131.4	223.3	204.5	146.3	58.4	5.2
1870/74	15.2	134.1	224.8	192.2	132.0	51.4	4.5
1875/79	16.1	140.9	217.8	175.3	116.8	44.8	3.8
1880/84	18.4	145.4	201.7	158.0	102.2	37.7	2.9
1885/89	21.7	143.0	181.1	142.4	86.1	29.4	2.1
1890/94	24.2	131.2	167.7	124.0	70.2	22.9	1.6
1895/99	23.2	124.3	153.0	105.0	60.6	20.5	1.6
1900/04	23.3	116.6	133.3	95.8	59.7	21.7	1.4
1905/09	24.2	106.8	129.4	102.3	67.3	19.8	1.1
1910/14	23.2	106.4	139.6	115.1	60.9	14.9	0.8
1915/19	23.4	122.4	155.7	109.4	46.5	12.0	0.7*
1920/24	26.6	147.2	157.6	95.4	40.7	10.0*	0.6*
1925/29	32.4	156.1	149.8	89.8			
1930/34	37.6	158.8	153.8				
1935/39	38.9	166.0					
1940/44	42.7						

* Extrapolated

The 'raw' age-specific fertility rates from 1860 to 1900 can now be used to construct the gross reproductive rate (GRR) and the net reproductive rate (NRR) over this forty-year period. The 'raw' age-specific rates include both male and female births. A comparison of the total fertility rate and the gross reproductive rate for the period 1901 to 1929, from published information [15],

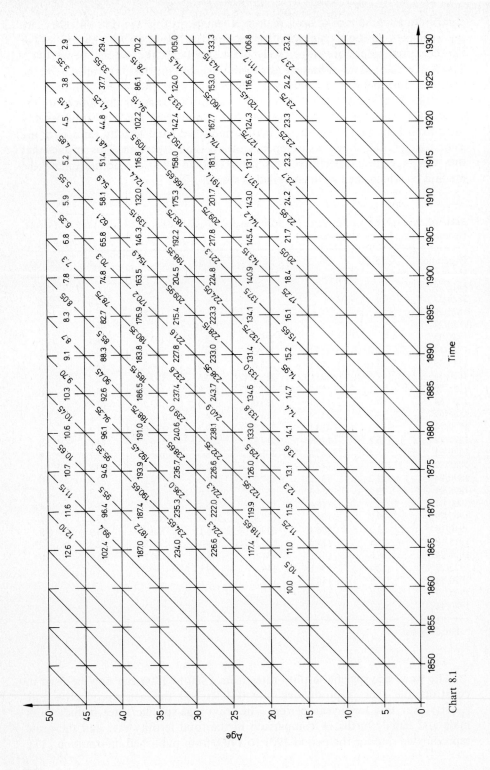

Chart 8.1

shows that 48.72 females are born out of every 100 births. Scaling the 'raw' age-specific fertility rates by this factor generates values for the discrete maternity function for the time period 1860 to 1900. Since life tables do exist over this forty-year period at ten-year intervals [16], the values for the net maternity function can be calculated for this same time period. The sum of the values of the discrete maternity function over the seven age categories multiplied by 5, the width of each age interval, is the gross reproductive rate. The

Table 8.3. Age-specific fertility rates per 1000 females for time periods 1860/64 to 1895/99, Denmark, compiled by author

Time period	Births per 1000 females per age class ——————————————— Female birth per 1000 females ———————————————— Survivorship from birth to age x ———————————————— Net maternity function ————————————————							Tot. fer. GRR – NRR
	15–19	20–24	25–29	30–34	35–39	40–44	45–49	per 1000
1860–64	10.50	117.40	226.60	234.00	187.00	102.40	12.60	4452.5
	5.12	57.20	110.40	114.00	91.11	49.89	6.14	2169.3
	0.7217	0.7005	0.6766	0.6505	0.6335	0.5932	0.5627	–
	3.70	40.07	74.70	74.16	57.72	29.59	3.45	1416.9
1865–69	11.25	118.65	224.30	234.65	187.20	99.40	12.10	4437.7
	5.48	57.81	109.28	114.32	91.20	48.43	5.90	2162.1
	0.7217	0.7005	0.6766	0.6505	0.6335	0.5932	0.5627	–
	3.95	40.50	73.94	74.37	57.78	28.73	3.32	1412.9
1870–74	12.30	122.95	224.30	236.00	190.65	95.50	11.15	4464.2
	5.99	59.90	109.28	114.98	92.88	46.53	5.43	2175.0
	0.7485	0.7256	0.7017	0.6752	0.6458	0.6143	0.5841	–
	4.48	43.46	76.68	77.63	59.98	28.58	3.17	1469.9
1875–79	13.60	129.50	232.35	238.65	192.45	95.35	10.65	4562.7
	6.63	63.09	113.20	116.27	93.76	46.45	5.19	2222.9
	0.7485	0.7256	0.7017	0.6752	0.6458	0.6143	0.5841	–
	4.96	45.78	79.43	78.51	60.55	28.53	3.03	1503.9
1880–84	14.40	133.80	240.90	239.00	188.75	94.35	10.45	4608.2
	7.02	65.19	117.37	116.44	91.96	45.97	5.09	2245.1
	0.7586	0.7369	0.7148	0.6888	0.6621	0.6349	0.6060	–
	5.33	48.04	83.90	80.20	60.89	29.19	3.08	1553.1
1885–89	14.95	133.00	238.35	232.60	185.15	90.45	9.70	4521.0
	7.28	64.80	116.12	113.32	90.21	44.07	4.73	2202.6
	0.7586	0.7369	0.7148	0.6888	0.6621	0.6349	0.6060	–
	5.52	47.75	83.00	78.05	59.73	27.98	2.87	1524.5
1890–94	15.65	132.75	228.15	221.60	180.35	85.50	8.70	4363.5
	7.62	64.68	111.15	107.96	87.87	41.66	4.24	2125.9
	0.7812	0.7630	0.7446	0.7240	0.7008	0.6751	0.6479	–
	5.95	49.36	82.76	78.16	61.58	28.12	2.75	1543.4
1895–99	17.25	137.50	224.05	209.95	170.20	78.75	8.05	4228.7
	8.40	66.99	109.16	102.29	82.92	38.37	3.92	2060.2
	0.7812	0.7630	0.7446	0.7240	0.7008	0.6751	0.6479	–
	6.56	51.11	81.28	74.06	58.11	25.90	2.54	1497.8

sum of the values of the net maternity function over the seven age categories multiplied by 5 is the net reproductive rate. Table 8.3 shows a summary of these calculations as compiled by the author. An illustration of these calculations, together with the published values, are shown in Figs. 8.4 through 8.11**. Figures 8.4 through 8.10 demonstrate the age-specific fertility rates from 1860 to 1983. Figure 8.11 shows both the gross reproductive rate and the net reproductive rate over the same 123-year time period; the convergence of these two rates is obviously due to the declining rate of mortality through the twentieth century. It is worth mentioning that the construction of a table, such as Table 8.3, is not an uncommon exercise in demography.

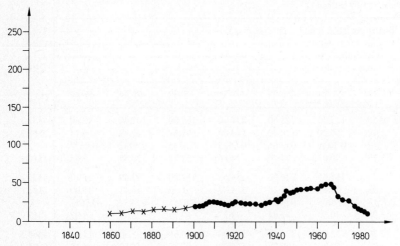

Fig. 8.4. Fertility distribution, Denmark, 1860 to 1983, ages 15–19

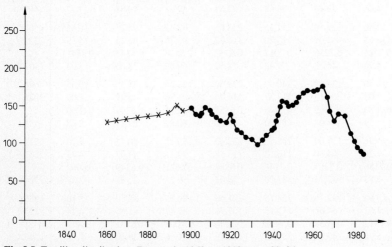

Fig. 8.5. Fertility distribution, Denmark, 1860 to 1983, ages 20–24

** These curves do not exist as published works and were calculated solely by the author. Years 1860 to 1899 illustrate the results from Table 8.3. Years 1900 (1901) to 1983 are from publications of the Danish government. Data retrieved from [18], [19] & [20].

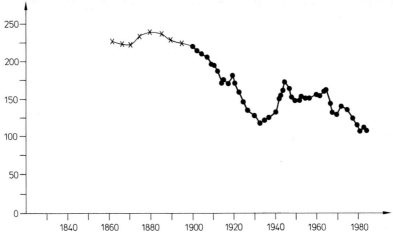
Fig. 8.6. Fertility distribution, Denmark, 1860 to 1983, ages 25–29

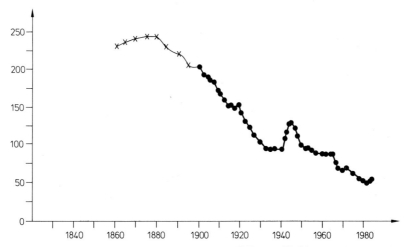
Fig. 8.7. Fertility distribution, Denmark, 1860 to 1983, ages 30–34

Unlike migration and fertility, information concerning Danish mortality is substantial, and can be traced back as far as the year 1735. In a publication by Andersen [17], life tables including life expectencies have been constructed from the year 1800 to the year 1839 in 10-year age classes, and for the period 1835 to 1839 in 5-year age classes. Age-specific death rates are available in five-year age classes beginning with the year 1840. Samples of age-specific death rates from 1840 to 1982 are shown in Figs. 8.12 through 8.16, where the natural logarithm of these rates shows a steady decline. Specifically, during the nineteenth century this decline is uniform, that is, of relative constant slope, as compared to the decline during the twentieth century.

167

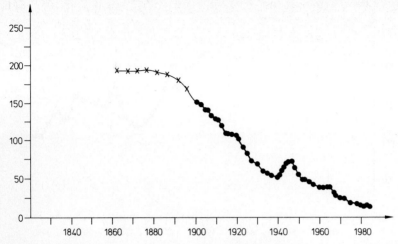

Fig. 8.8. Fertility distribution, Denmark, 1860 to 1983, ages 35–39

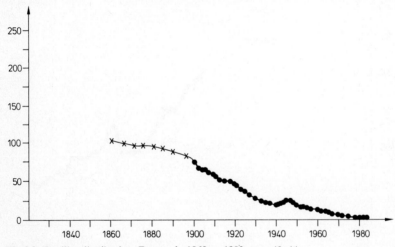

Fig. 8.9. Fertility distribution, Denmark, 1860 to 1983, ages 40–44

In summary, investigation of migration, fertility and mortality of the population of the Kingdom of Denmark, when viewed over two centuries, leads to the obvious conclusion that this population does not satisfy the premises of stable population theory. However, for a long period before the year 1880, the population was relatively closed to migration, had age specific fertility rates that were time independent, and had a small decline in age-specific death rates. Thus, for this period, Denmark satisfied the conditions for a quasi-stable population. This is manifested by the exponential pattern of growth of the population through the early part of the twentieth century as shown in Fig. 8.17. This pattern is disrupted by the rapid decline in both fertility and mortality through the twentieth century. As a result, after more than one and

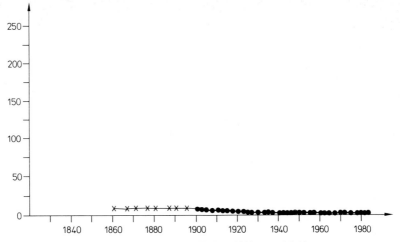

Fig. 8.10. Fertility distribution, Denmark, 1860 to 1983, ages 45–49

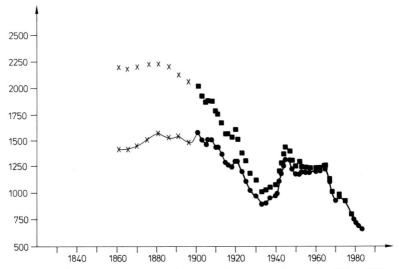

Fig. 8.11. Gross reproductive rate and net reproductive rate, Denmark, 1860 to 1983

one-half centuries of growth, the total population of Denmark showed a decrease as of 1 January 1982.

A further manifestation of the effects of a changing pattern in mortality and fertility is shown in Fig. 8.18 [21]. Here, the quasi-stable pattern of the nineteenth century is reflected by a uniform population pyramid for the year 1901. For the year 1975, however, the pyramid reflects a high percentage of older people and a very low percentage of younger people, due primarily to the rapid decline in mortality and fertility. Clearly, the present demographic situation in Denmark makes the direct use of stable population theory inapplicable.

169

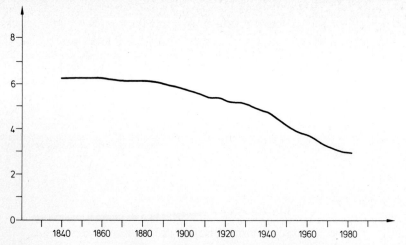

Fig. 8.12. Mortality distribution (scaled by ln function), Denmark, 1840 to 1982, ages 0–4

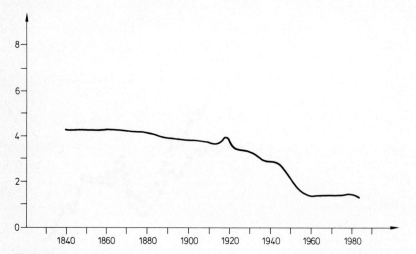

Fig. 8.13. Mortality distribution (scaled by ln function), Denmark, 1840 to 1982, ages 20–24

However, should Denmark enter into a demographic transition where the premises of stable theory do apply, then this theory would be a most viable tool in population analysis.

8.4 Conclusion

The population of the Kingdom of Denmark over two centuries served as a useful basis for demographic discussion. The country, for more than three

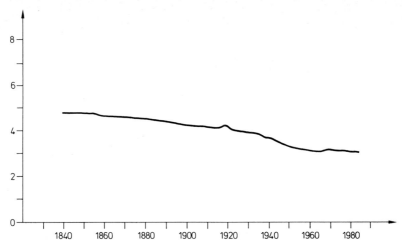

Fig. 8.14. Mortality distribution (scaled by ln function), Denmark, 1840 to 1982, ages 40–44

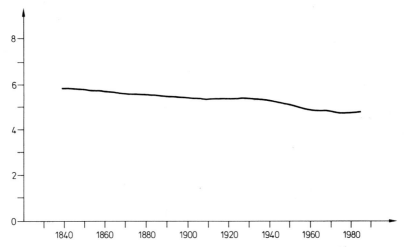

Fig. 8.15. Mortality distribution (scaled by ln function), Denmark, 1840 to 1982, ages 60–64

centuries, has demonstrated its concern for demographic information, from the requirement that the clergy keep records of births deaths and marriages in the year 1645, to its continuous registration of statistical data via the CPR of today. The Danish population could not serve as a "living" example of stable population theory when viewed over two centuries. It does, however, satisfy the conditions for a quasi-stable population during the nineteenth century. One may even speculate that population stability did exist in the eighteenth century, but little evidence exists to support such a claim.

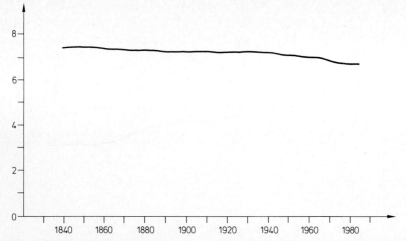

Fig. 8.16. Mortality distribution (scaled by ln function), Denmark, 1840 to 1982, ages 80–84

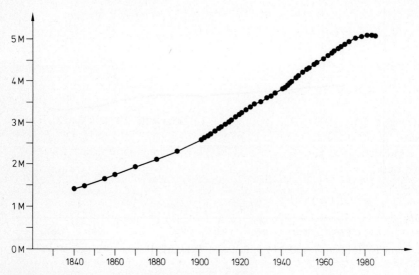

Fig. 8.17. Population profile*, Denmark, 1840 to 1984

It is hoped that the presentation of the demographic discussion on the Danish population will stimulate the reader to generate further discussion on the topic of mathematical demography, and to develop insights so that newer mathematical models can be created not only for this population, but for other biological populations as well.

---

* Adjusted to accommodate the transfer of Sønderjylland to Denmark on 15 June 1920.

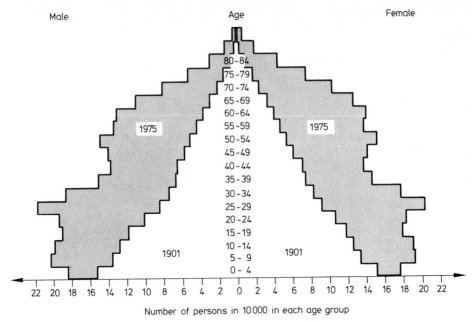

Fig. 8.18. Population pyramids, Denmark, 1901 and 1975 (Credit to O. Andersen)

8.5 Notes for Chapter Eight

[1] Andersen, Otto (1977), The population of Denmark. 1974 – World Population Year, United Nations.

[2] Matthiessen, P.C. (1970), Some aspects of the demographic transition in Denmark.

[3] Danmarks Statistik (1978), Personal identification numbers and population statistics in Denmark.

[4] Danmarks Statistik (1982), Building a register-based statistical system: Preconditions, consequences and perspectives.

[5] U.S. Department of Health and Human Services (1980), The person-number systems of Sweden, Norway, Denmark, and Israel. Data Evaluation and Methods Research, Series 2, No. 4.

[6] Andersen, O. (1977), op. cit., pp. 48–49.

[7] Matthiessen, P.C. (1970), op. cit., Table 8.1, p. 86.

[8] Andersen, O. (1977), op. cit., p. 14.

[9] Andersen, O. (1979), The development of Danish mortality: 1735–1850. Scandinavian Population Studies, no. 5, pp. 9–21.

[10] Det Statistiske Departement (1966), Befolkningsudvikling og sundheds-forhold 1901–60 (Population development and health conditions 1901–60). Statistiske Undersøgelser, no. 19, p. 67.

[11] Danmarks Statistik (1982), Befolkningens bevægelser 1980 (Vital statistics 1980). Statistiske Meddelelser, Lene Skotte, editor, 1982:1, p. 39.

[12] Vielser, Fødsler og Dødsfald i Kongeriget Danmark i Aarene 1865 til 1869 (1873), Statistisk Tabelværk, p. 22.

[13] Vielser, Fødsler og Dødsfald i Aarene 1875–1879 (1882), Danmarks Statistik, Statistisk Tabelværk, p. 10.

[14] Matthiessen, P.C. (1970), op. cit., Table II.1, p. 134.

[15] Det Statistiske Departement (1966), op. cit., p. 67.

[16] Ibid., p. 18.

[17] Andersen, O. (1973), Dødelighedsforholdene i Danmark 1735–1839 (The mortality conditions in Denmark 1735–1839). Nationaløkonomisk Tidsskrift, vol. 2/1973, p. 304.

[18] Det Statistiske Departement (1966), op. cit.

[19] Statens Statistiske Bureau (1905), Befolkningsforholdene i Danmark i det 19 aarhundrede (Population conditions in Denmark in the 19th century). Statistisk Tabelværk, VA, no. 5.

[20] Danmarks Statistik, Nyt fra Danmarks Statistik (News from Danmarks Statistik). Various publications, February, 1980, 1981, 1982.

[21] Andersen, O. (1977), op. cit., p. 53.

Appendix

The Continuous Time Model
According to McKendrick – von Foerster

The continuous time model as presented in Chapter Four can be developed by an alternate approach. This approach, which was first introduced in 1926 by A.C. McKendrick [1] and later in 1959 by Heinz von Foerster [2], makes use of a partial differential equation model. Part of their reasoning will be presented in this appendix together with the equivalence of this model to that of Lotka. For the sake of the reader some concepts and definitions will be repeated.

Consider Fig. 4.2 of Chapter Four. Let h denote equal increments of the continuous variables t (time) and x (age). The number of females whose age lies between x and $x+h$ at time t is denoted by $F(x, t)h$. On the age interval $[x, x+h)$ at time t the mean number of females alive can be represented by

$$F^*(x, t) = (1/h) \int_x^{x+h} F(y, t) dy. \tag{A.1}$$

Likewise, on the age interval $[x-h, x)$ at time $t-h$ the mean number of females is

$$F^*(x-h, t-h) = (1/h) \int_{x-h}^{x} F(y, t-h) dy. \tag{A.2}$$

The expression

$$F^*(x, t)h - F^*(x-h, t-h)h = \Delta F^*(x, t)h \tag{A.3}$$

obtained from (A.1) and (A.2) represents the average net loss of females that occurred between times $t-h$ and t as they aged from interval $[x-h, x)$ to interval $[x, x+h)$.

Under the assumptions of stable population theory the age-specific birth and death rates are time independent and migration is not considered. Therefore, the net loss expressed by (A.3) is due to the deaths that may have occurred on the interval. Since in this model $h = \Delta t = \Delta x$, the average rate of

175

change on the interval can be written as

$$\frac{\Delta F^*(x,t)}{\Delta t} = \frac{F^*(x,t)-F^*(x-h,t)}{\Delta x} + \frac{F^*(x-h,t)-F^*(x-h,t-h)}{\Delta t} \tag{A.4}$$

In the limit as $h \to 0$, $F^* \to F$ from (A.1) and (A.2), and expression (A.4) becomes

$$\frac{dF}{dt} = \frac{\partial F}{\partial x} + \frac{\partial F}{\partial t}. \tag{A.5}$$

If the population experienced a null death rate, then $dF/dt = 0$ and the model would take the form

$$\frac{\partial F}{\partial x} + \frac{\partial F}{\partial t} = 0$$

whose solution is trivial.

Populations, however, do experience mortality. Thus the difference expressed in (A.3) must be negative and $dF/dt < 0$. The force of mortality (defined by Definition 1.9) expresses the annual rate of mortality at exact age x. Using information from Sect. 1.4, the number of deaths that occur on the age interval $[x-h, x)$ is expressed as

$$\mu(x-h)F(x-h,t-h)h.$$

In the limit as $h \to 0$ the rate of change of females over interval width h is

$$\frac{dF}{dt} = -\mu(x)F(x,t). \tag{A.6}$$

Combining (A.5) with (A.6) results in

$$\frac{\partial F(x,t)}{\partial x} + \frac{\partial F(x,t)}{\partial t} = -\mu(x)F(x,t). \tag{A.7}$$

An expression similar to (A.7) was first presented by McKendrick [3] in 1926 and later by von Foerster [4] in 1959. Other references to this equation can be found in Rubinow [5] and Streifer [6].

The complete solution of (A.7) necessitates that the birth trajectory (or birth rate) be known as well as the initial population distribution. These are expressed as

$$F(0,t) \quad \text{and} \quad F(x,0) \tag{A.8}$$

respectively, and act as boundary conditions to (A.7).

The partial differential equation of (A.7) can be simplified to an ordinary differential equation. It can be easily verified by substitution that the solution to (A.7) is

$$F(x, t) = F(0, t - x) \exp\left[-\int_0^x \mu(y)dy \right].$$
(A.9)

Note that the birth trajectory appearing in (A.9) must be specified at time $t-x$ as illustrated in Fig. 4.2. The relationship between the survivorship function l and the force of mortality μ was given by Equation 1.29 of Chapter One as

$$\mu(x) = -[\ln(l(x))]'.$$

Therefore,

$$\int_0^x \mu(y)dy = -\ln[p(x)]$$
(A.10)

where $p(x) = l(x)/l(0)$. Thus (A.9) reduces to

$$F(x, t) = F(0, t - x)p(x).$$
(A.11)

By Definition 4.1, $B(t)$ represents the female birth rate at time t, which is the same interpretation as $F(0, t)$. The rate at which females are born at time $t - x$ is

$$B(t - x) = F(0, t - x).$$

Substitution into (A.11) yields

$$F(x, t) = B(t - x)p(x).$$
(A.12)

For the age-specific birth rate function m, Lemma 4.5 shows that

$$B(t) = \int_0^\omega F(x, t)m(x)dx.$$
(A.13)

Combining (A.12) with (A.13) results in

$$B(t) = \int_0^\omega B(t - x)p(x)m(x)dx$$
(A.14)

which is the familiar population renewal equation attributed to Lotka. Letting $\phi(x) = p(x)m(x)$ and using Theorem 4.6, (A.14) becomes the fundamental integral equation for the continuous, one-sex, deterministic population model. This is expressed as

$$B(t) = \int_0^t B(t - x)\phi(x)dx + G(t)$$
(A.15)

where $G(t)$ is obtained by use of the second of the boundary conditions expressed by (A.8), and represents the contribution of births by women already alive at time $t = 0$. The solution and ramifications of (A.15) was the principal subject of Chapter Four.

177

Notes for Appendix

[1] McKendrick, A.C. (1926), Applications of mathematics to medical problems. Proceedings Edinburgh Mathematical Society, vol. 44, pp. 98–130.
[2] von Foerster, H. (1959), Some remarks on changing populations, in the kinetics of cellular proliferation. Grune and Stratton, New York.
[3] McKendrick (1926), op. cit., p. 122.
[4] von Foerster (1959), op. cit., p. 394.
[5] Rubinow, S.I. (1968), A maturity-time representation for cell populations. Biophysical Journal, vol. 8, pp. 1055–1073.
[6] Streifer, W. (1974), Realistic models in population ecology. Advances in Ecological Research, vol. 8, pp. 199–266.

References

Acsadi and Nemeskeri: History of human life span and mortality. Budapest, 1970. Cited from Royal Statistical Society, News and Notes, Rosamund Weatherall, Editor, vol. 8, no. 10, London, June, 1982.

Andersen, Otto: Dødelighedsforholdene i Danmark 1735–1839. Nationaløkonomisk Tidsskrift, vol. 2/1973, Statistisk Institut, Københavns Universitet, 1973.

Andersen, Otto: The population of Denmark. 1974 – World Population Year, United Nations, CICRED Seris, 1977.

Andersen, Otto: The development in danish mortality 1735–1850. Scandinavian Population Studies, no. 5, Oslo, 1979.

Anderson, R.M. and R.M. May: Population biology of infectious diseases, Part I. Nature, vol. 280, 1979.

Bernardelli, Harro: Population waves. Journal of the Burma Research Society, vol. 31, part 1, 1941.

Bernoulli, Daniel: Essai d'une nouvelle analyse de la mortalité causée par la petite vérole et les avantages de l'inoculation pour la prévenir. Histoire de l'Académie Royale des Sciences, Année 1760, 1766.

Coale Ansley J.: How the age distribution of a population is determined. Cold Spring Harbor Symposia on Quantitative Biology, vol. 22, 1957.

Coale, Ansley J.: Estimates of various measures through the quasi-stable age distribution. Emerging Techniques in Population Research, Thirty-nineth Annual Conference of the Milbank Memorial Fund, New York, 1962.

Coale, Ansley J.: The growth and structure of human populations – A mathematical investigation. Princeton University Press, Princeton, New Jersey, 1972.

Cole, Lamont C.: The population consequences of life history phenomena. The Quarterly Review of Biology, vol. 29, no. 2, June, 1954.

Danmarks Statistik: Statistisk tabelværk, vielser, fødsler og dødsfald i kongeriget Danmark i aarene 1865 til 1869, København, 1873.

Danmarks Statistik: Statistisk tabelværk, vielser, fødsler og dødsfald i aarene 1875–1879, Fjerde Række, Litra A, nr. 2, København, 1882.

Danmarks Statistik: Personal identification numbers and population statistics in Denmark. Danmarks Statistik, Copenhagen, February, 1978.

Danmarks Statistik: Befolkningens bevægelser 1980. Statistiske Meddelelser, vol. 1982:1, Lene Skotte, kontorchef no. 1, editor, Danmarks Statistik, København, 1982.

Danmarks Statistik: Nyt fra Danmarks statistik, nr. 39, 'Befolkningen pr. 1 januar 1982, 25 feb 1982, et al.

Danmarks Statistik: Building a register-based statistical system: Preconditions, consequences and perspectives. Danmarks Statistik, Poul Jensen, director, Copenhagen, March, 1982.

Davis, Harold T.: Introduction to nonlinear differential and integral equations. Dover, New York, 1962.

DeMoivre, A.: Annuities on lives: Or, the valuation of annuities upon any number of lives; as also, of reversions. London, 1725.

DeMoivre, A.: The doctrine of chances, or, a method of calculating the probabilities of events of play. Third Edition, Printed for A. Millar in the Strand, London, 1756.

de Parcieux, A.: Essai sur les probabilités de la durée de la vie humaine .... Paris, 1760 (1746).

Det Statistiske Departement: Befolkningsudvikling og sundhedsforhold 1901–60. Statistiske Undersøgelser, no. 19, det Statistiske Departement, København, 1966.

DeWit, Johan: Waardye van Lyf-renten naer proportie van Losrente. The Hague, 1671.

Dobbernack, W. and G. Tietz: Die Entwicklung von Personengesamtheiten vom Standpunkt der Sozialversicherungstechnik. Twelfth International Congress of Actuaries, vol. 4, 1940.

Duvillard, Émmanuel Étienne: Analyse et tableaux de l'influence de la petite vérole sur la mortalité à chaque age …. Paris, 1806.

Easterlin, R.A.: The American baby boom in historical perspective. American Economic Review, vol. 51, 1961.

Easterlin, R.A.: The current fertility decline and projected fertility changes. Population, labor force and long swings in economic growth: The American experience. Chap. 5, Columbia University Press, New York, 1968.

Euler, Leonard: Recherches générales sur la mortalité et la multiplication du genre humaine. Mémoires de l'Académie Royale des Sciences et Belles Lettres, vol. 16, 1760.

Feller, Wilhelm: On the integral equation of renewal theory. Annals of Mathematical Statistics, vol. 12, 1941.

Fergany, Mader: On the human survivorship function and life table construction. Demography, vol. 8, no. 3, August, 1971.

Fisher, R.A.: The genetical theory of natural selection. Oxford University Press, London, 1930.

Foerster, H. von: The kinetics of cellular proliferation. F. Stohlman, Jr., Ed., Grune and Stratton, New York, 1959.

Frauenthal, James C.: A dynamic model for human population growth. Theoretical Population Biology, vol. 8, 1975.

Frobenius, G.: Über Matrizen aus nicht negativen Elementen. Sitzungsberichte der Königlich Preussischen Akademie der Wissenschaften, Berlin, 1912.

Gantmacher, Feliks, R.: Applications of the theory of matrices. Interscience Publishers, New York, 1959.

Getz, Wayne M. and John Pickering: Epidemic models: Thresholds and population regulation. American Naturalist, vol. 121, 1983.

Godwin, William: Enquiry concerning political justice and its influence on morals and happiness (1793, 1798). Three volume variorum edition with introduction and notes by F.E.L. Priestley, University of Toronto Press, Toronto, 1946.

Godwin, William: Of population – An enquiry concerning the power of increase in the numbers of mankind (1820). Reprint, Augustus M. Kelley, New York, 1964.

Goldberg, Samuel: Introduction to difference equations, with illustrative examples from economics, psychology and sociology. John Wiley and Sons, Inc., New York, 1958.

Gompertz, Benjamin: On the nature of the function expressive of the law of human mortality. Philosophical Transactions, vol. 27, 1825.

Graunt, John: Natural and political observations mentioned in a following index, and made upon the bills of mortality. London, 1662, Republished in the Journal of the Institute of Actuaries, vol. 90, 1964.

Greville, T.N.E.: Short methods of constructing abridged life tables. Record of the American Institute of Actuaries, vol. 32, 1943.

Hajnal, John: Weak egrodicity in nonhomogeneous markov chains. Proceedings of the Cambridge Philosophical Society, vol. 54, part 2, 1958.

Hale, Jack and Alfredo Somolinos: Competition for fluctuating nutrients. Journal of Mathematical Biology, vol. 18, Springer-Verlag, Heidelberg, 1983.

Hall, H.S. and S.R. Knight: Higher algebra, a sequel to elementary algebra for schools, London, 1887. Reprint, Macmillan & Co., Ltd., London, 1957.

Hildebrand, Francis B.: Finite-difference equations and simulations. Prentice-Hall, New Jersey, 1968.

Hoppensteadt, Frank: The equations of population dynamics, Mathematical theories of populations: demographics, genetis and epidemics. Society for Industrial and Applied Mathematics, Philadelphia, 1975.

Jacquard, Albert: The genetic structure of populations. Biomathematics, vol. 5, Springer-Verlag, Heidelberg, 1974.

Jordan, Chester Wallace, Jr.: Life contingencies, second edition. Society of Actuaries, Chicago, 1967.

180

Keyfitz, Nathan: Introduction to the mathematics of population (1968) with revisions. Addison-Wesley, Reading, Mass., 1977.

Keyfitz, Nathan: Applied mathematical demography. John Wiley & Sons, New York, 1977.

Keyfitz, Nathan and Wilhelm Flieger: Population-facts and methods of demography. Freeman Press, San Francisco, 1971.

Lee, Ronald: The formal dynamics of controlled populations and the echo, the boom and the bust. Demography, vol. 11, no. 4, November, 1974.

Lefkovitch, L.P.: The study of population growth in organisms grouped by stages. Biometrics, vol. 21, no. 1, Biometric Society, Tucson, Arizona, 1965.

Leslie, P.H.: On the use of matrices in certain population mathematics. Biometrika, vol. 33, 1945.

Levin, Simon A.: Age-structure and stability in multiple-age spawning populations. Renewable Resource Management, T.L. Vincent and J.M. Skowronski, Eds., Lecture Notes in Bio-Mathematics, vol. 39, Springer-Verlag, Heidelberg, 1981.

Levin, Simon A. and C. Phillip Goodyear: Analysis of an age-structured fishery model. Journal of Mathematical Biology, vol. 9, Springer-Verlag, Heidelberg, 1980.

Lewis, E.G.: On the generation and growth of a population. Sankhya, vol. 6, 1942.

Lexis, Wilhelm: Einleitung in die Theorie der Bevölkerungs-Statistik. K.J. Trübner, Strasbourg, 1875.

Lopez, Alvaro: Problems in stable population theory. Office of Population Research, Princeton University, Princeton, 1961.

Lotka, Alfred J.: Relation between birth rates and death rates. Science N.S., vol. 26, 1907.

Makeham, William M.: On the law of mortality. Journal of the Institute of Actuaries, vol. 13, 1867.

Malthus, Thomas Robert: An essay on the principle of population as it affects the future improvement of society with remarks on the speculations of Mr. Godwin, M. Condorcet, and other writers (1798). Reprinted with notes by James Bonar, Macmillan, London, 1926.

Matthiessen, Poul Chr.: Some aspects of the demographic transition in Denmark. København Universitets Fond, Copenhagen, 1970.

May, Robert M.: Mathematical aspects of the dynamics of animal populations. Studies in Mathematical Biology, Part II: Populations and Communities. S.A. Levin, editor, Mathematical Association of America, 1978.

May, Robert M. and R.M. Anderson: Population biology of infectious diseases, Part II. Nature, vol. 280, 1979.

McCann, James C.: A technique for estimating life expectancy with crude vital rates. Demography, vol. 13, no. 2, May, 1976.

McFarland, David D.: On the theory of stable populations: A new and elementary proof of the theorems under weaker assumptions. Demography, vol. 6, 1969.

McKendrick, A.G.: Applications of mathematics to medical problems. Proceedings of the Edinburgh Mathematical Society, vol. 44, series 1, 1926.

Meyer, Walter: Notes on mathematical demography: Stable population theory. Department of Mathematics, Adelphi University, 1978.

Meyer, Walter: Asymptotic birth trajectories in the discrete form of stable population theory. Theoretical Population Biology, vol. 21, no. 2, April, 1982.

Miller, Kenneth S.: An introduction to the calculus of finite differences and difference equations. Dover Publications, New York, 1960.

Miller, Kenneth S.: Linear difference equations. W.A. Benjamin, Inc., New York, 1968.

Milne, Joshua: A treatise on the valuation of annuities and assurances on lives and survivors. London, 1815.

Mitra, Smarendranath: Comment on N. Fergany's 'On the human survivorship function and life table construction'. Demography, vol. 9, no. 3, August, 1972.

Mitra, Smarendranath: On the efficiency of the estimates of life table functions. Demography, vol. 10, no. 3, August, 1973.

Moore, John T.: Elements of linear algebra and matrix theory. McGraw-Hill Book Co., New York, 1968.

Noble, Ben: Applied linear algebra. Prentice-Hall, New Jersey, 1969.

Perron, Oskar: Zur Theorie der Matrizen. Mathematische Annalen, vol. 64, 1907.

Petersen, William: The Malthus-Godwin debate, then and now. Demography, vol. 8, no. 1, February, 1971.

Pick, James B.: Computer display of population age structure. Demography, vol. 11, no. 4, November, 1974.

Pielou, E.C.: An introduction to mathematical ecology, Wiley-Interscience, John Wiley & Sons, New York, 1969.

Pollard, J.H.: Mathematical models for the growth of himan populations. Cambridge University Press, London, 1973.

Reed, Lowell J. and Margaret Merrell: A short method for constructing an abridged life table. American Journal of Hygiene, vol. 30, 1939.

Ross, Shepley L.: Differential equations. Second Edition, John Wiley & Sons, New York, 1974.

Rubinow, S.I.: A maturity-time representation for cell populations. Biophysical Journal, vol. 8, 1968

Schoen, Robert: Calculating life tables by estimating Chiang's a from observed rates. Demography, vol. 15, no. 4, November, 1978.

Sharpe, F.R. and A.J. Lotka: A problem in age-distribution. Philosophical Magazine, Ser. 3, vol. 21, 1911.

Sherbert, Donald R.: Difference equations with applications. UMAP, Unit 322, Modules and Monographs in Undergraduate Mathematics and its Applications Project, Newton, Mass., 1979.

Smith, David and Nathan Keyfitz: Mathematical demography – selected papers. Biomathematics, vol. 6, Springer-Verlag, Berlin, 1977.

Spengler, Joseph J.: Malthus on Godwin's 'Of population'. Demography, vol. 8, no. 1, February, 1971.

Spiegelman, Mortimer: Introduction to demography, Revised edition. Harvard University Press, Cambridge, Mass., 1968.

Statens Statistiske Bureau: Befolkningsforholdene i Danmark i det 19 aarhundrede. Statistisk Tabelværk, VA. no. 5, 1905.

Streifer, William: Realistic models in population ecology. Advances in ecological research, A. Macfadyen, Ed., vol. 8, Academic Press, New York, 1974.

Süssmilch, Johann Peter: An illustration of population growth. Die gottliche Ordnung, vol. 1, Berlin, 1761.

Trenerry, C.F.: The origin and early history of insurance including the contract of bottomry. P.S. King & Son, Ltd., London, 1926.

United States Department of Heath and Human Services: The person-number systems of Sweden, Norway, Denmark and Israel. Data Evaluation and Methods Research, Series 2, no. 84, DHHS Publication No. (PHS) 80–1358, Office of Health Research, Statistics and Technology, Hyattsville, MD, June, 1980.

Verhulst, Pierre-Francois: A note on the law of population growth. Correspondence Mathématique et Physique Publiée par A. Quetelet, vol. 10, Brussels, 1838.

Volterra, Vito: Variazioni e fluttuazioni del numero d'individui in specie animali conviventi. Memorie della R. Accademia Nazionale dei Lincei, anno CCCXXIII, II, 1926.

Westergaard, H.: Contributions to the history of statistics (1932). Mouton, The Hague, 1969.

Wunsch, Guillaume: La théorie des événements réduits: Application aux principaux phénomènes démographiques. Recherches Economiques de Louvain, vol. 34, no. 4, 1968.

Wunsch, Guillaume and Marc G. Termote: Introduction to demographic analysis – Principles and methods. Plenum Press, New York, 1978.

Zuev, G.M. and Soroko, E.L.: Mathematical description of migration processes. Avtomatika i Telemekhanika (USSR), Evolving Systems, Plenum Publishing, New York, 1978.

Index

185

186

Biomathematics

Volume 12
R. Gittins

Canonical Analysis

A Review with Applications in Ecology

1985. 16 figures. Approx. 320 pages.
ISBN 3-540-13617-7

Contents: Introduction. – Theory: Canonical correlations and canonical variates. Extensions and generalizations. Canonical variate analysis. Dual scaling. – Applications: General introduction. Experiment 1: an investigation of spatial variation. Experiment 2: soil-species relationships in a limestone grassland community. Soil-vegetation relationships in a lowland tropical rain forest. Dynamic status of a lowland tropical rain forest. The structure of grassland vegetation in Anglesey, North Wales. The nitrogen nutrition of eight grass species. Herbivore-environment relationships in the Rwenzori National Park, Uganda. – Appraisal and Prospect: Applications: appraisal and conclusions. Research issues and future developments. – Appendix 1: Multivariate regression. – Appendix 2: Data sets used in worked applications. – Appendix 3: Species composition of a limestone grassland community. – Index of plant and animal names. – Author index. – Subject index.

Volume 11
B. G. Mirkin, S. N. Rodin

Graphs and Genes

Translated from the Russian by H. L. Beus
1984. 46 figures. XIV, 197 pages.
ISBN 3-540-12657-0

Contents: Graphs in the analysis of gene structure. – Graphs in the analysis of gene semantics. – Graphs in the analysis of gene evolution. – Epilogue: Cryptographic problems in genetics. – Appendix: Some notions about graphs. – References. – Index of genetics terms. – Index of mathematical terms.

Volume 10
A. Okubo

Diffusion and Ecological Problems: Mathematical Models

1980. 114 figures, 6 tables. XIII, 254 pages
ISBN 3-540-09620-5

Contents: Introduction: The Mathematics of Ecological Diffusion. – The Basics of Diffusion. – Passive Diffusion in Ecosystems. – Diffusion of "Smell" and "Taste": Chemical Communication. – Mathematical Treatment of Biological Diffusion. – Some Examples of Animal Diffusion. – The Dynamics of Animal Grouping. – Animal Movements in Home Range. – Patchy Distribution and Diffusion. – Population Dynamics in Temporal and Spatial Domains. – References. – Author Index. – Subject Index.

Volume 9
W. J. Ewens

Mathematical Population Genetics

1979. 4 figures, 17 tables. XII, 325 pages
ISBN 3-540-09577-2

Contents: The Golden Age. – Technicalities and Generalizations. – Discrete Stochastic Models. – Diffusion Theory. – Applications of Diffusion Theory. – Two Loci. – Many Loci. – Molecular Population Genetics. – The Neural Theory. – Generalizations and Conclusions. – Appendices. – References. – Author Index. – Subject Index.

Springer-Verlag
Berlin
Heidelberg
New York
Tokyo

Biomathematics

Managing Editor: S.A.Levin

Editorial Board: M.Arbib, H.-J.Bremermann, J.Cowan, W.M.Hirsch, J.Keller, K.Krickeberg, R.C.Lewontin, R.M.May, L.A.Segel

Volume 8
A.T.Winfree

The Geometry of Biological Time

1980. 290 figures. XIV, 530 pages
ISBN 3-540-09373-7

Contents: Introduction. – Circular Logic. – Phase Singularities (Screwy Results of Circular Logic). – The Rules of the Ring. – Ring Populations. – Getting Off the Ring. – Attracting Cycles and Isochrons. – Measuring the Trajectories of a Circadian Clock. – Populations of Attractor Cycle Oscillators. – Excitable Kinetics and Excitable Media. – The Varieties of Phaseless Experience: In Which the Geometrical Orderliness of Rhythmic Organization Breaks Down in Diverse Ways. – The Firefly Machine. – Energy Metabolism in Cells. – The Malonic Acid Reagent ("Sodium Geometrate"). – Electrical Rhythmicity and Excitability in Cell Membranes. – The Aggregation of Slime Mold Amoebae. – Growth and Regeneration. – Arthropod Cuticle. – Pattern Formation in the Fungi. – Circadian Rhythms in General. – The Circadian Clocks of Insect Eclosion. – The Flower of Kalanchoe. – The Cell Mitotic Cycle. – The Female Cycle. – References. – Index of Names. – Index of Subjects.

Volume 7
E.R.Lewis

Network Models in Population Biology

1977. 187 figures. XII, 402 pages.
ISBN 3-540-08214-X

Contents: Foundations of Modeling Dynamic Systems. – General Concepts of Population Modeling. – A Network Approach to Population Modeling. – Analysis of Network Models. – Appendices: Probability Arrays, Array Manipulation. Bernoulli Trials in the Binomial Distribution.

Volume 6
D.Smith, N.Keyfitz

Mathematical Demography

Selected Papers
1977. 31 figures. XI, 514 pages
ISBN 3-540-07899-1

Contents: The Life Table. – Stable Population Theory. – Attempts at Prediction and the Theory they Stimulated. – Parameterization and Curve Fitting. – Probability Models of Conception and Birth. – Branching Theory and Other Stochastic Processes. – Cohort and Period, Problem of the Sexes, Sampling.

Volume 5
A.Jacquard

The Genetic Structure of Populations

Translators: D.Charlesworth, B.Charlesworth
1974. 92 figures. XVIII, 569 pages
ISBN 3-540-06329-3

Volume 4
M.Iosifescu, P.Tăutu

Stochastic Processes and Applications in Biology and Medicine

Part 2: Models

1973. 337 pages. ISBN 3-540-06271-8

Contents: Preliminary Considerations. – Population Growth Models. – Population Dynamics Processes. – Evolutionary Processes. – Models in Physiology and Pathology.

Volume 3
M.Iosifescu, P.Tăutu

Stochastic Processes and Applications in Biology and Medicine

Part 1: Theory

1973. 331 pages
ISBN 3-540-06270-X

Volume 2
E.Batschelet

Introduction to Mathematics for Life Scientists

3rd edition. 1979. 227 figures, 62 tables.
XV, 643 pages
ISBN 3-540-09662-0

Springer-Verlag Berlin Heidelberg New York Tokyo